FREEDOM
FALLACY

FREEDOM FALLACY

THE LIMITS OF LIBERAL FEMINISM

EDITED BY

MIRANDA KIRALY & MEAGAN TYLER

connorcourt
PUBLISHING

CONTENTS

PART III: SEXUALITY

PART IV: ACTIVISM AND CHANGE

ACKNOWLEDGMENTS

The editors would like to, first and foremost, express their deep gratitude to the contributors. Without these women having dedicated their precious time to this project, it obviously would not have been possible. We would also like to thank those who undertook the peer-review of this publication. In addition, the editors would like to acknowledge the many feminist activists, academics and writers, who have paved the way for collections such as this to be written.

We would also like to extend our thanks to Dr Anthony Cappello, of Connor Court Publishing, for his role in enabling this collection to be published. Anthony has been most generous with his time and encouragement for our work, despite being persistently bemused by its content.

Miranda would particularly like to thank Meagan for agreeing to come on board and join her on this ambitious project. Meagan's wit, wisdom and insight have been invaluable towards shaping the book's vision and bringing it to fruition. Miranda is also grateful to Jessica Cohen for her editorial feedback, and Murray Greenway for his remarkable research skills and patience.

Meagan is indebted to Sheila for her guidance, over the years, in navigating the often rough waters of feminist politics, and to Dan for his editorial and sounding-board skills, not to mention his exceptionally patient and loving care. Meagan would also like to offer her heartfelt thanks to Miranda, who not only came up with the great idea for this project in the first place, but also kept it on track. Finally, Meagan wants to thank the staff at various Melbourne cafés, especially Trotters, for putting up with our hours-long editorial meetings and loud laughter.

I'm a feminist, not the fun kind.

— Andrea Dworkin

INTRODUCTION

Miranda Kiraly and Meagan Tyler

Something is happening. For all the talk of a 'postfeminist' era over the last decade, there are now ever-increasing signs of a feminist resurgence. The visibility of feminist activism has led everyone from female singers and celebrities, to male political leaders, to start talking about the f-word, and even to start claiming the label 'feminist' for themselves. Something is definitely happening but what, exactly, is it?

With the rising tide of interest in all things feminist, there has been a rush to promote a popular brand of 'feminism-lite' or 'fun feminism' that does not offend or overtly threaten existing power structures. The mainstreaming of the feminist brand has left 'feminism' as little more than a sticker that anyone and everyone can now apply, largely because it has lost all sense of intellectual rigour or political challenge. This version of populist feminism embodies notions of empowerment, choice, and the individual above all else. It has been shaped, primarily, by liberal feminism, and the contributors in this volume also refer to it as third wave feminism, popular feminism, or choice feminism.

Individualism lies at the heart of liberal feminism, championing the benefits of 'choice' and the possibility that freedom is within reach, or occasionally, that it already exists should women choose to claim it. It also pushes – sometimes overtly and sometimes covertly – the fallacy that substantive equality has already been achieved and that the pursuit of opportunity lies solely in women's hands. Liberal feminism has helped recast women's liberation as an individual and private struggle, rather than one which acknowledges the systemic shortcomings of existing systems of power and privilege that continue to hold women back, as a class. Women's liberation has been reduced to a series of personal statements about whether women like or dislike particular aspects of themselves or their lives.

This problem is not new. In 1990, contributors to *The Sexual Liberals and the Attack on Feminism* bemoaned essentially the same thing: that 'feminism' had moved from a critique of – and collective resistance to – patriarchal oppression, towards an individualised, liberal model of 'choice'. Indeed, Catharine MacKinnon, in a piece titled 'Liberalism and the Death of Feminism', for that collection, posited that liberalism is the very antithesis of a movement for women's liberation. As she put it:

> Where feminism was collective, liberalism is individualist ... Where feminism is socially based and critical, liberalism is naturalistic, attributing the product of women's oppression to women's natural sexuality, making it 'ours'. Where feminism criticises the ways in which women have been socially determined in an attempt to change that determination, liberalism is voluntaristic, meaning it acts like we have choices that we do not have. Where feminism is based on material reality, liberalism is based on some ideal realm in the head. And where feminism is relentlessly political, about power and powerlessness, the best that can be mustered by this nouveau movement is a watered down form of moralism: this is good, this is bad, no analysis of power of powerlessness at all. [1]

These comparisons seem just as relevant and compelling as when they were first published, some 25 years ago. Many of our contributors pick up these issues again and consider them in the current context; a context in which the kinds of liberal feminism that MacKinnon was critical of have taken centre stage and seem to have become, in the coverage of much of the mainstream media, the be all and end all of feminist thought.

As Natalie Jovanovski notes in her chapter, it should not be surprising that liberal feminism has risen to prominence. It is generally seen to be less threatening to the status quo and reassures mainstream audiences that feminists are not a scary 'other'. But far from occupying some middle ground of inoffensiveness, the emphasis on 'choice' in much liberal feminist writing is actually rather extreme. It strips women's lives of context and makes it sound as though our 'choices' are made in a political and cultural vacuum. Each of our contributors, therefore, seeks to talk about the importance of power, context and culture, rather than individual choice and agency alone. Understanding and acknowledging the environment of women's inequality goes to the heart of what is meant by the 'freedom fallacy' of this collection's title. That is, there can be no freedom, no liberation, when the available choices are only constructed on the basis of gross inequity. More 'choice', or even a greater ability to choose, does not necessarily mean greater freedom.

Amid this dominance of liberal feminist orthodoxy, resistance is forming among a wide range of women. There is even talk of an emerging 'fourth wave' of feminism breaking in the United Kingdom and the United States; a movement that seeks to engage collective action and to address structural inequality, subjugation, and exploitation of women and girls, often at a grassroots level. Media outlets are struggling to conceptualise this emerging wave of feminism, and continue to attempt to simplistically slot it into a left–right, or generational, divide. Like many feminist movements before it, this new wave does not comfortably fit the mould of traditional politics, because it recognises that women's interests have been neglected across the political spectrum. As a result, there is a wide variety of criticism that we have been able to draw on for this collection. What unites our contributors in this book is not a single perspective – there is a range of different feminist positions included – but rather, a unified belief that liberation cannot be found at a purely individual level, nor can it be forged from adapting to, or simply accepting, existing conditions of oppression.

Hopefully, if you have picked up this book, you already recognise the systemic conditions of women's inequality, but to summarise a number of the areas raised by our contributors: women still face unbearably high levels of sexual violence and millions of women around the world do not even have the limited protection that marital rape law affords. Activists are still fighting all around the world for the rights of girls and women not be mutilated and exploited. Pornography and the trafficking of women and girls are booming global businesses trading primarily in sexual exploitation. Our contributors write about these injustices as existing on a continuum with other issues of inequality such as the sexual division of household labour, identity and autonomy through the marriage contract, sexual harassment laws, and the viciousness of the beauty and diet industries. They each shape women's social, cultural, political and material subordination.

The fact that all these issues pose significant barriers to a world in which women are truly free should be obvious but, as many contributors point out, activities which were once held up as the archetypes of women's subordinate status are now held up as liberating personal 'choices'. Sexual harassment becomes reframed as harmless banter that women can enjoy too. Marriage becomes a pro-feminist celebration of love. Wage labour becomes the ultimate empowerment. Labiaplasty becomes a useful cosmetic enhancement. Pornography becomes sexual liberation. Sexual objectification becomes a barometer of self-worth.

As a nod to this rather odd situation, where people who claim the label 'feminist' have ended up essentially supporting structures that work against women's liberation, many of the chapters begin with epigraphs highlighting the kinds of statements that our contributors wish to contest. This is to help make clear the situation in which we are all working, and the kinds of arguments that need to be picked apart in order for any feminist movement to gain momentum and push for meaningful change. This collection aims to challenge the limits of key liberal feminist concepts and to critique the idea that it is possible to find freedom simply by exercising 'choice' in a world in which women, as a class, are still not considered to be of fully equal human worth to men.

While *Time* magazine may be questioning whether or not feminism is still needed in 2015, prominent figures from previous waves of the women's liberation movement are certain it is desperately needed now, perhaps even more than in previous decades. As Germaine Greer recently declared: 'Liberation hasn't happened ... Things have got a lot worse for women since I wrote *The Female Eunuch*.' [2] It is in recognition of the deep-seated problems that we still face, that several of our contributors emphasise the need for collective action to again be at the heart of feminist activism. This is crucially important and has been sidelined in popular discussions about whether or not certain women are 'bad feminists', or make acceptably feminist 'choices'. This simply operates to blame individual women for their circumstances instead of casting light on the issues of structural and material inequality that affect women as a class.

It is important to note that while many chapters in this book draw on the concept of women as a class, [3] several of the contributors also acknowledge that there are significant inequalities between groups of women, *as well as* an overall situation of women's inequality, relative to men. In line with this, we have included contributions from academics, activists and commentators on a range of topics and from women with differing perspectives and backgrounds. There is a focus on the Australian context but we have included chapters dealing with developments in the United Kingdom, the United States, South Africa and Canada. Some contributors have been writing on these topics for decades, others for months; some are publishing publicly, here, for the first time.

We wanted to include new voices to sit alongside contributions from those with longstanding experience and more established platforms. The inclusion of a number of women, relatively new to the movement, represents, in part, the fact that there is indeed something happening, and that there is a need for us to challenge the prevailing liberal feminist standard. It also illustrates the point made by Finn Mackay, in her chapter on the supposed generational division between second wave and third wave feminists, that chronology and age have little to contribute to enhancing our understandings of feminist theory and action. Instead, it is a question of ideology that distinguishes the different branches of feminist thought and action.

Overview of content

The chapters of this collection are grouped into sections dealing with several key themes: choice and the individual, feminism and freedom, sexuality and, finally, activism and change. In the first section, on the concepts of choice and the individual, we have chapters from Rebecca Whisnant and Meghan Murphy, dealing with some of the main conceptual limits of mainstream, liberal feminism. Natalie Jovanovski, Kaye Quek and Margaret Thornton each looks at the issues of individual choice and agency in the context of self-help books, 'mail-order bride' services and neoliberalism, respectively.

The second section deals with feminist conceptions of freedom. Miranda Kiraly examines the 'freedom fallacy' and how both sides of traditional politics, left and right, have betrayed women. Helen Pringle examines the meaning of freedom in the context of sexual harassment. Shakira Hussein and Camille Nurka look into the issue of 'othering' in our understandings of women's freedom. Kate Farhall and Laura McNally take issue with the rebranding and corporate whitewashing of feminism under capitalism.

The third section deals most explicitly with issues of sexuality, however, we should point out that almost all the chapters make mention of sexuality and sexual politics in some way. With the exception of Laura Tarzia's piece on sexual violence, we did not commission individual pieces on sexuality, nor did we encourage contributors to consider it specifically. That so many contributors have found this to be a focus or, at the very least, a critical element in understanding women's oppression, is telling. It is wholly in-keeping with the radical feminist claim that the social construction of sexuality is at the heart of women's inequality. To again quote MacKinnon: 'Sexuality is to feminism what work is to marxism: that which is most one's own, yet most taken away.' [4]

In this section, Laura Tarzia argues that we cannot successfully combat violence against women without confronting the eroticising of violence in certain sexual subcultures. Caroline Norma looks at the changing understandings of prostitution within the human rights group, Amnesty International. Meghan Donevan examines claims that pornography can be a useful tool for promoting healthy sexuality, and Julia Long asks why feminist critiques of heterosexuality seem to have all but disappeared.

The final section on activism and change brings together a diverse grouping of chapters outlining feminist campaigns and ideas for moving forward. Finn Mackay offers insights from her interviews with feminist activists on their perceptions of second wave and third wave feminism. Naela Rose and Teresa Edwards, respectively, offer fascinating first-hand accounts of activism on female genital mutilation in the United Kingdom, and prostitution legislation in Canada with a specific focus on the impact for First Nations women. This section finishes with a chapter from Meagan Tyler on rejecting marriage as an institution, and hopeful thoughts from Rebecca Whisnant about where we can go from this point forward.

This book is best understood as a radical challenge to the dominance of liberal feminist discourse in the public sphere. For some of our contributors this is imperative because, as they understand it, the liberal feminist model does not represent small steps in the right direction, but rather actively inhibits real change. For others, liberal feminism can still be seen to have made some contribution to the women's liberation movement. As Andrea Dworkin once quipped: 'I do think liberal feminists bear responsibility for a lot of what's gone wrong,' but she also added, 'I have a really strong belief that any movement needs both radicals and liberals. You always need women who can walk into the room in the right way, talk in the right tone of voice, who have access to power. But you also need a bottom line.' [5] We hope that this book demonstrates the limits of the liberal feminist approach and the importance of reinforcing that bottom line.

PART I:
CHOICE AND THE INDIVIDUAL

Not your father's *Playboy*, not your mother's feminist movement: feminism in porn culture

Rebecca Whisnant

We kind of realised ... that feminism is really just owning your shit and feeling good about your decisions and just being equal with men. [1] — Krystyna Hutchinson

This chapter is about the state of contemporary feminism and how it relates to the porn culture that surrounds us. This is important because whatever porn culture is, and there are a variety of definitions, it's not what feminists, or women, or anybody with a lick of sense, ever meant by 'sexual liberation'. There have, however, been contentious debates between radical and liberal feminists about the relationship between pornography, power and choice. I aim to unravel some of those debates here and highlight how liberal notions of 'choice', favoured by self-proclaimed 'third wave feminists', confuse and undermine our thinking not only about pornography, but about women's oppression and patriarchy generally.

Let me begin with a major caveat. Whenever we talk about patriarchy, either in general or any particular element, we need to bear in mind that the main problem is men: men's choices, men's ways of seeing and treating women and, in the case of pornography, the material that mostly men produce and sell mostly to other men. Nonetheless, women have to live and make our own choices in the world that men have made. That's unfair enough, but what's even more unfair is that, as with all forms of oppression, much of the burden of resistance inevitably falls on those who are oppressed. The resistance movement of, and for, women – against patriarchy – is called feminism, and its strength depends significantly on the cogency of the political analysis that underlies it.

With this in mind, I want to provide a bit of historical and conceptual backdrop for further conversations about pornography and contemporary feminism. Here, then, is my brief thumbnail history of United States ('US') feminist perspectives on, and political action around, pornography over roughly the last 40 years.

How we got here

The early women's liberationists in the late 1960s and very early 1970s did not think very much about pornography, or at least they didn't write much about it. But this changed in the mid- to late 1970s, no doubt due partly to pornography's increasing cultural visibility as well as to many feminists' growing focus on rape and other forms of male violence against women. To these early feminists, it was clear that pornography contained and conveyed the ideology of male supremacy in a particularly visceral and vicious form that, as Robin Morgan famously put it in 1974: 'Pornography is the theory, and rape is the practice.' [2] Susan Brownmiller took up a similar theme as part of her 1975 book on rape, asserting – presciently, as it turned out – that:

> There can be no equality in porn, no female equivalent, no turning of the tables in the name of bawdy fun. Pornography, like rape, is a male invention, designed to dehumanise women ... Pornography is the undiluted essence of anti-female propaganda. [3]

The first feminist conference on pornography was held in San Francisco in 1978, and in October 1979, 5000 women (accompanied by a few renegade men) marched on New York's Times Square to protest against industries of sexual exploitation. That same year saw the publication of Andrea Dworkin's searing and heartbreaking book *Pornography: Men Possessing Women*, and in 1980 Laura Lederer published *Take Back the Night*, the first major feminist anthology on the subject.

As feminists continued thinking about pornography, and observing how it functions in the social world, many became inclined to revise Morgan's original dictum, to assert that pornography was not only a theory but also, itself, a practice; often a practice of rape, and always a practice of harm and subordination. This understanding animated the groundbreaking legal approach to pornography that Andrea Dworkin and Catharine MacKinnon brought to fruition in their *Antipornography Civil Rights Ordinance*. The ordinance defined pornography as sex discrimination and allowed those harmed in and through pornography to sue for civil damages.

The *Dworkin–MacKinnon Ordinance*, as it became widely known, was passed by the Minneapolis City Council in 1983 and in several other municipalities thereafter, but higher courts later overturned it as unconstitutional. [4] There was then, and is now, room for reasonable and conscientious people to disagree about whether the ordinance was the best strategy for combating pornography's harms. What occurred, however, was something far beyond this: an organised and vocal campaign by some self-described feminists, in open cooperation with pornographers, not only to defeat the ordinance, but also to mock and discredit the feminist critique on which it was based. Thus was the early feminist consensus around pornography shattered, much to the shock and dismay of many who had put so much of themselves into developing it.

Meanwhile – and, I think, non-coincidentally – a conservative backlash movement in American political culture had started to gather steam. Remember, this was the 1980s: Ronald Reagan was in office, busily undoing various progressive gains of the 1960s and 1970s and overseeing a spectacular resurgence of both social conservatism and unrestrained capitalism. A backlash is meant to scare people and shut them up and, to some extent, almost inevitably, it succeeds. The whole point, after all, is to back us into a corner where we don't have much choice – or at least it seems to us that we don't have much choice – but to buckle under.

Now think about it: in this cultural and political context, a feminism that *acquiesces* to certain key male entitlements, while simultaneously presenting itself as bold and liberated and rebellious, is likely to be appealing to many women. A version of feminism that supports girls' and women's desired self-conception as independent and powerful, while actually requiring very little of them as far as confronting real male power, will similarly have wide appeal. It is my contention that the versions of feminism currently most popular in the academy and in US popular culture more broadly are of exactly this kind, and that the backlash dynamics I just described are on especially clear display with respect to the politics of pornography.

After all, in one important sense, what happened in the 1980s was good news: back then, the feminist critique of pornography had enough cultural, political, and intellectual momentum that an orchestrated campaign was required to defeat it. During the 1990s and early 2000s, however, despite the best efforts of many of us, that critique largely dropped off the radar screen, replaced in some quarters by a depoliticised faux-feminism that caters to, rather than challenges, porn culture.

In *The Bust Guide to the New Girl Order*, for example, Marcelle Karp and Debbie Stoller state that:

> We don't have a problem with pornography unless, of course, it doesn't turn us on. We realise that American porn culture is here to stay. So rather than trying to rid the world of sexual images we think are negative, as some of our sisters have done, we're far more interested in encouraging women to explore porn, to find out whether it gets them hot or merely bothered ... While the female market for fuck films is still far less than that of men, it's a central tenet of our version of feminism to acknowledge that it exists at all. [5]

At a certain level, the logic here is hard to fault: we can't defeat this beast, Karp and Stoller figure, so we might as well see if we can get our jollies from it too. If you can't beat 'em, join 'em.

This is a common and familiar phenomenon: we adjust our desires based on what's actually happening and on what we think is, and is not, possible. Philosophers have a useful term for the results of this process: 'adaptive preferences'. [6] The basic idea is simple: if I can't have something (or think I can't have it), then it behooves me not to want that thing. Conversely, if I'm going to get something whether I like it or not, then I'll be happier if I can get myself to want it and like it. So people adapt their desires to fit their situations, rather than vice versa, thus minimising the pain of continuing to want something that they don't think they can get.

The concept of adaptive preferences is indispensable to understanding the self-reproducing dynamics of oppressive systems. In particular, I think it can help us understand the brand of feminism of which I am, for the moment, taking Karp and Stoller as representatives, the brand that's sometimes called 'do-me feminism', but for which the less polite moniker is 'fuck-me feminism'. One blogger sums it up as follows (unsympathetically but still, I think, pretty accurately):

> Fuck-me feminism … is a school of thought that suggests [women] are empowered by reclaiming and controlling our own sexual objectification, by reclaiming the power of pornography and the sex industry for ourselves, and by flaunting our desire and willingness to have sex. In other words, being a man's sexual object can't hurt me if I want to be objectified; pornography and the sex industry can't degrade me if I enjoy it or if I profit from it; being used for sex can't devalue me if *I'm* using him too; being regarded as nothing more than a pussy to fuck can't dehumanise me if I *want* him to fuck my pussy.

Now we should note an important theme here: that on this view, as far as feminism is concerned, it's not *what* I'm doing that matters, but whether I really *want* (or choose) to do it. File this away; I'll come back to it.

So here is the situation we now face. Over the last 15 to 20 years, the pornography industry has exploded in size and reach, and its themes and messages have increasingly colonised the rest of popular culture. During that same period, mainstream commercial pornography has become steadily more suffused with overt degradation, humiliation, and violence. This much is disturbing enough. What's even more distressing is that, as pornography becomes both more brutal and more pervasive, we are offered a version of feminism that is less and less able to help us understand and resist it, a significantly depoliticised feminism inadequate to the task of challenging male power, especially (though not only) in its pornographic form. In the next section, I contrast this new version, or 'wave', of feminism to the version that preceded it, and that, thankfully, still persists alongside it.

'Wave'-ing goodbye to radical feminism

For those uninitiated to the 'wave' model of feminism, the feminist movement of the late 19th and early 20th century, which focused most centrally on women's rights in marriage, and then later on the right to vote, is usually called the 'first wave'. The radical women's liberation movement of the 1960s and 1970s, and to some degree into the 1980s, is called the 'second wave'. Starting in the early 1990s, some young feminists began to identify as part of what is often called the 'third wave'.

Now as many before me have pointed out, this 'wave' model has a number of shortcomings. For one thing, it tends to downplay important feminist work, particularly by women of colour, between, throughout, and independent of the 'waves'. Furthermore, at least as commonly deployed in feminist circles, it wrongly suggests that the differences under consideration are primarily generational rather than political. It seems to me, on the contrary, that the difference between the second and the third wave is not primarily a matter of age or generation but that, in fact, most of this much-vaunted difference ultimately reduces to the timeworn distinction between radical feminism and liberal feminism.

As an unrepentant (though generationally anomalous) second wave feminist, let me attempt to articulate three central themes of second wave radical feminism, contrasting each in turn with the perspectives of some self-described third wave feminists. [7] The first is the idea that women can be understood as a class, the second is the notion that the personal is political, and the third is the concept of sexual politics. I'll then return to the pornography issue with this rudimentary theory in hand; after all, in my opinion, the second wave got things right with respect to pornography *because* it got things right in its overall political analysis, in its understanding of how systems of oppression work and of how, therefore, such systems must be combated.

One claim central to second wave radical feminism is that women are a class sharing a common condition. This claim sets off a lot of people's alarm bells, sometimes with good reason, as it is subject to widely varying interpretations. If we take it to mean, for instance, that all women face the same problems, have the same beliefs, values, and priorities, make or ought to make the same choices in life, and so on, then it is clearly problematic. If we take it to mean that women are not also members of other politically important classes – racial, ethnic, economic, and so on – which multiply complicate their relationships to other women, to men, and to feminism, then it is clearly problematic. But the claim that women are a class sharing a common condition does not mean any of this. It means that there exist patriarchal forces and structures which, regardless of how any particular woman feels about them or chooses to relate to them, *objectively* function to uphold the power and privilege of men while keeping women as a group down. And this in turn means that, as Andrea Dworkin once put it: 'the fate of every individual woman – no matter what her politics, character, values, qualities – is *tied* to the fate of all women whether she likes it or not'. [8]

So understood, the claim that women are a class sharing a common condition suggests a particular aim and purpose for feminist endeavour: namely, to figure out as best we can what serves the interests of women *as a class* (not just our own personal interests) and then to try as best we can – imperfectly, messily, but in good faith – to do that, support that, be that. Or, to put the same point a different way: what we do as feminists is figure out what the institutions, ideologies, and practices are that keep women down, and then try as best we can to challenge them, chip away at them, withdraw from them, take a sledgehammer to them, or in any other way diminish their power to harm and to subjugate women.

It is instructive to contrast this approach with claims of 'essentialism' from the third wave, that is, the suggestion that radical feminist claims appeal to some innate sameness shared by all women. Again, it's important to clarify: charges of essentialism are often made in connection with the failure to recognise racial, class, and other such hierarchical differences among women. Although this is an important challenge, it is not the one I am targeting here. Rather I have in mind the oft-expressed reluctance among third wave feminists to, as Jennifer Gilley has put it: 'speak in an assumed – and potentially false – solidarity'. [9] In short, the idea seems to be this: if I say that some act or institution is bad, sexist, patriarchal, and so on, then I am implicitly assuming something about 'all women' (that's the essentialism part): namely that, as women, they don't like and thus would never freely choose to undertake that act or engage with that institution. But then what about some woman somewhere who *does*, apparently, like or choose these things? I must be saying she is stupid, self-deceived, and/or a bad feminist (or not a feminist at all), and that doesn't seem like a nice or sisterly thing to say.

Second wave feminists also famously developed the slogan: 'the personal is political'. Through formal and informal consciousness-raising, the women of the second wave discovered that various experiences that they had previously thought were unique to them – from sexual harassment to rape to feeling burdened by domestic labour – were in fact common to many women's lives. This discovery opened the door to seeing such experiences as having political and feminist significance, as revealing something about the condition of women as a group, rather than merely as unfortunate, but quirky, features of one's own personal life. Thus second wave feminists newly claimed certain 'personal' or 'private' areas of life – home, sex, marriage, relationships, household chores, and more – as the domain of politics. This is great, in that it enables the expression of righteously political outrage about all manner of things previously suffered in silence. But there's a flip side to it, too: in recognising the personal as political, second wave feminists also recognised and embraced responsibility for the broader implications and consequences of their own 'personal' choices around everything from work, family, and parenting to beauty, sexuality, and self-defence.

Compare this perspective to that of third wave author/activists Jennifer Baumgardner and Amy Richards, who write in their book *Manifesta* that: 'feminism isn't about what choice you make but the freedom to make that choice'. [10] It follows on this view that, in order to establish that a choice in any given situation is a feminist one, we need only show that it is, in fact, really and authentically, one's own choice, that whatever one is doing, one has freely chosen to do it.

Now I'm going to ask you to indulge me in a bit of heavy theory here. Structurally speaking, as a person facing oppression of whatever kind, one has two choices: resist or obey. One can resist the oppression – in general, or in any particular instance – in which case one is likely to get viciously slapped down. Alternatively, one can obey, that is, act in ways that please the oppressors, perhaps in hopes of gaining some limited reward (or at least of avoiding the oppressive system's very worst consequences). As you may have noticed, neither option is altogether attractive; as the feminist philosopher Marilyn Frye points out, oppression systematically puts oppressed people in double binds, catch-22s, situations in which they 'can't win for losing'. [11] But the crucial point for our purposes here is that one way, arguably the central way, in which oppressive systems perpetuate themselves is by giving individual members of the oppressed group an apparent stake in toeing the line. At the very least, we 'go along to get along' in many situations, and we may find that the more we curry favour with those in power, the more we are rewarded on an individual basis.

Because of this dynamic, if a particular role or practice harms women as a group, in that it sustains and reinforces patriarchy, it is utterly predictable that some women will choose to engage in it. Thus, again, the fundamental feminist question is not whether some individual women 'like' or 'choose' that role or practice but whether the overall *effect* of the role or practice is to keep women as a group subordinate to men.

The third defining element of radical feminism I'll discuss here is the notion of sexual politics. In the English language, the word 'sex' is ambiguous: there's sex in the sense of male and female, and also in the sense of sexuality. Second wave feminism named 'sex' in both senses as an arena of politics, that is, an arena in which power is exercised. In short, patriarchy makes sex (as male/female) into an unjust power hierarchy, which then manifests itself in many mutually reinforcing ways, including in and through sex (as sexuality). Whatever supports and maintains that power hierarchy is, from a second wave point of view, problematic and wrong. If this includes, as it is almost sure to, certain ways of understanding and practising sex (as sexuality), then these understandings and practices should be resisted and transformed. Furthermore, in second wave thinking, challenging the sex-based power hierarchy itself requires challenging the very definitions of manhood and womanhood, of masculinity and femininity, on which it is premised: namely, masculinity as dominance and aggression, femininity as submission. These roles themselves are taken to be problematic, not just their coercive association with biological males and females respectively. Thus, on this view, for a woman to be sexually dominant (or a man submissive) does not constitute liberation or resistance.

The third wave also has a take on sexual politics, that is, on the connections between power and sex (both sex as male/female, and sex as sexuality). They too believe that the power hierarchy placing men above women is unjust, but they have different ideas about what counts as challenging that hierarchy, particularly as it is expressed in sex-as-sexuality. On this view, for instance, a woman challenges the hierarchy when she plays a dominatrix role, or when she becomes a sexual consumer (for instance, using pornography or getting a lap dance at a strip club) – that is, when she adopts a standardly masculine set of sexual roles and activities. A woman also resists, on this view, when she uses the 'power' of femininity – her beauty, her sex appeal and 'hotness' and so on – to her own perceived advantage. According to third wave feminists, then, a woman can enact a liberatory and feminist sexual politics by adopting *either* a typically feminine *or* a typically masculine sexual role and persona, and running with it, as long as she does so freely and with the right attitudes and intentions.

'Feminist porn'?

These elements of third wave feminist thought are in evidence virtually everywhere in contemporary feminism, but perhaps nowhere so clearly as in third wave responses to the pornography issue. Consider, for instance, the idea that what we need to do is to make our own, alternative and feminist pornography. This has become such a standard response to radical feminist criticism that it is worth our attention. I don't take a stand here on whether it is possible or desirable to create sexually explicit material that expresses feminist values. Rather I look at some of the people who claim to be doing that, at some of the materials they have produced and promoted, and at the *grounds* on which they claim those materials to be feminist ones.

Some claims made on behalf of purportedly-feminist pornography sound reasonable enough as far as they go – for instance, that by making and/or consuming pornography one asserts that it's okay for women to be sexual and to want sex, that women are not merely passive recipients of male sexual desire, but have sexual desires of our own. Furthermore, in 'alt.' (alternative) or feminist pornography we do occasionally see women with something other than the Hollywood-prescribed body size and shape. But when we look at the statements of self-described feminist pornographers, the utterly liberal, even libertarian, politics at the core of this enterprise become unmistakable. It turns out that this pornography is said to be feminist because it is made by women, who are freely choosing to make it. For instance, Joanna Angel, a self-described feminist pornographer, has said that 'you could do a porn where a girl is getting choked and hit and spit on, the guy's calling her a dirty slut and stuff and ... that can still be feminist as long as everybody there is in control of what they're doing'. [12]

Also clearly in evidence here, is the idea that women can enact a liberatory sexual politics by embracing either standardly feminine or standardly masculine sexual roles and activities. Without an overriding critique of sexualised dominance, the perfectly reasonable claim that it's okay for women to want and seek sexual satisfaction shades easily into claiming women's right to be sexual dominators and consumers. And of course, at the core of the 'feminist pornography' enterprise is the idea that women can and should redefine the feminised, pornographised sexual-object role as, itself, a form of power. Thus in

2007, prominently featured on the website of 'feminist pornographer' Nina Hartley, was a film entitled, *O: The Power of Submission*. Perusing Hartley's list of favourite links, one finds a site called Slave Next Door, which carries the tagline 'real sexual slavery'. The portal page of this website reads, in part: 'Slave Next Door is the graphic depiction of a female sex slave's life and training for sexual slavery. It contains extreme BDSM situations and ... sadistic training.'

I am not saying that all of what goes under the banner of 'feminist pornography' is this bad, but I will say that I have never once read or heard an account of what *constitutes* feminist pornography – that is, of what makes it feminist – that does not conform to the analysis I've described here as liberal and third wave. That analysis, I contend, is mistaken and dangerous in that it encourages a wilful myopia with respect to the role of one's choices in a broader system of sexualised dominance. That myopia, in fact – with the freedom it grants us to pretty much do as we please like good consumers – is precisely its appeal. That's why it's hard to combat. And that's why we must find ways to articulate a radical feminist vision that can move and inspire people while also challenging them to take themselves seriously as agents of change.

'I do what I want, fuck yeah!': moving beyond 'a woman's choice'

Meghan Murphy

'A woman's choice' is, without a doubt, a central tenet of feminist discourse. Creating options and choices – real choices – for women, not simply the illusion of choice within the very narrow confines of capitalist patriarchy, is a fundamental and appropriate goal for the feminist movement. But what we've seen evolve from that notion over the past 20 years is something of a different beast.

The 'I do what I want, fuck yeah!' ethos of '90s riot grrrl feminism, which some attribute as the beginnings of the third wave, is appealing, especially to younger women. It can feel very empowering to imagine you are throwing off society's chains, embracing and rejecting, all at once, restrictive, misogynist labels such as 'slut' and 'whore', as Bikini Kill lead singer, Kathleen Hanna famously did, taking off her top at her shows, to reveal the word 'slut' written across her stomach. Before Hanna, Madonna became a feminist icon of sorts during the '80s in a similar way, embracing 'sexy' clothing and imagery. She was seen as representative of a woman taking control of her sexuality and using her femininity to gain power. But while this kind of reclaiming of traditionally sexist or male-defined imagery and language might feel temporarily liberating, the question of whether, for example, we can 'reclaim' the word 'slut' or make sexualisation or objectification our own, simply by choosing to, is less straightforward.

In 2011, a Canadian police officer suggested to students at Osgoode Hall Law School in Toronto that 'women should avoid dressing like sluts in order not to be victimised'. These comments instigated the first 'SlutWalk' march, which took place in Toronto on 3 April 2011. The marches spread around the world to places such as Las Vegas, Melbourne, Bhopal, and Sao Paulo. 'SlutWalk' was heralded as the third wave incarnation of Take Back the Night. A blogger for *Ms. Magazine* wrote about the march that took place in Los Angeles in 2012: 'It's that third wave-y feel – that individualistic empowerment – that has made "SlutWalk" popular among young women,' adding that the marches were 'less emotionally intense than anti-rape rallies such as Take Back the Night, "SlutWalk" is more for spectacle.' [1] This is a pretty accurate assessment, but 'popularity' and a lighter message do not necessarily translate into 'better', when it comes to radical movements.

Rather than focusing on attacking male violence against women and rape culture, the marches seemed performative, and prioritised media attention. From the outset there was a focus on personal, individual notions of empowerment and the 'right' to wear sexy clothing – that 'I do what I want, fuck yeah!' mantra dominated. Performing to the male gaze was positioned as a positive thing, so long as women were choosing objectification.

It didn't take long before the marches began promoting the sex industry as an empowering personal choice for women, many of them actively advocating for the legalisation of prostitution. In New York City, the march featured lingerie-wearing pole dancers, and 'SlutWalk' Las Vegas created a slogan that described 'sex work' as something women enjoyed: 'Slut isn't a look, it's an attitude. And whether you enjoy sex for pleasure or work, it's never an invitation to violence.' What was erased by 'SlutWalk's focus on 'choice' and personal empowerment was the context within which women make 'choices', particularly with regard to their 'choice' to work in the sex industry or to 'self-objectify', whether in a strip club, on Instagram, or on the street.

In 2011, 'SlutWalk' organisers in Washington DC planned a fundraiser at a strip club. [2] From a feminist perspective, the idea of holding a fundraiser for a supposedly feminist event in a place that exists to further entrench the image of women as sexy objects that exist for male pleasure seemed odd, to say the least. When challenged, the organisers responded: 'This is a non-judgmental movement that embraces all choices a woman wishes to make.' But what does that mean, exactly? Are we so 'supportive' of 'women's choices' that we are incapable of understanding and being critical of the context of sexism and classism that might lead women to 'choose' to work in a strip club? And that, rather than criticising 'women's choices' when we challenge the sex industry, we are actually challenging male power and men's choices to objectify and exploit women for their own pleasure/gain and an economy that fails to offer women opportunities to make a decent living that does not involve stripping, prostitution, or pornography.

In the face of severe lack of choice, 'SlutWalk' opted, not to push back, but to simply reframe the conversation. 'If you can't beat 'em, join 'em' was the message; as though if we can convince women (and society at large) that the sex industry can empower them, or if a few individual women claim they enjoy their work as strippers or escorts, then everything will be fine.

In the face of ongoing and virulent misogyny, sexual harassment, rape culture, porn culture, and violence against women, liberal feminism and the third wave seem to have taken the easy route, focusing on 'choice' and personal identity rather than confronting the root of the problem: patriarchy.

Choice became a key part of feminist discourse and action as an integral aspect and rallying call within the fight for reproductive rights – the right to choose whether or not we wanted to give birth and to choose what we wanted for our bodies and lives. This choice was, and is, a fundamental aspect of the feminist movement because it impacts our ability to be empowered and autonomous, not only in the home and as individuals, but in other, more public, aspects of life and society. Having reproductive rights means we get to make real choices about what happens to our bodies, real choices about education, work, marriage, family, and our day-to-day lives.

'Choice' is, therefore, not a bad concept, in and of itself. Women's right to choose, for example, whether or not they wish to give birth, marry, go to university, and so on, are successes achieved by the feminist movement and are nothing to scoff at. There was a time when women could do none of those things and, even today in some parts of the world, our reproductive rights are being chipped away at while in others women have few rights when it comes to marriage. The United Nations estimates that 2.5 billion women live in countries where marital rape is not a criminal offence. [3] There is still much to struggle against but despite the power of 'choice' in feminist discourse, using the word ad nauseam seems to have achieved very little and has been co-opted in a way that is weakening, rather than strengthening, the feminist movement.

Of late, it has become standard to talk about 'choice' in terms of individual choice rather than collective choice (and collective freedom), as though 'my choice' could not possibly affect anyone in the world except me. And, as though 'her choice' can somehow negate any justifiable criticism or questioning of said choice or the context within which said choice was made. Used in this context, it is a way a shutting down the conversation. And where would feminism be (and where will it go) without conversation and critique? We can be critical of choices without actually shaming women. We *need* to think critically about our choices if we are to understand and challenge the larger systems of power that impact our choices.

Many critics do see this 'anything goes'/'I do what I want' mantra as being one the more significant weaknesses of the third wave, and of 'postfeminist' discourse; and while this attitude is not universally applicable to the entire wave, it certainly seems to have built considerable momentum. Does anything and everything count as 'feminist' just because we choose it?

While making choices for ourselves can most certainly be empowering, and while I would never advocate against a woman's right to choose to wear stilettos, take her husband's name in marriage, or even to sell sex, that she can or does make this choice does not equate to 'feminism'. To make a choice for oneself – no matter how good or strong or fulfilled it might make us feel – does not necessarily advance the rights or status of women globally and it does not push back against the system of patriarchy. While feeling good is great, it does not constitute political change. In other words, feminism is a movement, not a self-help book.

Sexism is defined as 'prejudice or discrimination based on a person's sex or gender', but this definition leaves out a key aspect: systemic power. If sexism were simply about gendered bias, then theoretically sexism against men would be an equal problem to sexism against women. But what patriarchy does is to create a dominant group (men) that holds systemic, individual power over an oppressed group (women), creating a system wherein sexism keeps women, as a class, in a vulnerable and subordinate position. Without an acknowledgement of patriarchy as the foundation for sexism, we are left with a neoliberal understanding of gendered discrimination and, therefore, women's liberation, wherein empowerment and discrimination alike, is evaluated on a case-by-case basis. This is done so purely on the personal feelings and experiences as individuals, without taking into account the larger historical, cultural, and social context of male power.

If not for that context – a history of oppression of and violence against women as a class – sexism would not exist as a concept. It is for this reason that individual choices, divorced from that context, do not equate to feminist acts. Beyond that, the fetishisation of individual choice actually erases that context and the fact that patriarchy is a system of power. If we pretend that a woman's choice to, say, get breast augmentation surgery is a feminist choice because it is a woman who is making that choice, we ignore the context behind that choice – objectification, body-hatred, capitalism, porn culture – all things that contribute to the oppression of women as a whole.

Conveniently for capitalism and patriarchy, if any choice a woman makes is viewed as liberating or 'feminist', she can even 'choose' to support both systems and no one has the right to challenge her. In 'choice feminism', if a woman 'chooses' to produce pornography which, in turn, contributes to the oppression and objectification, not only of the women acting in pornography, but of women as a class and contributes to the billion-dollar pornography industry, her choice remains untouchable because she is a woman making a choice that empowers her. Maybe she even identifies as a feminist! Even better. Now pornography is feminist – just like that.

Famous burlesque performer, Dita Von Teese, is quoted as saying, in defence of critics who call her act disempowering for women: 'How can it be disempowering when I'm up there for seven minutes and I've just made $20 000? I feel pretty powerful.' [4] This statement embodies the problem with today's 'choice feminism', making 'power' about the individual at the expense of others. Beyond that, if money is the primary basis upon which we decide what empowers women and what does not, we are in danger of colluding with a system that is responsible for the exploitation and oppression of millions of people worldwide. If women are compensated in exchange for their objectified bodies or in exchange for sex acts, that doesn't actually challenge the sexist ideas behind that objectification and exploitation. We're left in the same position we started, despite the fact that Von Teese can buy a few more pairs of Louboutins.

'Choice', and the feminist context within which it was born, has been co-opted by dominant systems and the ideology of liberal feminism, and they have made it their own. We are now being told what choice and freedom looks like by those who have no particular interest in feminism or in ending gendered oppression. Those systems are the ones who tell us that being radical, or revolutionary or feminist even, is bad. That we will be picked on and attacked if we ask for too much or the wrong kind of freedom and empowerment. They offer us their version of choice, and tell us that empowerment is easily available to us – it's just got to be pleasant. And sexy. And, hey guess what! We don't even need the feminist movement anymore! We can 'choose' to objectify ourselves now because we are free. Slap an 'empowering' label on it and voilà! It's freedom and everyone else needs to shut up because 'it's a choice'.

Well, no. It isn't as simple as that. Feminism is about resisting patriarchy, not about being able to just join in. We don't 'win' because we can act in oppressive ways just as men do. When we argue either that sexism will happen with or without us, so we may as well participate and make the best of it, or that if women can profit financially, this will somehow erase sexism. Presenting a radical challenge to patriarchy is not just going along with it, it is not being told by *Girls Gone Wild* producers what freedom looks like or that because one woman is getting rich from strip shows we are all, consequently, emancipated.

Choice without politics or theory behind it doesn't hold power. 'Choice' at the expense of others – particularly the marginalised – is not radical nor does it promote equality. 'Choosing' to objectify ourselves, for example, is not what our second wave sisters meant when they fought for the 'right to choose'. And empowerment, through choice, was never intended to be about individual women, but rather about empowerment on a large scale, and freedom from oppression for all marginalised people.

Our focus on 'supporting women's choices' has made us fearful and has stifled critical thought. We've turned 'critique' into 'judgment', forcing us to separate the political from the personal. The risk in continuing down this path is enormous: we lose the ability to confront sexism and patriarchy and continue to have to work within a system that consistently treats women as less than human. Individualism is what supports neoliberalism: an ideology that has and continues to wreak havoc on collective struggles, social safety nets and services, and more generally, the poor and otherwise marginalised. If our goal, as feminists, is to address structural inequality and end the global pandemic that is violence against women and girls, we need to move beyond individualist discourse and concern ourselves with a collective empowerment that confronts this increasingly depoliticised version of 'choice'.

Depoliticising the personal: individualising body image and disordered eating in *The Beauty Myth*

Natalie Jovanovski

I am not attacking anything that makes women feel good; only what makes us feel bad in the first place. We all like to be desirable and feel beautiful. [1] — Naomi Wolf

One issue that tends to unite feminists adopting a variety of perspectives, from radical to liberal, from socialist to poststructuralist, is the dominant cultural representation of women's bodies by the diet and beauty industries. There is almost unanimous criticism from feminists regarding the way in which these industries operate to reinforce women's insecurities and, at the more radical end, women's subordination. One of the most famous examples of this criticism, and its ability to seemingly bridge different branches of feminism, is Naomi Wolf's book *The Beauty Myth: How Images of Beauty are Used Against Women*, first published in 1990. The analysis Wolf presents in *The Beauty Myth*, is frustratingly difficult to align with the traditional separation of radical and liberal feminist theory. While the book undoubtedly draws on more radical feminist notions of structural oppression, I argue here, that when it comes to providing solutions and potential ways forward, Wolf's work, disappointingly, falls back on a kind of unhelpful, liberal individualism that verges on blaming women for their own situation. While *The Beauty Myth* is still seen as one of the most important feminist texts on body image and disordered eating, it also represents a missed opportunity, as it ignores the possibility of collective action, agitating for women's liberation, and an end to patriarchy, as ways forward for helping women to develop healthier relationships with their bodies.

The influence of *The Beauty Myth*

Naomi Wolf has become seen as iconic, even in the mainstream media, due partially to the novelty and political potency of her arguments in texts such as *The Beauty Myth*, but also because of the marketability of her public persona. It is worth noting that feminist authors – like Wolf – espousing liberal ideas of the individual, constitute a certain type of feminist figure, one that is more public and accessible to mainstream audiences than other feminist sources, particularly those that may be more radical or challenging. This can be explained, at least in part, by the recourse to a rhetoric of individualism, but also a (rather paradoxical) reliance on antiquated stereotypes of femininity. As American academics Brenda Helmbrecht and Meredith Love [2] explain, particular pop culture feminists become 'iconic' precisely because their image conforms enough to existing patriarchal standards to hold broad appeal. Therefore, the impact of *The Beauty Myth* upon its release, and its subsequent influence on popular understandings of feminist critiques of beauty, cannot be fully understood without also accounting for the media interest in Wolf, herself. We cannot separate the interest in the text, entirely, from Wolf's charismatic public persona, her famous argument with libertarian feminist Camille Paglia, and the mass media's obsession (rather ironically) with her conventional attractiveness. It is also important to note that while *The Beauty Myth* is still seen as a foundational feminist text on the problems of body image, it has managed to garner popular appeal by returning to notions of individual choice and shying away from directly challenging or dismantling structures of patriarchal power.

The radical feminism of *The Beauty Myth*

The foundation for Wolf's initial analysis in *The Beauty Myth*, draws heavily on radical feminist concepts of patriarchy and male dominance, which rose to prominence during the so-called 'second-wave' of the 1970s. Her understanding of beauty practices, and the social influences that compel women to conform to them, is underpinned by recognising that under patriarchy, 'beauty' is just another symptom of a cultural disease that creates and reinforces a gender hierarchy of male dominance and female subordination. A critical feature of this, drawn from radical feminist theory, is the notion that gender is determined, not by some innate or individual feeling or sense of self, but by socially constructed norms that dictate appearance and behaviour and which (re)create women as a subordinate sex class. Wolf adds to this by arguing that the continuing prominence of normative, feminine beauty practices, such as dieting, can be seen as a reaction to the gains made for women by feminists in the 1970s and early 1980s. She writes, for example, that 'we are in the midst of a violent backlash against feminism that uses images of female beauty as a political weapon against women's advancement; the beauty myth'. [3] Central to Wolf's thesis, then, is the idea that beauty is used to harm women's advancement and that the notion of beauty itself is a form of political sedative, keeping women in their place.

Wolf also places these ideas in historical context, stating that 'every generation since about 1830 has had to fight its version of the beauty myth'. [4] Wolf's critical engagement with women's historical subordination, as well as men's dominance, situates her voice within a kind of feminism that explicitly politicises women's inequalities and locates a system of male dominance as a critical factor behind women's reliance on 'beauty' as a cultural arbiter of success. Like many who came before her, most notably Andrea Dworkin, [5] Wolf problematises dieting as a primary symptom of women's subordination. Rather than focusing on the individual woman, which is what psychological literature has always tended to do, Wolf focuses on how cultural institutions encourage and reinforce 'thinness' in women as a disciplinary mechanism.

The focus on the cultural obsession with the emaciated and 'controlled' female body, in *The Beauty Myth,* is in stark contrast to the way that women's disordered relationships with food are typically presented in mainstream psychological or non-feminist work. Her repositioning of eating 'disorders' as symptoms of sick culture rather than a sick individual woman shares much in common with more radical works. Indeed, later in the book, Wolf goes as far as to say that 'women must claim [eating disorders] as political damage done to us'. [6] This emphasis on the political origins of women's personal psychopathologies gives Wolf's work quite a radical flavour. She conveys her position as one that is firmly aligned with previous second wave feminist sentiments on beauty, and gives the impression that her solutions to the problem will be political, too.

The liberal feminism of *The Beauty Myth*

Liberal feminism has been described as a combination of liberal political theory and feminist analysis; a study of the 'rights, autonomy and reason' [7] of the individual woman. While the blending of liberal and feminist politics can be perceived as a progressive step for women in the 21st century, some feminist writers, especially those with radical politics, have been vocal about their distrust of individualistic perspectives in feminist theory. The staunch liberal tradition of championing 'rationality' in the individual has been one of the dominant criticisms launched against liberal feminist writings by radical feminists. In *Toward a Feminist Theory of the State*, radical feminist legal theorist Catharine MacKinnon discusses the notion of 'rationality' in liberal feminist politics as being built on a framework of cultural and institutional sexism. Central to MacKinnon's argument, is the understanding that 'rationality' could only be conceived of within the context of male dominance and, thus, any 'rational' conclusion made by women within this landscape was based on their cultural objectification. MacKinnon's work therefore explicitly problematises the liberal feminist notions of 'rationality' and 'choice'.

From MacKinnon's perspective, the notion that women can use

their 'rationality' to make truly informed or free decisions about beauty practices is flawed because, in reality, the existing cultural landscape only provides women with limited choices. Under a system of male dominance, women either become complicit in their own objectification or become objectifiers of others. In *The Beauty Myth*, Wolf calls on the rationality of the female reader through the implicit encouragement of a liberal feminist position and, in some ways, fits between being both the objectified and the objectifier. In the concluding chapter of *The Beauty Myth*, entitled 'Beyond the Beauty Myth', she explains how a change in media images addressing thinness is not enough to curb the problems she has outlined in the preceding chapters:

> While we cannot directly affect the images, we can drain them of their power. We can turn away from them, look directly at one another, and find alternative images of beauty in a female subculture ... We can lift ourselves and other women out of the myth – but only if we are willing to seek out and support and really look at the alternatives. [8]

Wolf's suggestion that women can 'turn away' from harmful cultural images is contradictory to the more radically informed feminist angle of the critique she presents in the early part of the book, where her key argument is centred around the pervasiveness of the beauty myth and its harmful grip on women's lives. The implication that women should merely 'find alternative images' of femininity is simplistic and contradictory, as the majority of the book actually demonstrates how difficult it is for women to avoid the stronghold of the beauty myth. Wolf's liberal feminist position in terms of solutions offered to improve women's relationships with their bodies and eating/food can be seen as a fitting example of MacKinnon's assertion that liberal feminist 'rationality' is implicitly couched within male-centred politics that espouse objectification. Rather than challenging these politics, Wolf places ultimate trust in women's 'rationality' to change their own harmful relationships with food and, in doing so, shifts the burden onto women themselves, revealing an overreliance on individual, as opposed to political and institutional, change.

The notion that liberal feminist politics falls short of providing women with the adequate tools for emancipation is not new. Referring to the tensions between liberal politics and feminist analysis, Ruth Groenhout explains that: 'if liberalism, viewed accurately, is simply male dominance writ large, feminist liberalism is an oxymoron'. [9] Wolf's liberal feminism, in relation to women's relationships with their bodies, is therefore, from Groenhout's perspective, a contradiction in terms. On the one hand, it suggests that the broader culture and structures of power are responsible for disseminating the beauty myth, yet it relies on the individual to find the solution.

This seeming contradiction between structure and individual agency is also evident in Wolf's use of the term 'choice' to describe women's engagement with alternative forms of 'beauty':

> Women will be free of the beauty myth when we can choose to use our faces and clothes and bodies as simply one form of self-expression out of a full range of others. We can dress up for our pleasure, but we must speak up for our rights. [10]

Wolf's use of the term 'choice' is somewhat superficial, however, as the concept of 'choice' with regard to beauty practices can, in reality, only ever be understood within the pre-existing cultural scripts of ideal femininity. Given that Wolf herself argues that cultural standards of beauty are predicated upon the ideology that women are 'worth less', it is surprising that she relies on the individual woman to 'choose' to 'feel worth more'. [11] Wolf's decontextualised use of the term 'choice' can be seen as an implicit reinforcement of body-consciousness in women, as it idealistically resituates power (and responsibility) as residing in the mind of the individual woman rather than within the social and political structures that shape her.

One of the major criticisms levelled against the proclamations of 'choice' found in *The Beauty Myth*, comes from radical feminist scholar Sheila Jeffreys. In her book *Beauty and Misogyny*, Jeffreys refers to the assumption that women have the power to 'choose' their beauty practices as erroneous and ill-conceived. According to Jeffreys, 'the absence of any alternative culture within which women can identify a different way to be a woman enforces oppressive practices'. [12] When women are confronted with a cultural landscape that psychologically and physically inflicts beauty practices onto them, and they participate in these practices, at least in part because of a conscious or unconscious fear of social stigma and ostracism, then their actions cannot be simply conceived of as 'choices'. As a result, I argue that Wolf's depiction of 'choice' inadvertently strengthens the shame that women already feel about our bodies and our lack of control over defining our relationships with our bodies.

The now-popular notion that women freely 'choose' to engage in beauty practices, such as dieting, is painted by some feminists, like Jeffreys, as a failure to acknowledge how gender norms operate to oppress women and to situate them within the social hierarchy as the denigrated 'other'. Wolf, presents an alternative depiction of women's choices to engage in beauty regimens when she almost apologetically states: 'I am not attacking anything that makes women feel good; only what makes us feel bad in the first place. We all like to be desirable and feel beautiful.' [13]

Wolf's proclamation that she is not 'attacking [what] makes women feel good' is a powerful statement; one that inadvertently reflects how her reliance on liberal feminism means that she then hesitates to politicise women's engagement with beauty practices on a personal level. Rather than continuing to view dieting and beauty practices as part of an overarching system of harmful gender norms, Wolf reverts to individualistic thinking in an attempt to avoid alienating her readers. This stance, however popular, is also problematic. In shifting the discussion from structures of subordination and oppression that create beauty norms, to individual feelings about beauty and essentialist notions that all women must want to 'feel beautiful', the conclusion of *The Beauty Myth* mutes the strong critique that comes before it.

The idea that beauty practices, such as dieting, can be reduced to a discussion of what makes women 'feel good' has also been criticised in a range of psychological and sociological literature. Some psychological research, has pointed to the danger of relying on women's 'enjoyment' of dieting practices as an indicator of psychological wellbeing. A study on women's 'positive' experiences of restrictive eating, found that in their sample of 18 clinically-diagnosed participants, anorexic symptoms were viewed as holding both personal and social benefits. Among some of these benefits, women reported gaining enjoyment from their restrictive eating behaviour as it gave them a sense of control and made them feel more attractive. [14] The researchers argued that the aspects of eating disorders that these women perceived as positive, carry clues into the culturally-seductive nature of starvation in women; something which Wolf largely overlooks in her encouragement of women's engagement with beauty practices, as long as it makes them 'feel good'.

Another factor that Wolf overlooks is how women are encouraged to view beauty practices as positive, and even 'feminist', experiences in some popular cultural discourses. In her article on beauty advertising, 'Entitled to Consume: Postfeminist Femininity and a Culture of Post-Critique', literature professor Michelle Lazar analysed the content of contemporary beauty advertisements. Examining discourses on the basis of their objectifying messages, she found that part of the seduction of engaging in beauty practices is the social and cultural promise it offers women. Lazar argues that engaging in beauty practices has been constructed in contemporary advertising as 'women's *right* to be beautiful' shown most prominently in the tagline for cosmetic giant L'Oréal, 'because you're worth it' – and reflects how beauty advertisers have appropriated feminist language about women's rights and subverted it to reinforce pre-existing norms of women's unhealthy relationships with their own bodies. [15] Wolf's encouragement of Western beauty practices that make women 'feel good', therefore, decontextualise how women are taught to value themselves in the first place. Her use of liberal feminist analysis in terms of moving forward does not offer any truly viable solutions for change. Rather, in reverting to a decontextualisation of women's 'choices', and suggesting women can simply think or wish away the power of *The Beauty Myth*, Wolf shifts the blame for women's ongoing subordination back onto women themselves.

Beyond 'body-consciousness'

The appropriation of feminist language to sell beauty products and the individualisation and depoliticisation of beauty and weight loss are still very prominent. Size acceptance arguments have become a new and popular way of addressing a culture that is obsessed with women's weight and diets. The aim of these arguments is to try and diversify images of women in the media, giving women a range of body shapes to identify with, in an effort to promote a positive body image. Rather than trying to overcome the objectified representations of women's bodies, the solution is presented as providing a greater range of women's bodies to objectify. In 2003, the international beauty company, Dove released its 'The Real Truth About Beauty' campaign targeting women aged 18 to 64. The campaign, marketed extensively throughout both Western and non-Western countries, set out to expose the digital airbrushing techniques of contemporary beauty advertisements and to redefine what 'real' women look like. Dove later went on to launch their 'Campaign for Real Beauty', which used a diverse range of body shapes and sizes to emphasise what they referred to as 'real' women; women who were traditionally seen as overweight, or had freckles, age lines, and so on. While commercially successful, there has been little evidence to suggest that the promotion of 'different' bodies, in campaigns such as Dove's, reduce women's surveillance over their bodies and, subsequently, improves their relationships with food. In fact, in one recent study looking at the promotion of 'plus-size' bodies in fashion and beauty discourses, it actually appears that these attempts reinforce body-conscious attitudes among women. The researchers explain that, 'comparing oneself to a plus-size model may have deflating effects if one feels rather similar to the model'. [16] Indeed, placing more attention to the weight and shape of the body appears to indirectly reinforce body-policing and restrictive eating behaviours in women, regardless of whether or not the image in question has been modified to meet 'realistic' standards.

The answer then, cannot lie in believing that beauty companies, out to sell products, can produce any kind of pro-woman revolution. Nor can the answer lie in hoping that some women can find solace in particular beauty practices, despite their oppressive underpinnings, or that individual women should, on their own, attempt to shut out all the cultural conditioning about dieting, food and beauty. Moving beyond the individual, and moving beyond body-consciousness, to reclaim forms of collective action, for a change away from judging women by their bodies, whatever their shape and size, and placing this as part of the larger struggle for women's equality, would truly be a step in the right direction.

Questioning 'choice' and 'agency' in the mail-order bride industry

Kaye Quek

Like sex workers, mail-order brides are commonly depicted as victims of patriarchy and the ultimate symbol of female oppression ... Instead, [agency] allows us to see how women assert dignity, express strength, and in doing so resist and transform the role and image of passive sex object and submissive wife. [1] — Nicole Constable

In much recent feminist writing on the mail-order bride ('MOB') industry, there is an assumption that to identify MOB marriage as exploitative of women is also to imply that women are incapable of resisting oppression in its various forms. To describe the industry as premised on gender inequality – in that it involves far greater risks for women than for men, and draws on sexist (and racist) stereotypes – is held to 're-victimise' women, to overlook individual 'choice', and above all, to deny the expression of female 'agency'. [2] In this chapter, I examine the growing number of feminist analyses which suggest that the MOB industry should be understood first and foremost in terms of individual agency and choice. The chapter seeks to illuminate the shortcomings of this type of argument, which misattributes the 'robbing' of female agency to feminist scholars critical of the MOB trade, [3] rather than to the practice of MOB marriage itself. I show that, far from being based on an equal partnership or reciprocity of care, the MOB industry promotes and facilitates a particular kind of marriage that is characterised by sexual, racial and class inequalities between the men and women it involves. In this context, representing MOB marriage as simply a matter of individual 'choice' risks normalising a form of marriage that is essentially servile in its basis, and whose features feminist activists, since the period of the 1850s, have sought to eradicate from marriage as whole.

Mail-order bride marriages can be described as unions arranged through for-profit marriage agencies, between women in the developing world and men in developed or industrialised states. In a typical case of MOB marriage, men pay a fee to an agency in order to communicate with women whom they have selected as potential brides after having viewed an agency's online catalogue of women. [4] Once a man has chosen a bride and obtained her consent to marriage, MOB agencies will often take a leading role in facilitating the migration of women for an additional fee, by completing visa applications and organising the transportation required for their relocation abroad. Women advertised on MOB websites are typically young, with varying levels of education, and from regions of the world experiencing political instability or economic hardship. [5] In contrast, male users are most often middle-class, middle-aged, divorced and white; as well as between 20 to 50 years older than the woman they are marrying. [6] They predominantly come from countries such as the United States ('US'), Canada, Germany, Australia and Japan. [7] There are no MOB websites advertising men as available for marriage to women in the non-West, nor are there sites promoting the marriage of women in the West to men in developing states. [8] Rather, the MOB industry bases its business on global structures of gender and economic inequality, seeking to pair men specifically from the industrialised world with women from economically impoverished states.

Against this backdrop, it is perhaps surprising that an increasing number of self-identified feminists seek to conceptualise the MOB trade as, primarily, a matter of female agency and choice. Yet, in contemporary feminist scholarship on the issue, it is these liberal and poststructuralist perspectives that are now dominant. The work of feminist anthropologist Nicole Constable is one such example. [9] Constable charges feminist scholars, who are critical of the industry, with causing harm to women, by representing them as 'accept[ing] of their own subservience' effectively 'rob[bing] women of their ability to express intelligence, resistance, creativity, independence, dignity and strength'. [10] In her view, a more useful approach is to focus on women's 'agency', or the 'subtle and complex renderings of power' which counter 'the sorts of homogenising images that construct women as victims and men as agents'. [11] Constable's discussion directly links analyses of female exploitation in the MOB industry with a form of racism on the part of feminist critics; such works are seen to reflect 'a highly problematic Orientalist, essentialist, and universalising feminist approach' and are said to constitute 'a bad feminist argument'. [12]

Similarly, the human rights theorist Nora Demleitner argues that 'mail-order brides' should be seen as 'choosing' the type of marriage they are entering into. Drawing on the language of individual choice, she contends that women 'voluntarily choose to come to a foreign country, to marry a foreign man who is also often a stranger ... "mail-order brides" are neither pawns nor goods'. [13] Like Constable, Demleitner identifies works that focus on the limitations on women's choices and exercise of agency as a form of oppression against the women themselves. She asserts that by 'characteris[ing] the women as incapable of helping themselves', these structural analyses 'revictimise the women and turn them truly into objects'. [14]

A fundamental flaw in these discussions is their tendency to position feminist scholarship as the chief source of women's subordination, rather than the practice of MOB marriage, itself. Indeed, in these works, the type of marriage marketed by the MOB industry is largely unexamined or assumed to be neutral; in other words, little attention is paid to the relations of power between men and women that the MOB trade seeks to facilitate. In contrast, an examination of the content of MOB websites brings into focus the shortcomings of choice- and agency-based analyses. Far from promoting a form of marriage based on mutual companionship and equality, the MOB trade can be seen to advocate a type of marriage that is purposefully *unequal*, and which seeks to advance the interests of men while actively minimising and constraining women's ability to exercise agency and resistance.

The particular concern of the industry to match men from wealthy states of the global North with women from economically poorer countries – with no interest shown for any other combination or pairing – points to the inequality that is built into MOB marriage. On MOB websites, male buyers are encouraged to view 'foreign women' as especially easy to exploit, through the use of racist and sexist stereotypes or with reference to the vulnerabilities women are likely to face upon migration. Women who migrate to the US for marriage, for example, are required to stay married for at least two years, before they obtain permanent residency or are allowed recourse to public funds. They are also likely to suffer from a lack of knowledge of local laws, customs, and language; and from the absence of a support network in the country to which they have migrated. [15]

The position of power that these circumstances afford male buyers is not lost on the industry, but used to promote this type of marriage to men in the West. One agency, for example, encourages its male users to take advantage of women's tenuous migration status, stating 'there will be fewer tedious discussions about the "relationship" when your fiancée's vocabulary is limited to yes, sex, and Green Card!' [16] In other cases, women are represented on MOB websites in terms of racial and ethnic stereotypes. Sites often make reference to Asian women's (supposedly) small physical stature and allude to their sexual submissiveness. The agency Heart of Asia describes Asian women thus: 'They are normally Petite [sic] and slender with delicate bone structure. They typically have smooth, silky, hairless skin.' [17] In contrast to the 'smallness' attributed to Asian women, women from Latin American countries are marketed as 'exotic' and sexually inviting. One business states: '[Latin] women will look you in the eyes with a lust and

hunger you have never seen outside Latin America. Its [sic] nature at
its finest with the beach girls of Rio Brazil.' [18] As feminist scholars of
prostitution industries note, the use of such racially-based stereotypes
serve to encourage men to view 'foreign' women as less than fully
human, and therefore, as 'legitimate targets for exploitation'. [19] Where
the core business of the MOB trade is to pair men with women who
are compromised in their ability to meaningfully resist exploitation,
it can be seen that the industry itself – far more so than feminist
scholarship – limits and constrains women's capacity to effectively
exercise agency.

Further examination of how women are represented in the
industry gives lie to the characterisation of MOB marriage merely as
a matter of individual 'choice'. One major difficulty with the current
focus on 'choice' and 'agency' in much feminist scholarship is that
it only relates to one half of the equation – the supply side – and
does not take into consideration why this form of marriage may be
attractive to some men. On MOB websites, however, the benefits to
men are made plain as foreign women are portrayed as submissive,
subservient, and accepting of very traditional gender roles. The site of
MOB agency Manila Beauty, for instance, seeks to promote marriage
to Filipino women by contrasting their attentiveness to men's 'needs',
with the less caring approach that is supposedly common to Western
women. It states:

> While many women that you are used to would never cater to
> you like in old-fashioned times, a filipina [sic] will insist that
> she make you more comfortable ... She will do everything
> to shows [sic] that she appreciates having you as her man.
> There are not too many girls like this anymore (especially
> domestically), but rest assured this character trait is ingrained
> in the mind of the average filipina [sic]. [20]

This same theme of female subservience is apparent across the industry, with another agency, Chance for Love, similarly promoting the idea that foreign-born wives are particularly amenable to inequality in marriage. The agency explains: 'In Russia, she doesn't have a choice to stay home to take care of her husband, house and her children – for her, it is a dream ... she is the weaker gender and she knows it.' [21] Notably, the promise of providing men with a 'traditional' wife, made by MOB sites, appears in line with the demands made by male users of the industry. It is pointed out by male consumers in contexts such as online discussion forums that 'it can be much less expensive to purchase a wife than to pay for prostitution services, which don't also include housekeeping and cooking'. [22] The point here is not to suggest that women are unequivocally without any 'choice' or 'agency' in this form of marriage. Rather, it is to illustrate that representing the MOB trade principally in terms of agency is to overlook the extent to which these expressions are constrained by the very nature of the practice. In this context, the almost exclusive focus on female 'agency' in current analyses might itself be considered 'a bad feminist argument', as the language of choice serves to normalise and legitimise a form of marriage based on inequality and female servility.

Lastly, it is worth considering the degree to which the industry itself promotes the objectification and commodification of women involved in MOB marriage. The issue of commodification is important to examine in the context of the present discussion, given that feminist critics of the trade are often charged, by those who favour focusing on 'choice', with treating women as objects. [23] As before, the argument can be made that such criticism is misdirected, and better made in relation to the MOB trade itself.

The websites of MOB agencies provide clear examples of the industry's objectification and commodification of women. In one sense, this is reflected in the increasing use of online purchasing icons and processes on MOB sites. On the websites of businesses such as Anastasia Russian Brides, the appearance of online shopping prompts, such as 'shopping cart' features, [24] situate women as the implied goods for purchase, which can be bought in the same manner as books or furniture can be bought through an online store. Although some supporters of the MOB trade argue that it is services (such as introductions to women or their contact information) that are being sold on MOB sites rather than women themselves, [25] the language used to describe women in the industry undermines the notion that it is only services, and not persons, that are being sold. Several businesses, for example, liken the process of obtaining a 'mail-order bride' to the practice of ordering food. The agency A Foreign Affair ('AFA') states, 'luckily, AFA has made searching its voluminous database as easy as ordering a pizza' [26] while another agency describes its online site as 'a candy store'. [27] As several women's organisations point out, the construction of women as consumable objects for purchase by male buyers is significant, as men often believe that they own and, therefore, have a right to exert control over a woman and to place specific demands on her person. [28] The fact that women have managed to escape such situations of harm resulting from MOB marriages attests to the resilience feminist scholars have long known and shown women to possess. However, to represent the practice principally in terms of its 'expressions' of 'female agency' is to *misrepresent* the gendered power dynamics at the heart of the trade.

Feminist analyses that focus on women's exercise of 'choice' and 'agency' in the MOB industry risk normalising, and even romanticising, a form of inequality and abuse. MOB marriage represents a particular type of marriage; one that is founded on the economic, social and gender inequality of the women it involves. Rather than providing an introductory service for two equal, consenting adults, the purpose of the MOB industry is to source women specifically from developing regions of the world to be wives for men in the West, *because* such women are seen to be especially lacking in agency and the means to subsist. Although it is possible that in some individual cases women may not experience direct harm from their husband, and may even enjoy better living conditions than prior to their migration, it remains that the objective of the industry itself – clearly shown on MOB websites – is to provide men with women who will fulfil the role of a subservient wife. To suggest that it is feminist critics of the trade who are 'robbing' women of their agency and resilience is both misleading and highly problematic. A more useful approach would be to consider the type of relationships being promoted by the trade in seeking to understand the numerous constraints that are often imposed upon women's freedom.

Feminism and the neoliberal state

Margaret Thornton

The state of things

'The state' is an ambiguous and vexed concept for feminist scholars. Bringing women into the state was the primary focus of first and second wave feminism, which meant that feminist campaigns for justice had to be directed to the instrumentalities of the same masculinist state that legitimated the injustices in the first place. That a demonstrably hostile entity was expected to transmute itself miraculously into a beneficent one has been a central paradox perennially besetting feminist reformism. Indeed, Wendy Brown suggests that the notion of women seeking protection *from* masculinist institutions *against* men is more in keeping with a politics of feudalism than freedom. [1] The state must nevertheless *appear* to be fair in order to maintain its legitimacy, [2] and despite misgivings, this veneer of fairness initially acted as a spur to feminist campaigners. The need for the liberal state to accommodate divergent interests also attests to the fact that it is not a unitary entity.

The state that Marx critiqued, for example, was a centralised state 'with its ubiquitous organs of standing army, police, bureaucracy, clergy, and judicature' which served middle-class society in its struggles against feudalism. [3] Typically, Marx paid no attention to the gendered or raced character of the state. The Marxist critique fell out of favour with the collapse of Communist regimes in Europe, and the anti-essentialist swing induced by post-modernism. 'The state' came to be viewed as old-fashioned and one-dimensional. Foucault's concept of governmentality shaped a more comprehensive and fluid understanding in accordance with new ways of seeing that focused on the way fields of action are structured through discourse. [4] Rather than the state being understood as a discrete sphere as in conventional political theory, every nook and cranny of society, including the family and the self, are viewed as productive sites of meaning. Governmentality also stresses the importance of power, which has struck a chord with feminist poststructuralist accounts of the state. [5]

Nevertheless, an understanding of the dispersal of power does not mean that we should go to the other extreme and regard the state as having 'withered away'. Neomarxist scholars believe that postmodernists have gone too far in disaggregating the state:

> The postmodernist call to reject unitary or 'grand' theoretical perspectives (metanarratives) has inspired 'governmentality' theorists to move closer to an understanding of power as an almost ethereal force, so dispersed throughout the body of society that it has little relation to the traditional centres of political and economic decision making in capitalist social orders. [6]

While I accept that the state is not a static entity, it is not ethereal either, for it remains a powerful masculinist force that is also raced, heterosexed, able-bodied and classed. However, the contemporary deployment of a range of discourses around individual freedom, choice and success under the rubric of 'the market' may convey the impression that the state is ethereal.

It is notable that the time 'the state' fell out of favour coincided with the collapse of the category 'woman'. This centrepiece of second wave feminism began to be attacked, like the state, as cumbrous, old-fashioned and essentialist. 'Engagement with the state' also lost its intellectual appeal for feminist scholars seduced by the micropolitical and the seductiveness of bodies, sexualities and popular culture.

At the same time, women's studies centres in universities came under attack and were either closed down or replaced by configurations such as gender, sexuality and diversity. Despite the importance of acknowledging the variegated and heteroglossic nature of women, the disintegration of a unifying subject weakened the political commitment to feminism. Once women had been 'let in' to public life, it became fashionable within popular and political discourses to aver that feminism was passé. Even former conservative prime minister, John Howard, entered the fray by referring to the 'postfeminist age'. [7]

The project of first and second wave feminism to place women in the state *qua* public life could be said to be reflective of an epistemic moment where a particular construction of 'woman' was politically and strategically necessary. This unidimensional woman also provided a point of contestation for those who felt excluded by virtue of their race, class or disability. While feminist theorists, such a Gayatri Chakravorty Spivak [8] or Judith Butler, [9] have alluded to the way that the category 'woman' has been invoked epistemically to challenge its surface essentialism, a focus on the capillaries has served to deflect attention away from the insidious power of the state. It is arguable that the fragmentation of the state in feminist theory, while itself a by-product of postmodernism, has also contributed to the marginalisation of a politics of economic justice for women.

By the millennial turn, the embrace of neoliberalism had caused virtually all traces of feminist influence to be erased from official discourses, including government policies, other than in so far as subordinate, dependent, entrepreneurial or commodified subject positions were concerned. The 'femocrat', for example, a distinctive Australian neologism, has now virtually disappeared from feminist discourse, apart from the occasional allusion by an overseas scholar. [10]

Taken unawares while preoccupied with 'the capillaries', feminists have discovered that they lack either a politics or a theory to deal with the neoliberal swing that has pulled the rug from under our feet. Catharine MacKinnon famously postulated well over two decades ago that 'feminism has no theory of the state'. [11] Governmentality theory, with its multiple discourses and sensitivity to the play of power, does provide a way of understanding the dynamic constitution of the state in regard to gender, but this may not go far enough in capturing the facilitative role of the neoliberal state in relation to the market within a global economy.

In the late 1980s, Franzway, Court and Connell asked with considerable prescience: 'Will the state be captured by the New Right and transformed into a monetarists' heaven with devastating consequences for feminism including the femocrats?' [12] The answer must be an unequivocal 'yes'. The issue has acquired a singular urgency as feminist scholarship in the academy is contracting as a result of ever-increasing government intervention in universities, which includes pressure to teach 'relevant' skills and satisfy specified research priorities. In a neoliberal environment that has fostered a resurgence of benchmark masculinity and the privileging of applied knowledge, critical theory of any kind is regarded as a luxury.

From social liberalism to neoliberalism

While freedom and equality are the key features of liberalism, they are counterpoised against one another. Freedom is maximised when conservativism is in the ascendancy, equality when progressivism triumphs. As a result of the tension between them, Brown suggests that liberalism perennially produces a Nietzschean notion of *ressentiment* within one side or the other as a result of its paradoxical promise of freedom *and* equality:

> A strong commitment to freedom vitiates the fulfilment of the equality promise and breeds *ressentiment* as welfare state liberalism – attenuations of the unmitigated licence of the rich and powerful on behalf of the 'disadvantaged'. Conversely, a strong commitment to equality, requiring heavy state interventionism and economic redistribution, attenuates the commitment to freedom and breeds *ressentiment* expressed as neoconservative anti-statism, racism, charge of reverse racism, and so forth. [13]

Thus, when the liberal pendulum swings to the left, embracing collective good and equality, it arouses *ressentiment* on the part of conservatives, who believe that their freedom is inhibited. Once the pendulum swings to the right, the *ressentiment* of the left is roused, for the untrammelled freedom to satisfy individual desire prevents the realisation of equality. I do not wish to overstate the pendulum metaphor by suggesting that the responses are automatic as, like all discourses, they are necessarily marked by discontinuities, breaks, thresholds and limits. [14]

Feminist critiques have long unmasked the universal citizen of the liberal state as male. [15] He is the autonomous inhabitant of the public sphere who has been able to slough off the domestic sphere and its particularities of relationality and care, which are compatible with neither freedom nor equality. Despite the best endeavours of feminist scholars to stress the importance of the symbiotic relationship between public and private life, relationality and care remain marginal to liberal state theory. The social liberalism that is associated with the inchoate welfare state of the 20th century nevertheless took halting steps to respond to feminist claims that freedom and equality be reconceptualised, but the modest gains achieved have now been largely eviscerated.

Under social liberalism, the untrammelled play of individual freedom was tempered by a notion of collective good. State regulation and progressive taxation were employed to effect a modicum of distributive justice, bolstered by a vibrant civil society. In contrast, the cluster of values associated with neoliberalism maximises the individual freedom associated with the masculine, and minimises the feminised values of collective good and distributive justice, thereby signalling what Marian Sawer refers to as a 'sex change' in the state. [16] Under neoliberalism, we find that deregulation is the order of the day as the state purports to have devolved the management of the economy to the market. The public sphere, *qua* government, has contracted and public goods, such as utilities, transport, health and education have been privatised and commodified. Nothing is of significance unless it has use value in the market.

It was under the social liberalism of the late 20th century that women were grudgingly accepted by the state as legal subjects after decades of struggle. In terms of liberal theory, exclusion and the most blatant inequalities could then be treated as aberrations that needed to be corrected because they did not comport with the liberal commitment to (formal) equality between citizens. Measures such as equal pay, no-fault divorce, the proscription of family violence, changes to sexual assault laws, the setting up of women's advisory units within state and federal governments, and the passage of sex discrimination legislation, were all notable examples of reformist initiatives designed to remedy the anomalies of the past. The recognition of the category 'woman' coincided with the high point of social liberalism under prime minister Gough Whitlam in the early 1970s but at that very moment, the first seeds of neoliberalism were sown when Whitlam cut tariffs on imports by 25 per cent. [17] Since that time, neoliberals have set out with a vengeance to reassert their freedom and neutralise the gains of social liberalism.

Instead of the social state, an ethic of individualism prevails, in which citizens are expected to take responsibility for the course of their own lives. If they do not succeed, they have only themselves to blame. The concept of individual responsibility has been popularised and made palatable by stressing the liberal rhetoric of individual freedom, autonomy and choice. In contrast, the ethic of care associated with social liberalism is dismissed pejoratively by neoliberals as a manifestation of the 'nanny state'. [18] The feminised language alerts us to the reassertion of the masculinity of the neoliberal state and its latent hostility towards the feminine. Rather than equality and distributive justice as the fundamental underpinnings of the state, there has been a discernible shift in favour of *in*equality, exemplified by the emphasis on competition policy, entrepreneurialism and the market. While inequality has always been an undeniable dimension of a free enterprise society, its potential for excess was formerly reined in by state regulation.

It should not be thought, however, that the state has opted out altogether under neoliberalism. While market freedom, deregulation and privatisation are the hallmarks of the neoliberal political economy, it is the state that remains the driver of policy. While the state may have ostensibly devolved responsibility for the good of the economy to the market, it retains power by operating insidiously through the market; there is no invisible hand at work here. The appearance of self-regulation through the market is one of the most successful ploys of neoliberalism. It highlights the cogency of Foucault's governmentality thesis, for the discourse of the free market does not emanate from a discrete sphere, but represents the voices of the powerful operating through multiple sites.

Thus, the state has not self-destructed under neoliberalism. It remains firmly in control, albeit behind the scenes, single-mindedly pump-priming the economy and suppressing social justice policies that are regarded as an 'impost on business'. The state *qua* government works to boost the market by restricting social welfare policies for individuals but sponsoring 'corporate welfare' in order to tempt profitable ventures away from global competitors. In this marketised and privatised incarnation of the state, social justice and gender equality are passé. The market has transformed citizens into consumers obsessed with lifestyle and the visible markers of success. What sense do vestigial egalitarian measures make in a state committed to competition policy and inequality?

Neoconservatism

Hand-in-glove with neoliberalism is neoconservatism. While a conservative morality is not the necessary corollary of a conservative economic policy, there is a convenient ideological intersection between them. The state's adoption of a conservative stance has resulted in the unravelling of the feminist agenda in conjunction with an anti-feminist discourse. 'Women' have once again become *passé* as a category of analysis as the *ressentiment* of the right is realised.

Instead of 'women', 'feminism' or 'gender', the political focus now tends to be on 'the family'. The transition has occurred as a result of the intersection of economic neoliberalism and social conservatism borrowed from the American religious right, a conjunction which has been brilliantly exposed by Marion Maddox. [19] The revived discourse of 'the family' refers to the traditional two-parent heterosexual family, although not necessarily the norm in contemporary Australia. It is nevertheless recognised by moral conservatives that it is not feasible for them to continue to corral women with children behind the white picket fence 1950s style. Contemporary conservatism has had to acknowledge that women are now a legitimate part of the paid workforce, even if they have young children. Neoliberalism has deployed this reality to its own ends. Full-time work is still frowned upon, but women with (school-age) children have been seized upon as the ideal flexible workers. Echoing the reserve army theory of women's labour long identified by feminist scholars, [20] women can be brought out of the home at times of high demand, such as the need to work in retail for two or three hours in the middle of the day and be home again in time to collect the children from school.

The preference theory of labour market theorist, Catherine Hakim, [21] has struck a chord with neoliberals and neoconservatives alike, for it naturalises the assignation of both paid precarious work and unpaid caring work to women in ways that crucially serve the state, thereby underscoring the symbiosis between public and private life of liberal theory. In brief, Hakim's thesis is that the differences between men's and women's labour market experiences and pay are explicable in terms of the lifestyle choices women make, including electing to work less hours or part-time, or choosing different work from men. She argues that 'work-centred women' can be equal at work because of initiatives such as anti-discrimination legislation but, by the same token, 'home-centred women' should not be denied equality because of the choices they have made. The third group, to which most women now belong, comprise the 'adaptive women' who fit in paid work around the needs of the family.

While many women may opt for flexibility at work, particularly when they have family responsibilities, this does not mean that they favour precarious jobs that are exploitative. They appear to consent to poor working conditions because there are no alternatives or they lack bargaining power. Rational choice theory underpins the neoliberal notion of individual responsibility, which conveniently glides over structural discrimination. Rational choice theory disguises the way in which increasing numbers of unskilled women workers and those from non-English-speaking backgrounds are subordinated through precarious work. By a certain sleight of hand, freedom and equality thereby appear to be reconciled in the case of precarious workers.

While a great deal of attention is presently being paid to work/life balance, the assumption is that it is women, the 'marginalised care givers', [22] who are expected to do the balancing. Precarious work, as the descriptor graphically implies, denotes insecurity, inadequate pay, dependency and/or poverty, both at the time of working and in old age. Work/life balance confirms that substantive equality remains a chimera for women. The low status accorded the bearing of life and caring for it, compared with the destruction of life and the endangering of it, as in war, again signifies the way a gendered dichotomy is mapped onto the priorities of the neoliberal state. Child care workers are so low paid that agencies encounter difficulty in recruiting and retaining qualified staff. [23] In contrast, war service is extolled as heroic and carries connotations of good citizenship. [24]

Neoliberalism and neoconservatism have colluded in the

development of an anti-feminist agenda that has seen a sharp turn away from the concerns of social liberalism. It is only in the last decade or so – as neoliberal policies have taken hold – that neoliberalism and neoconservatism have begun to coalesce and the masculinist character of the state has been able to expose itself with confidence once again. Anne Summers' book, *The End of Equality*, shows graphically how social liberal policies designed to benefit women rapidly unravelled under the Howard regime. [25] Notable examples were the downgrading of the Office of the Status of Women and dramatically increased child care costs. [26] A particularly bizarre illustration of the discounting of women's interests was the despatch of an official 12-person delegation to an ILO conference on pregnancy and the workplace in Geneva in 2001 that did not include a single woman. [27] Indeed, one could go so far as to say that gender justice was rendered both unseeable and unsayable in neoliberal discourse.

The discourse of freedom as rational choice has complemented the more overtly masculinist discourses to deflect attention away from the struggles of second wave feminism. The new incarnation of the feminine that is acceptable is a commodified form that serves the market. 'Girl power' has been deployed to sell style in designer clothing, makeup and household goods. Packaged as 'third wave feminism', it is sexy, trendy and superficial. Second wave feminism, with its trenchant exposé of the gendered partiality of the liberal state, can now be dismissed as so cumbrous and old fashioned that it is best consigned to mothballs.

Conclusion

Far from there being a contraction of the state – as ostensibly appears to be the case with devolution, deregulation and privatisation – we are seeing a boosting of the power of the state through neoliberalism that includes a renewed emphasis on the construction of gendered subjects. Clothed in the language of flexibility and choice, we are once again being spun a story of a neutral and progressivist liberal state in which things are always getting better. The ostensible devolution of responsibility for the economy to the market tricks us into believing that the state has disappeared. Just because it is less visible does not mean that it is now ethereal. It is not the invisible hand of the market that is at work, attenuating the inchoate commitment to equality, but the invisible hand of the state working through the market. By effecting an intimate liaison with the market, the state has played a key role in sustaining and intensifying the neoliberal project.

There is little space for social justice and the constellation of feminist values in the neoliberal state's single-minded pursuit of the interests of capital accumulation. As Sawer points out, markets are incapable of delivering equal opportunity 'which is why welfare states were introduced in the first place'. [28] Competition and the bottom line, however, are all that matters to the players on the global economic stage. Equity for those who continue to undertake the preponderance of care is of little consequence when not measured in economic terms. The success of neoconservative ideology means that the neoliberal state has been saved from having to expend energy in accommodating divergent interests, leaving it free to proceed with its agenda largely unimpeded. Distributive justice and gender equality can be effected only by the state *qua* government; they cannot be realised through the market alone. The swing from social liberalism to neoliberalism occurred as a result of pressure from the business sector and exponents of the free market, together with the *ressentiment* of the right generally. A swing in the other direction is unlikely to occur without significant energy being expended by feminist and social justice activists. Engagement with the state is fraught as it always carries with it the danger of co-option, to say nothing of posing the ubiquitous conundrum of 'who speaks for whom?' It can nevertheless serve 'both as a brake on the negative externalities of capitalism and as a positive force for material redistribution'. [29]

The fickle and treacherous character of the neoliberal state poses an ongoing challenge, but there is too much at stake to ignore it. The absorption of feminist energies by the capillaries has deflected attention away from the market metanarrative. The change in the relationship of feminism and the state is so dramatic that it calls for a new episteme of feminist theory. I am not exhorting gender mainstreaming or a revival of femocracy in the vain hope of securing an instantaneous panacea, but critical engagement with the insidious workings of the anti-feminist neoliberal state. It may be our only hope for developing the necessary groundswell to push the political pendulum back towards social justice again.

* * * * *

Some of the content of this chapter has been developed from an earlier work published in the journal *Australian Feminist Studies* (2006) under the original title, 'Feminism and the Changing State: The Case of Sex Discrimination' and is reproduced here with permission from Taylor & Francis.

PART II:
FEMINISM AND FREEDOM

The illusion of progress: a betrayal of women from both ends of the political spectrum

Miranda Kiraly

There seems to be a general misconception that liberal feminism is a politically left-wing ideology because many of its champions are seen as 'progressive' women. In reality, both left and right have been responsible for failing women, [1] and liberal feminism often engages the worst elements of both ideologies, ultimately staggering and halting meaningful progress for women. Liberal feminism is both illiberal and neoliberal, selectively, in its ideological parameters. It seeks to work within the confines of the existing liberal sphere, yet liberal feminism is not typically 'liberal' in a classical sense. [2]

On one hand, liberal feminism borrows from the left by relying heavily on rights and regulation without seeking to address the underlying root of the issue. The left's approach is steeped in the idea that governments can use law alone to target a social problem and effect change. Many such reforms are not groundbreaking but symbolic, and are presented under the rhetoric of justice and equality, which means that systemic injustice remains intact but women are led to believe that progress has been achieved. Liberal feminism fails to acknowledge that equality under the law does not always equate to substantive equality for women.

On the other hand, liberal feminism concurrently borrows from the more extreme elements of the neoliberal right in terms of sexual politics, under the more palatable guise of left-wing equality and sexual liberation rhetoric. Additionally, liberal feminism seeks to revive the neoliberal individualist 'public–private' divide to ensure that the personal again becomes private, rather than political, and women's liberation becomes an individual, rather than a collective struggle. Neoliberal individualism seeks to undo the work of more radical strands of feminism: feminism which fundamentally aims to overturn the status quo and address the root of the issues that obstruct women's progression.

This chapter considers two main areas where liberal feminism has been at the forefront of public discussion: liberal legal reform and the politics of sexual freedoms. It outlines the way that changes which may appear 'progressive' in principle, have actually limited the vision of women's equality and constrained progress. I argue that men of the left and the right benefit from the dominance of liberal feminism, as it does not fundamentally challenge male power, but rather grants women conditional participation in the liberal sphere, on men's terms. I conclude that women should not be divided by traditional notions of left–right politics, and stress that any movement for women's liberation must transcend such barriers if it is to be effective.

Men of the left: hollow notions of 'equality' in the liberal sphere

Liberal feminism has typically focused on addressing inequality by seeking to remove 'the explicit, state-sanctioned barriers that kept women from competing in the public sphere'.[3] Its advocacy for political liberalism has consequently provided opportunities for women via common law rights, freedom of expression and participation in the workforce. The extension of liberal, legal rights to women has been gradual in terms of equal opportunity and anti-discrimination laws; and has been typically resisted by men in areas that threaten their professional and personal dominion over women. One such example is marital rape, which was only acknowledged as a crime in recent decades in Australia and in the United Kingdom.[4]

Liberal legal rights flourished for women, but primarily in areas that could still be of benefit to men. Men can grant women conditional rights in areas such as education, employment, equal pay and opportunity, and childcare, so long as they do not substantially trample – or at least are not seen to substantially trample – the pre-existing rights of men. As Harvard Law professor, Catharine MacKinnon, has reflected on the passage of the *Equal Rights Amendment* in the United States: 'It presented an extraordinary spectacle – which I, frankly, found humiliating – of feminists ardently denying that sex equality would make much difference while urgently seeking it.' [5]

One of the landmarks of liberal feminist reform is the introduction of quotas and affirmative action in areas such as business and politics to help overcome the hurdles women face in terms of career progression. Such reforms dictate that company boards should be constituted by an arbitrary minimum percentage of women, such as 30 or 40 per cent, and that women should be installed in leadership positions in public life. Quotas and affirmative action are typically associated with a left-of-centre political ideology that sees merit in moulding society through the imposition of public policy, with the intended end result being a somewhat more balanced, but rarely equal, outcome.

While such reforms appear to be progressive or groundbreaking in principle, the reality is that such measures are still effectively dependent of men's willingness to grant women conditional access to professional and public life. Further, they equally rely on women's ability to litigate and/or enforce them. Had such affirmative action and quotas been effective in facilitating meaningful cultural change towards creating substantive 'equality of opportunity', they would have been seen as short-term measures to be removed once true 'equality of outcome' was achieved. Real progress is more than a matter of mere compliance, it is a matter of changing the culture; a fact which liberal feminism tends to overlook.

It is in the interests of men of the left to capitalise upon the liberal feminist trend of marketplace intervention, not to facilitate women's elevation but, rather, to ensure that true progress is kept at bay or is only ever granted on their terms. Further, when women are actually elevated to high positions on the back of such reforms, they are accused of being 'less qualified' and only there because of quota systems, rather than merit, at the expense of more 'capable' men – a criticism that was regularly thrown at former Labor prime minister Julia Gillard, even from those on her own side of politics. [6]

As MacKinnon argues, measures such as this simply reinforce a hollow notion of equality, which does not represent freedom and fairness at all. In models such as quota systems, the notion of equality which is invoked is 'premised not only on a meaningless symmetry, an empty equivalence but also that it [is] defined according to a male standard'. [7] She notes that such a system essentially only offers the option of 'being the same as men or different from men', [8] so you can be *equal*, but only ever on men's terms. There is no challenge to the overall system or set of norms which have been constructed under male dominance. It becomes painfully obvious then, that a liberal feminist approach, one that does not challenge the masculinised norms, is seen as a more palatable option for change by 'progressive' men.

Men of the right: the 'myth of merit'

While elements of the political right criticise 'token politics' and reject affirmative action and the imposition of quotas in business and politics, they do so as alternative means to halting progress for women. The political right's opposition to such artificial constructs is often based on criticisms that they are illiberal, unwarranted interferences in the marketplace. Instead, the right relies on the 'myth of merit', [9] the idea that capable women will always prevail on the basis of their own capabilities if they work hard enough. Jenny Turner characterised this 'trend' as the 'basic no-frills neoliberal package': [10]

> At the moment, the popular elements include 'empowerment',
> 'choice', 'freedom' and, above all, 'economic capacity' ... This
> young woman has been sold a deal, a 'settlement'. So long

as she works hard and doesn't throw bricks or ask awkward questions, she can have as many qualifications and abortions and pairs of shoes as she likes. [11]

The neoliberal aspiration of 'merit' may seem a worthy ideal, but its theoretical success is dependent on the premise of an even playing field for men and women; a misguided premise that disregards the insidious cultural problems that have typically hindered women's professional and personal progress. In reality, market forces empirically fail to achieve substantive equality, of either outcome or opportunity, for women – regardless of qualifications or capabilities – because neoliberal attitudes conveniently deny the existence of a 'woman problem'. Equality cannot be forged from an uneven playing field. The political right's overreliance on market forces means that meaningful progress is kept at bay, while concurrently, holding women responsible for their own 'failures' because, according to men, they evidently haven't yet met the requisite benchmark for success.

Women can rise up on so-called 'merit' in the marketplace, but only if men permit them to do so. One of the most recent examples of the merit myth in Australia was the composition of the conservative Abbott government's ministry, in 2013. Only one woman, Julie Bishop, was appointed to the 19-member Cabinet. Prime minister Tony Abbott faced criticism for the vast gender imbalance, particularly from the political left, for not adopting affirmative action policies to overcome the discrepancy. After the announcement, Abbott's new Cabinet members defended his distribution of portfolios. The minister for employment explained to media outlets that, 'at the end of the day we ... have always said that these positions should be based on merit rather than on quota'. [12] This demonstrated that if, on merit, only one woman out of 19 was deemed to be 'worthy' of Cabinet status, the women presently there lacked the requisite capabilities. If that were the case, a claim which few would agree, it must pose the question of why there were so few 'capable' women in conservative politics in the first place. It revealed the fact that neoliberal 'merit' does not always prevail in the face of other extraneous cultural factors that otherwise hinder 'capable' women from becoming elected members of public life at a root-and-branch level.

Both left and right manipulated the limits of liberalism to the detriment of women's interests. Men of the left have arguably never been true allies of liberal feminism, but see merit in controlling the market, as a means to shaping women's advancement on men's own terms, under the guise of 'gender equality'. While men of the right cling to the ideological idiom of 'merit', their strategic rejection of 'tokenistic' liberal feminist reform is equally about halting women's advancement, under the guise of neoliberal market forces. The end result of both firm positions is that women miss out, and the root of the problem remains unaddressed.

On men's terms: sexual liberalism is not liberation

While liberal, legal progress is looked upon with caution in terms of addressing systemic inequality; neoliberal deregulation is seemingly encouraged in areas that are of significant benefit to men, particularly in terms of sexual liberalism. Sexual liberalism or 'sex positivism' – 'a set of political beliefs and practices rooted in the assumption that sexual expression is inherently liberating and must be permitted to flourish unchecked' [13] – is another aspect evident in much liberal feminist writing, and another element which has proved to be appealing to men.

It seems that for such neoliberal ideas to become palatable to progressive women, sexual liberalism had to be rebranded as expressions of 'empowerment' and 'liberation'. This demonstrated 'how sexism [and sex inequality] can be embedded in the social fabric in ways that may not come to light without sensitising liberalism to its own blind spots'. [14] 'Sex positivism', essentially a neoliberal approach to sexuality, flourished on the back of left-wing politics in order to make it appear as a viable option for increasing women's freedom. Right-wing conservatism, on the other hand, was tacked to those who either resisted or questioned the 'sex positive' push. Historically, women who did not subscribe to 'sex positivism', many of them radical, lesbian feminists, rather ironically became branded as 'conservative' and 'anti-feminist'. The conservative movement was never a friend of liberal feminism in reality, other than its practical use as a tool to bully dissenting women into submission by use of reactionary or 'sex negative' rhetoric. It was, and still is, a clever ploy to pacify contrary opinion – and it worked. [15]

It should perhaps be unsurprising that some men became champions of sexual liberalism, vaguely masked under the banner of liberal feminism, in order to increase women's availability to men. For the first time, men of the left and the libertarian right, including the likes of *Playboy* founder Hugh Hefner, became joint ideological champions of the individualist 'my body, my choice' rhetoric and minimal state intervention in reproductive matters, particularly in regards to unrestricted abortion rights and the availability of contraception. [16] It was a page right out of the neoliberal handbook, and was not so much driven by a concern for bolstering women's self-determination and autonomy, but primarily by a self-interest in what they could gain from women in terms of (hetero)sexual accessibility of women. [17]

In fact, MacKinnon has made a similar argument with regard to abortion law reform in America. While the well-known *Roe v Wade* [18] case may have decriminalised abortion for women, it did so on the understanding that access to abortion was a privacy right. [19] That is, the change was not really achieved on women's terms, but rather on the basis of the 'male supremacist nature of the privacy right'. [20] She explains that: 'It is not that decriminalisation wasn't an improvement over jail. It is that getting a right to abortion as a privacy right without addressing the sex inequality of and in the private sphere is to assume that sex equality already exists.' [21] Which, of course it does not.

The liberal feminist collusion with neoliberal sexual politics has also been capitalised upon by the sex industry, [22] as a way to commodify the large-scale systemic abuse and subjugation of women on the basis that men and women are 'equal but different'. [23] According to MacKinnon, 'pornography turns sex inequality into sexuality and male dominance into sex difference'. [24] This has reinforced violence against women as a consequence of 'male biology' rather than conditioned behaviour, and has consequently allowed the consumption of pornography to be seen as a healthy and necessary outlet for male sexuality. It removes the responsibility of men for their actions against women on the basis of traditional and right-wing notions of 'human nature', and further serves to normalise pornographic culture into the mainstream. This follows the notion that if a woman is physiologically aroused, she therefore must be 'empowered' by that experience. [25] Pornographic culture transforms harm into sex and makes harm invisible [26] by recruiting women and girls into a sexual 'freedom fallacy', in order for men to reinforce their personal and psychological dominion over women, rather than to 'bolster' them through feminist liberation.

This is evidenced by the fact that while women are actively encouraged to explore the parameters of hypersexuality on the one hand; on the other, they are also denigrated for doing so. Men, as a class, benefit from this model of the increased sexual accessibility of women, but then revert to traditional right-wing and reactionary notions of 'immorality' and 'slut-shaming' in order to condemn women for their 'sexually liberal' behaviours. It is one of the most dangerous and insidious forms of misogyny; one which coerces women into the neoliberal sphere via 'choice' and 'agency', and then blames them for any harms they may suffer as a result.

Liberal feminism purports not to 'slut-shame' women who suffer harms at the hands of sexualisation. However, it does not adequately vindicate women and girls for their negative experiences because it merely sees that women are agents of their own choices.

Its firm ideological commitment to neoliberal individualism fails to acknowledge the pressures of a cultural context that inhibits a more substantive notion of women's consent and effectively shields men from any responsibility for their role in harming women. Michaele L. Ferguson acknowledges this trend under the category of 'choice feminism', which:

> fails to differentiate between those who can choose and those who cannot; analysis of how class, race, sexuality, and power affect women's choices is often missing. Since it represents choices as a matter of individual responsibility alone, choice feminism can be deployed to punish women who have 'made' the wrong choices. It also misleadingly suggests that since choices are individual, they have no social consequences; women are therefore relieved of responsibility for considering the broader implications of their decisions. Indeed, individual choices are figured as private matters of no one else's concern. [27]

In order to keep achieving its tactical goal, individualist 'choice' has to remain front and centre in liberal feminist rhetoric at any cost, and anyone who questions the limitations of liberal feminist 'choice' is to be excluded from the 'feminist' umbrella.

The 'wrong' versus the 'right' kind of feminist

Tacking 'choice' rhetoric and sexual liberalism to so-called progressive politics was not only about recruiting a larger pool of women to buy into the 'freedom fallacy', but was also to disenfranchise women of contrary views. As a result, one of the more divisive tactics of liberal feminism is in its illiberal adoption of what is, in effect, a strict 'party line' on what constitutes a feminist, or an acceptably feminist choice.

Women of *both* left and right are visibly barred from the 'feminist' label for questioning liberal feminist orthodoxy, particularly on the topics of sexual politics, pornography, abortion, freedom of religion, or even the decision of whether or not they wish to identify with the 'feminist' label at all. It goes to show that while liberal feminism often sees an end goal of empowering women to make choices, whatever they may be, some choices are seen as more equal than others. As a result, any woman who queries whether or not 'choice' *always* equates to freedom can be simplistically labelled 'anti-feminist' or 'conservative', by other liberal feminists, as means of quelling her views. While, to liberal feminists, it appears that such tactics are intended to preserve the purity of their 'progressive' ideology, it instead serves to divide women into 'the wrong' and 'the right' categories of feminist. Women of opposing views are turned against one another on the basis of their *differences*, rather than seeking to look to their commonalities, which consequently immobilises any meaningful action for women, and operates ultimately, to the benefit of men. As Andrea Dworkin once explained in her piece, 'Woman-Hating Right and Left':

> We have to go past the conventional political barriers, the lines that men have drawn for us. '*Our* girls over there ... we'll call them socialists ... we'll call them whatever we want to call them. *Those* girls over there; that's *their* girls. The girls on our side aren't allowed to talk to the girls on their side.' Well, if the girls on either side talked to the girls on the other side, they just might find out that they're being screwed the same way by the same kinds of men (emphasis in original). [28]

Women cannot move anywhere with such a divide. Feminism, or more accurately, a movement for women's liberation, cannot succeed if we only associate with, or advocate for, women on 'our side'. As Dworkin also pithily argued, it is not enough to simply call yourself a feminist: 'That's not what being a feminist is. Feminism is a political practice of fighting male supremacy in [sic] behalf of women as a class, including all the women you don't like.' [29]

Conclusion

Liberal feminism is neither progressive nor 'liberal' in reality. Instead, liberal feminism has become a piecemeal, watered down version of feminism that uses elements of both the political left and neoliberal right to manipulate the boundaries of liberalism in order to halt progress where it would be of meaningful benefit to women, while concurrently exploiting women's interests in ways that ultimately serve to benefit men. At an ideological level, the core flaw of liberal feminism is arguably that it fails to adequately acknowledge the underlying cultural problems that have historically excluded and oppressed women. Liberal feminism places an overemphasis on a legal rights-based agenda and symbolism in an attempt to highlight barriers facing women, but it arguably lacks the resources to address the fundamental root of the problem: a radical consideration of the deep-seated, underlying issues which constrain women's choices. 'Freedom' and 'equality' are worthy aspirations but they remain mere liberal feminist rhetoric until they can be freely exercised in an environment in which men are no longer the primary beneficiaries of women's 'choices'.

It also demonstrates that while the liberal sphere has not failed women, 'liberalism has reached the limits of its feminist potential'. [30] In order to demonstrate these limits, it is necessary to focus on the subsequent harms, rather than the benefits, of liberal feminism. True liberation is not possible by working *strictly* within the confines of the existing liberal sphere. 'Only by revealing the illiberal tendencies of liberalism can certain harms be made visible,' [31] and this is where the limits of liberal feminism become clear. The personal needs to remain political, now more than ever, and feminism must transcend traditional political lines in order to attack anti-woman forces from both sides of the left–right political divide.

The making of women's unfreedom: sexual harassment as harm

Helen Pringle

Sexual banter, the exchange of jokes and flirty comments can be the welcome spice of life for women, as well as men, and it's foolish to let the prudish in our midst determine what is appropriate behaviour. [1] —
Bettina Arndt

Women have joined the permanent workforce in large numbers over the last 40 years, a development that promises greater economic welfare and independence for women, and greater equality between men and women. But this promise has been betrayed by continuing high levels of hostility to working women. The most common form of hostility is no longer opposition to women taking up jobs, but harassment when they do. Such patterns of sexual harassment are not rearguard actions by reactionaries who believe women belong in the kitchen. Prominent claims of harassment and violation of women at work have involved men of high professional standing, among others, a president of the United States ('US'), a managing director of the International Monetary Fund, and a United Nations High Commissioner for Refugees.

In Australia, sexual harassment in the workplace has been unlawful for nearly 30 years. However, in 2012, one in four women reported to the Australian Human Rights Commission ('AHRC') third national telephone survey that they had experienced harassment. [2] A particularly troublesome finding of the AHRC survey, as of previous telephone surveys, is that around one in five of those who reported that they had *not* experienced harassment nevertheless said that they had experienced behaviour that appeared to meet the criteria of harassment set out in the *Sex Discrimination Act 1984* (Cth) (*'Sex Discrimination Act'*). To put the point another way, harassing behaviour is not always recognised, even by its targets, as harm. Women who are harassed in the workplace may now seek legal redress, but harassment is still not taken seriously as a restraint on women's freedom and an obstacle to full recognition of their standing and dignity as persons.

The actions and behaviour that the law and public policy now classify as harassment are still widely characterised as trivial matters between individuals, rather than as exercises of power by perpetrators acting out roles in a script of gender-based power in the service of sex discrimination. My argument in this chapter is that unless we address harassment fully and appropriately as *harm* to women, the existence of a wider range of choices as to work and career does not lead to greater freedom for women, but to one more form of unfreedom.

Unfreedom and invisible harms

Liberal writers have always recognised that freedom is not an absolute, that freedom does not include a right to harm others. In his classic work *On Liberty*, for example, John Stuart Mill argued that there is a 'very simple principle' that should govern the relation of society and individuals:

> That principle is, that the sole end for which mankind are warranted, individually or collectively in interfering with the liberty of action of any of their number, is self-protection. That the only purpose for which power can be rightfully exercised over any member of a civilised community, against his will, is to prevent harm to others. His own good, either physical or moral, is not a sufficient warrant ... The only part of the conduct of any one, for which he is amenable to society, is that which concerns others. In the part which merely concerns himself, his independence is, of right,

absolute. Over himself, over his own body and mind, the individual is sovereign. [3]

Mill's passage on the value of freedom is widely quoted, but often without an acknowledgement of the problem it raises, the problem of what counts as harm. My argument here is that an appropriate understanding of freedom must be accompanied by a full and robust understanding of harm, particularly if we are to maximise the sovereignty of women. It is easy enough, now, to recognise the exclusion of women from the workforce, or from particular jobs and industries, as the harm of sexual discrimination, but many people find it more difficult to place forms of sexually harassing behaviour at work within the framework of harm. And this difficulty is particularly acute where so much cultural emphasis is placed on the importance of sexual expression and freedom. Women's equal standing, safety and freedom in the workplace are compromised where harassing behaviour is viewed as 'just sex', or as 'just sexual banter'.

As noted above, Australian public policy and law do recognise that sexual harassment in the workplace is unlawful as a form of discrimination. For example, the Commonwealth *Sex Discrimination Act*, enacted in 1984 consequent to Australia's international human rights commitments, prohibits discrimination on the basis of sex, marital status, family responsibilities and pregnancy. The Act defines sexual harassment in terms of the making of an unwelcome sexual advance, or an unwelcome request for sexual favours, to the person harassed; or engaging in other unwelcome conduct of a sexual nature 'in circumstances in which a reasonable person, having regard to all the circumstances, would have anticipated the possibility that the person harassed would be offended, humiliated or intimidated'. [4]

This legal recognition of harassment as a form of discrimination capable of redress is fairly new. Until relatively recently, many actions that do harm were not recognised as such in our culture, in our politics, or in our law. In particular, many forms of sexual harm were not taken seriously, so much so that they were in a sense invisible. As an example, until approximately 30 years ago, a man who raped his wife did not commit a crime, that is, a man who forced his wife to have sex with him could not be charged with raping her. The law also generally turned a blind eye to wife-bashing, as long as it didn't go 'too far' and become murder. And there was little legal recourse for women (or men) who were sexually handled or pestered at work. Such actions had no legal names. Public policy did not name them: they were simply conditions of the sexual landscape that most men, as well as women, took for granted as natural and unchangeable aspects of 'sexual geography', of how we map our lives and of how we draw boundaries in accordance with the principles of permissible freedom. Harassment, such as marital rape, did not count as 'harm to others'. In other words, women's freedom was constrained by the failure to recognise harassment and other forms of sexual violation as harm.

This failure in recognition did not of course mean that women escaped being subject to harassing behaviour. Sexual violation at work was largely invisible to law, but not to working women themselves, even where it was presented by its perpetrators under the guise of an appreciation of women or solicitude for their interests. A notorious example of this in the early 20th century concerned the owner of a New York garment factory who said that he was acting as a 'fond father' in pinching his women employees – leading the labour organiser Rose Schneiderman to remark, 'we would rather be orphans' and to launch what became known as the 'orphan's strike'. [5] In the late 20th century, the UN High Commissioner for Refugees (and former prime minister of the Netherlands) Ruud Lubbers responded to an employee's allegation of groping by claiming that it was a 'friendly gesture' that the woman had misunderstood. [6] Where harassing behaviour was culturally visible, it was chiefly so as a form of bad manners, rudeness, or lechery, such as to raise questions of morality rather than of equality and of women's freedom. There was little legal, political or cultural advantage in reporting sexual harassment when it was not taken seriously or acted upon as a form of sexual injustice.

This 'sexual geography' has changed dramatically within my lifetime, so that when a woman now complains of harassment, her voice is not simply ridiculed or dismissed as an overreaction to trivial incidents. And she is not simply told that she had provoked what happened to her, by her dress or her looks, or what she did or said, or by what she didn't do or say. She is not always simply told, in short, that she had in some way 'asked for it'. And her voice is not simply dismissed on the basis that it raises a purely *private* matter, one of intimacy, sex and sexual freedom. However, many writers continue to frame harassment as a moral question, as simply bad manners. For example, Jeffrey Minson has argued that:

> sexual harassment may be likened to a more general class of inconsiderate behaviour or gross impoliteness which is commonly, but not exclusively, directed by men against women. It includes standing too close to another, presuming an inappropriate familiarity, staring at strangers, gate-crashing another's sphere of activities, and putting them in a position of having to say no. [7]

Writers such as Minson believe it is important to adopt this framework of morality in addressing harassing behaviour in part so that the law is precluded from an overregulation of sexual freedom. Grossly bad manners might be offensive, the argument goes, but they are not *harm* that should trigger legal regulation of the realm of sexual freedom and choice.

In some early test cases of sexual harassment, it was argued along such lines that only actions resulting in a tangible or economic detriment to their target (for example, a person losing her job as retaliation for her reaction to the incident) could count as legally actionable harassment. In the 1986 US case of *Meritor Savings Bank v Vinson*, [8] Mechelle Vinson claimed that she had been subjected to constant demands for sexual favours, as well as fondling, indecent exposure and rape by Sidney Taylor, the vice-president of the bank in which she worked, and that such actions were harassment that created a 'hostile working environment'. The US Supreme Court agreed that Taylor's behaviour was discriminatory and more than 'inconsiderate', and noted that the enactment of the US *Civil Rights Act* was intended 'to strike at the entire spectrum of disparate treatment of men and women' in employment. Unless the harassment of working women is recognised as *harm to women*, gendered harm, it is difficult to address the ways in which it curtails women's freedom, and the ways in which men's freedom is thereby left unbridled.

The distance between an approach to harassment as a moral infraction and to harassment as harm can be measured by contrasting the 'morality' approach against the terms of the 1993 United Nations *Declaration on the Elimination of Violence Against Women*. The preamble to the Declaration notes that 'violence against women is a manifestation of historically unequal power relations between men and women which have led to domination over and discrimination against women by men'. That is, gendered violence is not natural, biological or inevitable. Included in the declaration's definition of violence is 'any act of gender-based violence that results in, or is likely to result in, physical, sexual or psychological harm or suffering to women, including threats of such acts, coercion or arbitrary deprivation of liberty, whether occurring in public or in private life'. Such a definition comprehends a range of behaviour, including 'physical, sexual and psychological violence occurring within the general community, including rape, sexual abuse, sexual harassment and intimidation at work, in educational institutions and elsewhere, trafficking in women and forced prostitution'. [9] This striking placement of harassment as a form of violence on a spectrum of sexual assault emphasises that it is not only a criminal issue, but also a human rights problem, the wrong of which is identified in terms of how it 'violates, impairs or nullifies women's human rights and their exercise of fundamental freedoms'. As a question of human rights, harassment is something for which states are accountable. Article 4 of the declaration requires that:

> states should pursue by all appropriate means and without delay a policy of eliminating violence against women and, to this end, should ... exercise due diligence to prevent, investigate and, in accordance with national legislation, punish acts of violence against women, whether those acts are perpetrated by the state or by private persons.

In naming sexual harassment as a form of violence against women, the *Declaration on the Elimination of Violence Against Women* decisively ups the ante on behaviour towards women in the workplace. Sexual harassment is identified in terms of the pervasive acts and structures of violence that perform the oppression of women and accomplish their unfreedom. The inclusion of sexual harassment along a spectrum of violence against women is an acknowledgement that harassment is indeed harm, and harm of a particular kind. As noted by Harvard Law School professor, Catharine MacKinnon, sex harassment is:

> a practice of inequality on the basis of gender, an integral act of subordinate civil status because of sex, a practice of treating a person as less than fully socially human because that person is a woman or a man, a status-based treatment of hierarchy, of dominance, that is illegal. [10]

The threat of the 'fun police' to a culture of sexual impunity

However, such a human rights framework is far from forming the most common understanding of sexual harassment in Australia, or anywhere else, for that matter. The political and legal meaning, and the consequences of sexual harassment as harm through its creation of an intimidating, hostile or offensive working environment is not yet general. A conciliation officer with the NSW Anti-Discrimination Board used to tell the story of a man who contacted the board to complain that he had been dismissed from his job because of sexual harassment. The man insisted that it had not happened, saying: 'Sure, I squeezed her tits and I called her a slut, but I didn't harass her.' There is still a common perception that women enjoy sexual joking, 'banter', and contact, or at least that they view such behaviour as a form of flattery or appreciation. As Helen Garner noted in *The First Stone*, [11] her 1995 account of harassment at Melbourne's Ormond College, women should be very careful how they respond to such gestures of flirting and seduction by men so as not to betray a prissy and puritan opposition to sex (a 'mingy, whining, cringeing terror of sex', to use Garner's words). Those who harass women generally think they can get away with it under the guise of manly ways. And they are right. There is still a culture of impunity for sexual assault and abuse, which Garner's book simply accepted as the entitlement of men to access the bodies of women. This is what freedom means where it is not accompanied by an understanding of how harm is done to women.

A more recent example in this context is the 2010 claim of Kristy Fraser-Kirk that the company David Jones was responsible for the 'sexual misconduct' to her by its CEO Mark McInnes. [12] Ms Fraser-Kirk's action was widely scoffed at in the media and in popular conversations as 'absurd', and she was slimed as 'hysterical', a 'serial complainer', and 'a gold-digger'. [13] At the time, the fashion designer Alannah Hill notoriously described the case in these terms: 'it'll be a little glitch and then we'll move on from it'. The media reported further on Ms Hill's comments about the claim, made at a David Jones fashion show:

> 'I've sort of got a crush on Mark McInnes ... I've had a crush on him for four years. I wanted to be the girl who lived in the Bondi flat,' [Hill] told reporters. 'I wish he'd have touched

me up. I threw myself at him, threw myself at him. He told me he didn't want to mix business with pleasure.'

Fellow designer Alex Perry, who accompanied Hill into the event, tried to change the subject by asking her what colour dresses she had on the runway this season. Before she had a chance to reply, a reporter asked Hill if she was the 'brunette' referred to in former publicist Kristy Fraser-Kirk's $37 million lawsuit against the retail giant. Among her allegations, Fraser-Kirk says McInnes phoned her a day after a work function asking to meet with her for dinner or a drink, saying: 'I could have had guaranteed sex with that brunette last night but I wanted you.'

The reporter's question prompted Hill to press on with her comments. 'Yes I was the brunette, yes, yes I was the brunette,' Hill said. 'He could have bedded me but he chose the other one,' she added, laughing. 'I mean, can you imagine that,' Perry chimed in. 'I know, why would he chose her over me?' Hill continued. [14]

Hill's comments imply that women are generally 'up for it', that they are 'walking around this country in a state of constant consent to sexual activity', [15] upon which men are entitled to presume.

By referring to this case, I do not of course mean to imply that all harassment takes the form of erotic invitations. It is sufficient to peruse cases about the use of pornography in the workplace to realise that the detriment of harassment does not always come in such (dis)guises. McInnes invited Ms Fraser-Kirk to eat a dessert that he said tasted like 'a fuck in the mouth', [16] but such a phrase can refer not merely to a dessert but to an overt threat. The construction of workplaces as a man's world can be accomplished by an overtly hostile marking of territory with pornography, bodily fluids, graffiti, and even with fire hoses in one notorious case of discrimination in Western Australia. [17]

A single incident of harassing behaviour can be sufficient to create a hostile working environment. Even the implicit possibility of harassing behaviour can serve to remind women of the basis on which they have been admitted to the workplace, that is, that they are required to 'run a gauntlet of sexual abuse in return for the privilege of being allowed to work and make a living'. [18] Columbia University Law professor Katherine Franke has emphasised the pervasive harm of harassment as going beyond the detriment done to its individual targets, to a construction of the workplace as a man's world in which the violence of sexual harassment is a way of performing masculinity, or at least, a stereotypical version of virility. [19] Women are permitted to participate in this toxic theatre as long as they consent to give men pleasure while they are there by acting the part of a spectacle, not that of a person of dignity.

It is true that women, like men, are not entitled to have their own sense of themselves adopted by the world at large. A child who imagines that he is a volcano, or that he will grow up to be a fire engine, is not treated unjustly when he is disabused of these possibilities for his future life. But a person *is* entitled to be socially and culturally accepted by something more than a spectacle. In this context, feminist theorist Sandra Lee Bartky has written of the experience of being harassed by men on the street:

> While it is true that for these men I am nothing but, let us say, a 'nice piece of ass,' there is more involved in this encounter than their mere fragmented perception of me. They could, after all, have enjoyed me in *silence* ... But I must be *made* to know that I am a 'nice piece of ass': I must be made to see myself as they see me. There is an element of compulsion in this encounter, in this being-made-to-be-aware of one's own flesh; like being made to apologise, it is humiliating. It is unclear what role is played by sexual arousal or even sexual connoisseurship in encounters like these. What I describe

seems less the spontaneous expression of a healthy eroticism
than a ritual of subjugation. [20]

Such 'rituals of subjugation' are not merely forms of treating
individuals badly or discourteously, but of treating a woman as less
than a person, as chattel to be 'owned' (as the saying now goes). In
the past, such rituals of sexual ownership might have been, to some
extent, curbed by sexual puritanism or prudery, or by what are today
outdated notions of women's place in the world. Such rituals are now
often shrugged off as exercises of sexual freedom. However, such
rituals inscribe the workplace, as much as the street, as a space of
constraint and unfreedom for women, in which they are not free to
be themselves – whatever that might be.

Entitled to be free:
exposing the limits of choice

Shakira Hussein and Camille Nurka

Muslim women are widely represented as living in a state of unfreedom in comparison to the freedom enjoyed by their Western counterparts, and their bodies are similarly represented as radically different – covered rather than exposed, mutilated in ways that are not culturally sanctioned by hegemonic Western norms, and breeding to an excessive and threatening degree. The abject Muslim woman has become a trope of the post-9/11 sociopolitical landscape, but the discourse surrounding her has a far longer history, metamorphosing in obverse reflection to changing gender norms within Western societies. The unrelenting fascination with her alien body has remained constant from colonialism to postcolonialism and throughout various eras of feminism.

Despite the prevailing level of discomfort with 'other' bodies, we are assured that the relevant area of difference is one of ideology rather than biology and that social acceptance is open to all who choose to embrace hegemonic norms. This is particularly the case during discussion of anti-Muslim racism, which, we are assured, is not racism at all since Islam is a religion, not a race. However, the female body provides an important site for the reintegration of the biological with the cultural in contemporary forms of racism as the material expression of unacceptable, alien difference. Where traditional biologist accounts of racial difference rely on assumptions that attribute character and value to intraspecies (or racial) physiology, assertions of ethnic (for example, religious) difference may instead be made on the basis of body practices that make ethnicity both visible and material. The female body is a particularly contentious surface over which certain Western claims about the essence of modernity and freedom are persistently made. The commitment to freedom in the form of choice is rendered problematic by women who are conceptualised as making the 'wrong' choice, or as choosing in circumstances which are regarded as insufficiently autonomous.

The new Orientalism

Muslim women are conspicuously present in contemporary 'postfeminist' discourses that exploit feminist rhetoric to create new Orientalist boundaries between bodies that inhabit the spaces of freedom or unfreedom. As Christina Scharff argues, [1] the perceived success of Western feminism – which is based on the assumption of its widespread cultural and institutional integration – is indissociable from the perceived necessity of feminism in Islamic cultures in particular. She found that in her conversations with young German and British women, the 'trope' of the 'oppressed other woman' emerged as the figurative ground upon which their neoliberal claims to individualism and self-responsibility could be asserted. [2] Unhelpfully, feminism's apparent redundancy-through-victory in the West has become a convenient yardstick by which to measure the civilisational lag of others. This is not necessarily directly attributable *only* to contemporary 'postfeminism', a label which refers to the idea that feminism now has such broad social currency that it has become unnecessary. In fact, Western women's assumptions of superior freedoms have deep roots within a much longer history of feminist activism. The origins of modern Western liberal feminism are closely linked to white British and American women's involvement in anti-slavery campaigns in the mid-19th century and in later manifestations of imperial feminism whereby white women sought to save their oppressed colonised sisters. [3]

In contemporary 'postfeminist' accounts, the bodies of Muslim women figure prominently in this pre-established oppositional imaginary, as practices such as Islamic dress and genital cutting become the material point at which feminism is called into service as a necessary politics for the unenlightened. The narrative of rescue that Scharff found in her respondents' reflections on (what is commonly known as) female genital mutilation ('FGM') among Muslim women is, as she suggests, an Orientalist construction. Edward Said's landmark book *Orientalism* outlines the various ways that the 'Oriental' archetype was constructed within white frameworks of representation, which became the obverse foundation for European self-identity. Said's work contains little analysis of gender. However, *Orientalism* does discuss Flaubert's relationship with the Egyptian courtesan Kuchuk Hanem and the ways in which he 'spoke for and represented her'.[4] As he assured his lover, Louise Colet:

> Be convinced that she felt nothing at all: emotionally, I guarantee; and even physically, I strongly suspect ... The Oriental woman is no more than a machine: she makes no distinction between one man and another man. Smoking, going to the baths, painting her eyelids and drinking coffee – such is the circle of occupations within which her existence is confined. As for pleasure, it must be very slight, since the well known button, the seat of same, is sliced off at an early age.[5]

We suggest here that the imagined body of 'the Muslim woman' is crucial to representations of self and other in certain forms of white neoliberal (post)feminism and Western culture more broadly. For instance, the trope of the genitally defined oppressed Muslim woman was readily identifiable in a recent controversy involving renowned evolutionary biologist and spokesperson for the atheist movement, Richard Dawkins and feminist atheist blogger, Rebecca Watson, author of the *Skepchick* blog. Now dubbed 'elevatorgate', the controversy erupted over an incident which took place at an atheist conference in Dublin, Ireland, which Watson describes in her video blog. [6] As Watson relates, at four o'clock in the morning after post-conference drinks at a hotel bar, she took the elevator to go back to her room, during which time she was sexually propositioned by a fellow (male) conference attendee. This, for Watson, demonstrated the point she had made earlier in her conference panel that sexualisation of women by men in the atheist community is a problem as a form of unacknowledged sexism. She also implied that being trapped in a confined space (an elevator) by a drunken delegate making sexual overtures placed her in an uncomfortable zone of sexual vulnerability. [7] Watson was clearly using this incident as an illustration of her argument that male-dominated institutions such as the atheist movement tend to reproduce unequal gender relations through placing value on female members' sexual, rather than intellectual, capacities. This video blog, in which she advises men not to behave in this manner (as Watson herself put it: 'Guys, don't do that,') sparked an internet war notable for Richard Dawkins's infamous response in a facetious letter written to a fictitious character called 'Muslima'. We reproduce the Dawkins letter in full, as it appears on Watson's blog, here:

> Dear Muslima
>
> Stop whining, will you. Yes, yes, I know you had your genitals mutilated with a razor blade, and ... yawn ... don't tell me yet again, I know you aren't allowed to drive a car, and you can't leave the house without a male relative, and your husband is allowed to beat you, and you'll be stoned to death if you commit adultery. But stop whining, will you. Think of the suffering your poor American sisters have to put up with.
>
> Only this week I heard of one, she calls herself Skep"chick", and do you know what happened to her? A man in a hotel elevator invited her back to his room for coffee. I am not exaggerating. He really did. He invited her back to his room for coffee. Of course she said no, and of course he didn't lay

a finger on her, but even so ... And you, Muslima, think you
have misogyny to complain about! For goodness sake grow
up, or at least grow a thicker skin.

Richard. [8]

In an astonishing rhetorical feat, Dawkins' figuration of 'the Muslim
woman' manages to construct more than one 'other' against which
rational (white) man defines himself; it is illustrative of Orientalist
stereotyping which homogenises Muslim women's experiences and it
produces the unsavoury character of the 'whining' Western feminist.
This characterisation is consistent with neoliberal 'postfeminist'
assumptions that Western feminists are anachronistic because gender
equality has already been achieved. Importantly for our argument
though, in the Dawkins letter, genital mutilation is invoked as the
major signifier of what it is to be a Muslim woman (that is, you can't
be classified as a Muslim woman unless you've been 'mutilated'). It
could perhaps be that Dawkins implicitly draws on black, indigenous
and postcolonial feminist critiques that criticise Western feminism
for addressing white women's concerns only. Dawkins fails dismally
in this project, however, because he reproduces the very same racial
stereotypes that such feminists would denounce as unambiguously
racist. Instead, Dawkins presents a liberal conception of 'freedom'
– what this volume calls a 'freedom fallacy' – embedded in colonial
discourse that produces the Muslim woman's body as the inscriptive
surface of degeneracy. As Anne McClintock argues:

> In colonial discourse ... space is time, and history is shaped
> around two, necessary movements: the 'progress' forward of
> humanity from slouching deprivation to erect, enlightened
> reason. The other movement presents the reverse: regression
> backwards from (white, male) adulthood to a primordial,
> black 'degeneracy' usually incarnated in women. [9]

While Dawkins is certainly not suggesting that Muslim women are inherently, biologically inferior to white women, his brand of cultural racism is nonetheless 'incarnated' in the Muslim woman's 'mutilated' body, which signifies the refusal of Islamic cultures to progress. This discourse is affixed in a 'binary axis of time', [10] which opposes barbaric Islam, and its associated practices of genital mutilation, and secular civilisation. In reprising this logic, Dawkins eliminates the operations of power that racialise Muslim women to refocus our attention on the ways in which white, Western female bodies inhabit (or indeed abuse) freedoms made available to them through the passage of secular time. It makes a 'postfeminist' appeal to a linear model of history, in which the liberal freedoms assumed to have already been obtained by white women are instated through the passing of both feminism and oppression (in the West), where the persistence of gender oppression is defined through the covered and/or 'mutilated' body of the Muslim woman.

Abhorrent choices and abject bodies

Muslim women's bodies are regarded as abject, from the hair and skin – which are only rendered more visible by the garments intended to shield them from external scrutiny – to the mutilated and overly fertile sexual organs. The supposed need to rescue them from an alien religious patriarchy has seen them subjected to regimes of discipline and governance. Muslim spokeswomen have responded to this onslaught by describing their religious practices (in particular those relating to dress) through the now-mainstream feminist terminology of choice (although the word 'feminism' is a taken for granted element that is not necessarily explicitly stated). However, their entitlement to draw upon this well-established discourse is heavily contested, with their abhorrent 'choices' seen as infiltration of the West by an alien patriarchy.

Burqas and other forms of face covering are regarded as one of the most extreme of the abject choices that Muslim women may undertake in the name of their religious identity. The ability to see and be seen is described as an essential prerequisite in establishing their trustworthiness as citizens of liberal democracies, as well as a condition of freedom from the strictures of a medieval religion. A veiled woman's clothes may be used to conceal not only her identity, but also the weapons with which she plans to attack her fellow citizens. On a day-to-day level, veiling is described as unfriendly and rude. On a phenomenological level, it is seen to be an impediment to women's relationship with the outside world. The body beneath the veil is also imagined to be physiologically transformed for the worse: veiling as a risk factor for vitamin D deficiency and rickets in newborn children and breastfed children is described as a disease of backwardness, unseen in Europe since Victorian times until the arrival of Muslim communities. Yet despite widespread public health campaigns warning of the association between sun exposure and skin cancer, tanning continues to symbolise leisure and freedom.

The Muslim woman's body is, we suggest, narrativised in ways that mark it as 'unfree', in comparison to Western women. It thus obtains representational reality as an imagined body which can be made to stand in for forms of injury and oppression that Western liberalism seeks to disown through their projection onto the 'other' (body). One significant function of this imagined body is that it allows for the justification of female genital cosmetic surgery ('FGCS') as a *lifestyle choice* or healthful procedure in Western society to coexist with a zero-tolerance approach to FGM in non-Western cultures. Our problem here is with the way in which genital modification as practised upon Muslim women's bodies forms part of a larger – and, it must be said, hypocritical – discourse that positions non-Western FGM as barbaric, and Western FGCS as medically legitimate.

In 2012, the UN General Assembly adopted a resolution to eliminate female genital mutilation worldwide, with UN secretary-general Ban

Ki-moon stating that 'harmful practices, such as genital mutilation, constitute a serious threat to the health of millions of women and girls worldwide and violate their fundamental rights'. [11] The resolution itself is emphatic in its recognition that 'female genital mutilations are an irreparable, irreversible abuse that impacts negatively on the human rights of women and girls'. [12] It states further concern 'about evidence of an increase in the incidence of female genital mutilations being carried out by medical personnel in all regions in which they are practised', [13] indicating a zero-tolerance, rather than harm-reduction, approach to FGM, where, for instance, FGM may be tolerated if conducted in a sterile clinical setting. The World Health Organisation has also published a forceful statement condemning FGM in 2010 in its *Global Strategy to Stop Health-Care Providers from Performing Female Genital Mutilation*. [14] This document strongly advises medical professionals to refuse to participate in FGM, with the assertion that:

> Health professionals who perform female genital mutilation (FGM) are violating girls' and women's right to life, right to physical integrity, and right to health. They are also violating the fundamental ethical principle: 'Do no harm.' [15]

In Australia, FGM is outlawed, though the law itself is state-dependent. For example, in New South Wales, it is illegal to excise, infibulate or mutilate the whole or any part of the labia majora or labia minora or clitoris, with the exception of medically indicated surgery in connection with birth or labour, sexual reassignment surgery and, importantly, surgery that is deemed 'necessary for the health of the person on whom it is performed and is performed by a medical practitioner'. [16] Usually, ethical objections to FGM/FGCS are formed around the experiences of young girls, and the practice is rightly regarded as a child protection issue. However, the legal prohibition of 'cultural' FGM extends to adult women as well as to underage girls, regardless of consent. [17]

What is interesting to us is that, in legal terms, female genital cosmetic surgeries in Australia appear to be protected from criminal penalty because considered 'necessary for the health of the person'. This is particularly the case with vulvoplasty surgeries funded under the Medicare Benefits Schedule ('MBS'). According to MBS data, vulvoplasty surgeries claimed under Medicare had more than doubled in 2012 compared with 2002. [18] This item was subject to an MBS review in 2013, which described the medical justifications for surgery in the following way:

> Labioplasty corrects the clinical conditions wherein a woman presents labia minora that are disproportionately greater than her labia majora; the labioplastic correction of the disproportions creates less asymmetrical labia minora that are functionally and aesthetically satisfactory to the woman. A protruding labia minora may lead to psychological, cosmetic, or functional problems. Labial hypertrophy causes loss of self-esteem and embarrassment for some women. Even in the absence of psychosocial factors, enlarged labia minora can lead to functional difficulties. Issues that may arise secondary to labial hypertrophy include interference with sexual intercourse, chronic local irritation, problems with personal hygiene during menses or after bowel movements, and discomfort during walking, cycling, or sitting. [19]

Clearly, the legal and ethical waters are exceptionally muddy indeed with regard to what, exactly, makes FGCS socially sanctionable and 'what constitutes a medically necessary procedure', [20] especially in relation to the psychosocial constitution of vulval pathology. In Western contexts, the most popular form of genital surgery is labiaplasty, in which the inner labia (or labia minora) are excised. As outlined above, the reasons for surgery may include genital shame and low self-esteem, dyspareunia, chafing and problems with hygiene. Cosmetic surgery on the female genitals does not serve as a rite of passage and is therefore not as widespread a practice as in cultures where it is necessary for a girl's transition into womanhood. It is not generally performed on girls and mostly involves labiaplasty surgery, though there is a documented case of a woman who requested cosmetic labia and clitoral hood excision and later cosmetic clitoridectomy. [21] However, there are remarkable similarities to FGM in relation to female anxieties about normalcy, belonging and sexual desirability, especially where 'FGM is associated with cultural ideals of femininity and modesty, which include the notion that girls are "clean" and "beautiful" after removal of body parts that are considered "male" or "unclean"'. [22] Women seeking labiaplasty have offered comparable rationales: their genitals are seen to be unhygienic or unclean, ugly, asymmetrical, unfeminine, or like 'a willy'. [23] Yet, as Sullivan points out, a legal discrepancy between FGM and FGCS nonetheless exists, which 'establishes and polices boundaries and borders between "us" and "them", between proper and improper bodies'. [24] This boundary, Sullivan argues, is increasingly invoked in public discourse in relation to 'Islamic' practices (of which FGM is a highly visible and recognisable example) considered intolerable, abhorrent and disgusting to the Australian public. [25] The female body is a central site over which anxieties about the limits of multiculturalism are played out. As Susie O'Brien has written for *The Herald Sun*: 'There is no place in our civilised Australian society for female genital mutilation, forced marriage, honour killings and polygamy ... We do not want the barbaric practice of female genital mutilation to be acceptable in this country.' [26] And in a piece for British magazine *The Spectator*, Lara Prendergast drew on FGM to illustrate the limits of *feminism*, specifically intersectional feminism, which she characterised as 'left-wing jargon' too insipid to counter the 'barbaric practice' of FGM. [27] When the language of 'barbarism' is repeatedly applied to FGM, but not to FGCS, we are witnessing the discursive power of racialised norms simultaneously embedded within liberal rhetorical frameworks that have great trouble engaging with the political complexities of acknowledging radical difference.

In such a context, the cultural practice of FGCS remains invisible, while Muslim women's bodies continue to be the visible markers of female oppression. Indeed, we are apt to lose sight of the blurred ground between FGM and FGCS – as well as the experiences of real women – when the genitally altered body of 'the Muslim woman' is metaphorised as everything that's wrong with contemporary feminism, be it intersectionalist women of colour or, as in Dawkins' imagination, whiney white women who don't understand how *lucky* they are.

Nevertheless, while Muslim women are perceived to be vulnerable as the victims of a patriarchal rule the West has purportedly left behind, they are also depicted as genetically dangerous. The Muslim woman's body incorporates imagined threat, both to Western ideas of democracy and, importantly, to the reproduction of whiteness. Muslim women are accused not only of potentially concealing weapons under their garments, but of also harbouring a yet more sinister weapon within their bodies – their wombs. Reproductive rights in the form of safe access to contraception and abortion have played a central role in feminist campaigns. However, 'appropriate' reproduction (variously defined) also serves the interests of neoliberal economics and demographic politics, and has led to the 'othering' of women whose bodies are seen as reproducing too often and too early (or, on the other hand, too infrequently and too late). Muslim women are regarded as prime offenders in this form of reproductive transgression. Muslim communities in the West, particularly in Europe, have been represented as a demographic threat to the 'native population', with projected demographics or pseudo-demographics forecasting a 'Muslim takeover' through sheer force of numbers rather than arms. Despite having been widely debunked, alarmist forecasts continue to circulate through both mainstream and social media of non-Muslim Europeans reduced to a struggling minority as the countries of their citizenship and ancestral heritage are overwhelmed by a booming

Muslim population. Australia has not been immune to this type of demographic panic. As then-federal Liberal MP Danna Vale said in 2006 of the abortion drug RU486:

> I have read ... comments by a certain imam from the Lakemba Mosque [who] actually said that Australia is going to be a Muslim nation in 50 years' time ... I didn't believe him at the time. But ... look at the birthrates and you look at the fact that we are aborting ourselves almost out of existence by 100 000 abortions every year. [28]

As political theorist Kate Gleeson has suggested, anti-abortion politics in Australia is historically aligned with anxieties about declining birth rates among white Australian women. The conservative, Christian political tradition gained traction in the 1970s with B. A. Santamaria's National Civic Council and the contribution of abortion to declining birth rates of the 1960s was high on the agenda as a national threat. Santamaria expressed the view that pro-choice legislation was 'inviting race suicide'. [29] Tony Abbott's attempts to reinvigorate an abortion debate while minister for health under the Howard government, Gleeson says, was a revival of anxieties that had become remapped to suit the post-9/11 political landscape. Danna Vale's comments thus appeared in the context of a growing fear 'of a clash of civilisations that the West just might not survive'. [30] The fertility choices made by white Australian women, then, negatively contextualise the capacity and apparent willingness of Muslim women to prioritise childbearing ahead of other life choices, enabling the demographic conquest envisioned by Vale. Muslim women are not only transmitters of a dangerous ideology, but also repulsive breeders of the enemy horde. Such 'anti-feminist race panic' distracts from recent discussions on feminism and natalism that seek to expand the discussion of women's reproductive choices beyond the issues of contraception and abortion by analysing the impact of factors such as access to parental leave and childcare. [31]

Conclusion

Feminist freedom continues to be defined primarily in terms of 'our' access to choices supposedly denied to 'other' women and is inscribed upon the body through practices which are held to signify either agency or oppression. Muslim women in particular are represented as simultaneously endangered (by practices such as veiling and FGM) and dangerous (thanks to their reproductive capacity and ability to conceal their identity). The new Orientalism of the post-9/11 era revitalises old distinctions between East and West through casting the Muslim female body as injured, uncivilised and unfree while leaving the West's own injurious racist representations unexamined. Muslim women are viewed as needing feminism more than Western women and serve as convenient Dawkins-style tropes for the deflection of feminist criticism. The 'mutilated' Muslim body in particular is an especially arresting image against which the legitimate concerns of non-Muslim feminists can be disregarded as the complaints of 'killjoys', as Sara Ahmed phrases it. [32] Ahmed argues that:

> feminists might kill joy simply by not finding the objects that promise happiness to be quite so promising ... In the thick sociality of everyday spaces, feminists are thus attributed as the origin of bad feeling, as the ones who ruin the atmosphere, which is how the atmosphere might be imagined (retrospectively) as shared. [33]

In the rhetoric of the 'elevatorgate' persuasion, the feminist killjoy is dismissed as irrational and annoying for failing to agree to the happy state of gender relations in the West. Meanwhile, the figure of the 'oppressed Muslim woman' assumes a certain rightful proximity to unhappiness as the subject of unfreedom. The abhorrence of Islam synecdochally invoked in public commentary through the example of FGM is underwritten by a contrasting script that accepts FGCS on the basis that it brings psychological wellbeing (or *happiness*). Western freedom of choice, then, turns the bodily site of injury (surgically altered genitals) into one of happy transformation and a reinvented selfhood liberated from the shame of abnormality. Western, secular culture represents itself as both desired and desirable through determining the Muslim woman's body as intolerably marked and inimical to white freedoms. And yet it is under this threat of foreign genetics that Western feminists are expected to relinquish one of their most cherished freedoms – reproductive choice. If being free means being white, then Western women's freedom to choose turns to obligation when it comes into conflict with the desires and fears of the (white) nation. In this way, 'postfeminism' heralds the achievement of female success on the condition that it be traded off for the preservation of the nation. The Muslim woman's body is all too often the casualty of boundary-maintenance procedures underpinning 'choice', where to be feminist or unfeminist, free or unfree, happy or unhappy is largely dependent on a prefabricated Orientalism materially expressed through sex.

'We love make-up, romance, high heels and men, of course': the contradictions of 'pop feminism'

Kate Farhall

Being a sex object is a very good thing. If you're not a sex object, you're in trouble. [1] — Helen Gurley Brown, founder of *Cosmopolitan*

Recently there has been an explosion of a new, popular feminism. Feminism has been rebranded and marketed to a younger, more pop culture-oriented generation, with celebrity royalty such as Beyoncé leading the charge; to call oneself a feminist is no longer seen as social suicide. This re-emergence of what is essentially liberal feminism, repackaged for a 21st century audience, is reflected in the Australian versions of the women's magazines *Cleo* and *Cosmopolitan*. Contemporary editions of the magazines consciously align themselves with this popular feminism, lauding the achievements of openly feminist celebrities, explicitly engaging with feminist issues and applauding strong, empowered women. Yet the progressiveness of this iteration of feminism is tempered by its ongoing commitment to the objectification of women. Feminist research consistently shows the objectification of women and the pressure of feminine beauty ideals to be problematic and limiting to women. Consequently, the dual emphases of women's freedom and adherence to feminine beauty standards seemingly render this popular form of feminism, not only internally incoherent, but also counterproductive to women's equality.

Since the birth of the modern women's lifestyle magazine in the mid-20th century, such publications have had a complex relationship with feminism. In Australia specifically, both *Cleo* and *Cosmopolitan* emerged in the early 1970s at the height of second wave feminism and amid rapid social change. In this progressive political context, both *Cleo* and *Cosmopolitan* to varying degrees espoused a level of support for feminism, predicated upon women's individual freedoms, tempered by a concurrent emphasis on teaching women how to attract a man. Between the 1980s and the first decade of the 21st century, social commentary content declined and feminism all but disappeared from the pages of women's magazines. The recent resurgence of feminism as a popular movement with which mainstream women's magazines affiliate themselves is a noteworthy transformation. However, it is important to critically evaluate this shift in terms of what it means for the feminist movement, as well as what it says about the content of contemporary popular feminism.

Feminists have consistently identified women's magazines as producing or reproducing ideas that are problematic for women. Feminist scholars have been critical of the messages such magazines send women and girls regarding body image, beauty standards and self-esteem, sexuality and intimate relationships, as well as what it means to be a woman more broadly. [2] A plethora of research suggests that magazines such as *Cleo* and *Cosmopolitan* present a narrow band of acceptable femininity, while media effects research contends that popular media forms such as magazines can have a very real impact on the values and behaviours of those who read them. [3] Despite the rise of digital media, these magazines continue to have a wide audience, with the publisher of *Cosmopolitan*, Bauer Media Group, boasting that 'one in 10 Australian women' are 'reached' by the magazine. [4] In their attempt to sell magazines through providing content that is broadly appealing to young women, as well as tapping into social trends relevant in their lives, these magazines can be seen as both a barometer of popular culture and a conduit through which ideas, perspectives and values are potentially disseminated to their target demographic.

The sudden embrace of feminism by particular celebrities

and sections of popular culture, including one of the bastions of femininity, the women's magazine, begs the question of what this popular iteration of feminism means for the women's liberation movement more broadly. The question remains as to whether the goals of a movement for women's liberation can really be reconciled with mainstream celebrity and popular culture. While shining a spotlight on feminist concerns and growing debate and awareness surrounding these issues is encouraging, arguably there are internal inconsistencies in the contemporary liberal feminist movement. On the one hand, popular feminism applauds strong women and seeks to empower young women to achieve their goals, become educated and attain a greater level of self-respect. On the other hand, beauty ideals that are unattainable for most women are still held up as a standard to emulate and those who vocally support popular feminism are often those who also objectify themselves in order to conform to a male-driven understanding of what is 'sexy'.

Sexualised objectification, in line with meeting male desires, is central to the public persona of many of the proponents of popular feminism. In the wake of her controversial and hypersexualised MTV performance and *Wrecking Ball* film clip, Miley Cyrus declared herself to be 'one of the biggest feminists in the world'. [5] Meanwhile, pop icon Beyoncé danced at the 2014 MTV Music Awards in front of a huge illuminated sign that read 'feminist' only months after sparking controversy at the Grammy awards, during a performance of the duet *Drunk in Love* with husband Jay-Z. She enthusiastically sang a line that has been criticised as making light of the violence Tina Turner suffered at the hands of her ex-husband. [6] Feminism in its current, popular form, then, would seem reluctant to confront or criticise male power. These tensions between a 'sexy' popular feminism and more substantive challenges to the patriarchy are also played out in women's magazines.

Popular feminism in contemporary women's magazines

The 2013 editions of *Cleo* and Australian *Cosmopolitan* are littered with references to feminism. An article in the July 2013 edition of *Cleo* tackles the issue of the enduring gender pay gap, with a large headline on the front cover proclaiming, 'Sexism exposed!' and the editorial explaining that because feminism 'hasn't been cool since the '70s, we've stopped calling out misogyny and sexism when we see it'. An interview in the same issue with the writer, creator, director and star of the TV show *Girls*, Lena Dunham, asks whether she would 'describe [her] work and [herself] as feminist'. Her response, that 'any woman who doesn't describe herself as a feminist is crazy' is positioned as commendable. Beyoncé is similarly idolised for her feminist credentials in the November 2013 edition of *Cosmopolitan*. The 'first lady of awesomeness' is praised for her ability to 'influence the global conversation on feminism, race, sexuality, philanthropy, justice, marriage, love and friendship' via the 'booty-popping' way that she 'gets her fans involved in the politics of empowerment'.

It is this 'booty-popping' aspect of 'pop feminism' that is at the heart of its broad appeal, yet also arguably the heart of the problem. The article cites several quotes that demonstrate Beyoncé's feminist credentials, such as her assertion that women's financial independence is important because 'money gives men the power to run the show. It gives men the power to define value ... define what's sexy ... [and] define what's feminine.' It also highlights her support for 'women's rights' through her involvement in the 'Chime for Change' concert, raising money for women's health, education and justice initiatives. Yet alongside praising her commitment to putting 'women's rights in the spotlight', the article also gushes over Beyoncé's beauty and style, swoons at 'the way Jay-Z [her rapper husband] looks at her when they're together' and cites her position as 'lads' mag' *GQ*'s '#1 Hottest Woman of the 21st Century'. The fact that she 'still reserves the right to be a Feminist In Heels' (capitalisation in original) is presented as the main reason to love her.

This 'Feminist In Heels' sentiment is echoed throughout the 2013 editions of *Cleo* and *Cosmopolitan*. The July 2013 *Cleo* editorial mentioned above, despite positing a need for feminism, similarly decries its previously unfashionable nature, suggesting that women were reluctant to label themselves as feminist because 'it has ugly connotations of man-hating women with icky underarm hair – when we love make-up, romance, high heels and men, of course'. A column in the May 2013 edition of *Cosmopolitan* that discusses why feminism is still relevant similarly draws on the 'fashionable' image of new popular feminism to encourage women to identify as feminists. The author announces to 'all of the smart, savvy ladies reading *Cosmo*' that 'I'm an ordinary gen-Y woman. I shave my legs, I own red lipstick, I wear five-inch heels. I love my job and I love men.' She concludes her discussion by proclaiming: 'I'm a feminist and I'm proud of it. I hope you are too.' It is this blending of feminist objectives and stereotypical femininity that is central to the popular feminist movement. In this context, feminism is reconceptualised as something that centres on the choices of individual women, regardless of the conditions under which those choices are made or the long-term effects of making them. Popular feminism is rebranded as fun, flirty and feminine and actively placed in direct opposition to alternative iterations of feminism that are labelled as outdated and unattractive. This individualisation of feminism, and lack of critique of the structures and systems that limit women, leave popular feminism ill-equipped to tackle issues associated with racism, capitalism, pornography or compulsory heterosexuality, as the individual choice of each woman is seen as sacrosanct. It is difficult to see how conforming to traditional notions of heterosexual femininity will bring about equality.

Alongside the conscious references to feminism and the celebration of celebrities who are self-proclaimed feminists, these magazines also provide articles that tackle feminist issues or pay tribute to strong or intelligent women. The '*Cosmo* Reports' section of the May 2013 edition asks whether the topless protest strategy of Ukrainian feminist group FEMEN empowers or objectifies women. An article in the March 2013 edition of *Cleo* respectfully and appropriately addresses the problem of domestic violence, while a further piece in the November issue explores the idea of a federal government 'fantasy Cabinet' composed entirely of Australian women who are leaders in their respective fields. Yet despite this shift towards embracing the feminist label, in conjunction with topical articles exploring feminist issues and positive female role models, the majority of the content of *Cleo* and *Cosmopolitan* continues to be based around beauty, fashion and how to please men. The question remains, therefore, whether it is possible to reconcile the goals of popular feminism, as espoused by contemporary women's magazines, with popular culture as it is constructed within their pages.

Fashion, femininity and finding 'Mr Right'

Despite their recent engagement with feminist ideas, the majority of the content of contemporary women's magazines remains grounded in mainstream understandings of femininity with an emphasis on content relating to appearance and relationships. Approximately 65 per cent of the total number of pages in the editions of *Cleo* from 2013 are dedicated to beauty, fashion, celebrity and advertising content. As a point of comparison, in 1973, that figure was 35 per cent. Women's magazines are frequently critiqued for designing content explicitly to support their advertisers; feminist theorists contend that much of the editorial substance in mainstream women's magazines actually plays on women's insecurities, causing them to feel inadequate and thus serving to produce a purported need for the beauty, fashion and lifestyle products advertised within their pages. [7] Academics in the field argue that a significant portion of the content of commercial women's magazines centres on how to obtain and maintain a male partner, subordinating women's needs and desires to men's pleasure, both sexual and otherwise. [8]

A significant body of research that addresses women's magazines notes their focus on successful heterosexual relationships that lead to marriage as the ultimate goal for women. Feminist psychologists Janna Kim and L. Monique Ward identify 'women's beauty and their success in relationships' as the central tenets of women's magazines, asserting that:

> These magazines place young women's ability to establish and maintain heterosexual dating relationships at the *centre* of women's identities, to the exclusion of content about their education, their careers, or their participation in athletics and politics. [9]

Rhetoric surrounding the achievement of 'wedded bliss' and finding 'Mr Right' abounds, with men the ultimate source of 'women's fulfilment'. [10] This ultimate goal of obtaining a man is inextricably intertwined with achieving physical perfection; beauty, fashion tips and achieving the ideal body shape, are often positioned in service of this goal. [11]

An interview with *Cleo*'s 'cover girl' from its November 2013 magazine, ex-reality TV star Lauren Conrad, demonstrates this centrality of beauty and heterosexual relationships to the magazine's understanding of women. Of 11 interview questions that are posed to the now-fashion designer and author, seven relate to Conrad's tips on beauty, hair and makeup. The remaining four pertain to relationships, three of which directly request the celebrity's advice about how to handle 'guy[s]' or 'boyfriend[s]'. By consistently framing women with multiple talents or areas of interest, in terms of these two overriding criteria, the magazines suggest to female readers that their worth lies primarily in their physical beauty and their relationships with men.

The relationship between women's magazines, physical perfection and body image is one that has been extensively discussed within feminist literature. In recent decades, there has been a significant body of work linking representations of physical appearance in women's magazines and the media more broadly to negative body image in young, female consumers. [12] One study found that 78 per cent of the covers of popular women's magazines featured a message about physical appearance. [13] Not only was body image such an integral part of the magazines' messages, the authors of the study also concluded that the positioning of messages related to body weight 'may imply that losing weight or changing the shape of one's body will lead to a better life'. [14] Kim and Ward argue that women's magazines 'uphold traditional femininity ideologies that ... perpetuate physical beauty as the standard to judge women's worth'. [15] Moreover, it is not simply physical beauty that is prioritised in women's magazines, but a certain type of physical beauty: a homogenised, predominantly white, feminine beauty ideal.

Feminism and the objectification of women: incompatible goals

The cohabitation of feminist ideals and the objectification of women in contemporary popular feminism, as seen in *Cleo* and *Cosmopolitan*, requires analysis. Put simply, the goal of women's equality and the achievement of beauty ideals, as defined within a patriarchal system, are incompatible. It is not possible for women to advance, to become the empowered women popular feminism both applauds and envisages, if ultimately their value is still based on their physical appearance and sexual attractiveness to men. An emphasis on the achievement of feminine beauty ideals is thus incompatible with women's equality, as it actually serves to limit, rather than empower, women. It is important to accept this if feminism is to be truly effective in the

21st century. While the explosive success of popular, liberal feminism in recent years has been viewed as a cause for celebration, by failing to address the objectification of women as a cornerstone of the structural constraints that impact on women's lives, popular feminism becomes self-limiting and self-defeating. Such internal inconsistencies within popular feminism not only detract from the strength of the movement, but also serve to water down the term 'feminist' itself, stripping it of its potency and rendering it increasingly meaningless.

Unrealistic beauty standards have been shown to disadvantage women in various ways. Feminist philosopher Sandra Lee Bartky contends that women are continually self-critiquing against beauty standards driven by male desire. [16] Within this system, women's physical appearance routinely comes to represent their 'entire self'. [17] Under relentless pressure to present an appropriately feminine exterior, as exacerbated by media representations of flawless, photoshopped bodies, women and girls begin to self-objectify, dissociating from their bodies and instead viewing themselves as objects to be used and appraised by others. [18] Not only does this cause women to be more self-critical than their male counterparts, self-objectification also carries with it a host of negative emotional consequences, such as feelings of anxiety, shame and self-consciousness, as well as the disruption of mental functioning and inhibition of concentration. [19]

Research shows that women who read magazines primarily to glean beauty and fashion advice are also more likely to report 'objectifying their own bodies' alongside beliefs that 'women should be indirect and alluring when attracting men's interest'. [20] This is perhaps unsurprising given that content analyses of women's magazines have consistently found that they give 'specific instructions about the steps [women] can take to turn themselves into the kind of sexual object that will catch a man's eye'. [21] Although the 'booty-popping' rhetoric of popular feminism is associated with a sexually empowered representation of women, research suggests that this may be even more problematic than the objectification of more traditional, passive forms of sexualised representations of women. A 2011 study by Emma Halliwell, Helen Malson and Irmgard Tischner, showed that exposure to 'idealised images of women' framed as 'agentic sexual subjects', that is to say active and knowing in their sexuality, led to greater self-objectification and weight dissatisfaction than exposure to images framed more passively. [22] As such, the associations between popular feminism and the objectification of women are problematic for women's mental health, even when such objectification is framed in terms of women's sexual power.

Given the very real harms and limitations placed upon women by valuing them in terms of their physical appearance, the dual emphases of female empowerment and the objectification of women within popular feminism are in direct conflict. Without addressing the role of unattainable beauty standards and female objectification in maintaining women's inequality, popular feminism is unlikely to produce real change towards women's equality. Although the recent, mainstream interest in feminism remains grounds for celebration; without addressing the very real negative impacts of the objectification of women, as well as the function it plays in constraining women's ability to succeed, this victory remains hollow. Until popular feminism works to dismantle the significant constraints faced by women as a result of valuing them according to their physical beauty and their relationships with men, its success will remain limited by the patriarchal system in which it operates. Feminism should aspire to fight the overarching patriarchal structures that limit women, rather than teach women how to achieve success in a man's world. Thus, a popular liberal feminism that remains committed to objectification, ultimately cannot achieve women's freedom.

Business as usual, rebranded as ethics: the whitewashing of systemic injustice

Laura McNally

Recent decades have been challenging for women's rights. According to Germaine Greer, we've never had it so bad as women. [1] The proliferation of technology has resulted in the flourishing of pornographic culture and the male entitlement and misogyny it breeds. [2] Simultaneously, globalised consumer culture is at an all time high. In essence, sexist male entitlement has gone global.

From early liberal feminist campaigns such as the pro-pornography movement, to the recent global 'SlutWalk' campaign, there is a move to rebrand sexual objectification as feminist. Some liberal feminist scholars argue this is diversification or 'sex positivity'. However, more critical feminists see this as an ill-fated partnership with the capitalist exploitation of women.

Feminism is at a crossroad. Feminism can either fight to liberate women from growing male entitlement and the institutions that underpin it, or feminism can work to make patriarchy more acceptable by selling it as 'choice'. So how is it that liberal feminism has come to promote the very practices that our foremothers fought so hard to end?

This chapter will explore the effects of advanced globalisation on women's oppression, in particular, how globalisation amplifies the shortcomings of liberal feminist theory, analysis and praxis. Using examples such as sexual objectification and sexualised oppression, this chapter will demonstrate how liberal feminism develops the rhetoric of 'empowerment' that consequently bolsters systemic oppression. Ultimately such limitations result in liberal feminist collusion with industry and exploitation to the detriment of women. It's business as usual, rebranded as ethics.

Globalisation

The intensifying processes of globalisation means that consumers and corporations are no longer subject to national boundaries or robust state regulatory systems. Multinational firms can operate outside national legislative structures. These firms not only bypass the rules but can also partake in setting the rules, often yielding more economic and lobby power than nation states. Such an environment is fertile ground for misogynist and exploitative industry to take hold. The economic exploitation of women occurs on a fully global scale. Unethical industries can follow the 'downward spiral' to operate in locations with lower costs and less regulation.

Corporate ethics appear to be at an all-time low, yet we are led to believe corporate social responsibility ('CSR') will fill the void. Capitalism has long been charged with co-opting social justice, from cigarette companies marketing 'women's empowerment': 'You've come a long way, baby,' to today's 'Real Beauty' campaigns by Dove or Unilever. Some scholars see a trend toward 'conscious capitalism' while others see this as 'whitewashing' at best. By co-opting the language of social justice, corporations can perpetuate inequality, albeit concealed within a glossy CSR report.

Community members often find themselves in a bind with CSR; they may be pacified or gagged from speaking against corporate injustice through the provision of CSR funding. A company may be rapidly polluting rare ecologies but, at the same time, its CSR programmes may also fund scholarships for disadvantaged youth. A company can be implicated in violent civil unrest but, under its CSR remit, may also provide local roads and utilities.

Such CSR actions are not benevolent, but are political manoeuvres to legitimise capitalist exploitation. In effect, they may become a tool for compounding economic and political power away from nation states and into corporate enterprise. In this way CSR can be understood as a tool for promulgating ongoing colonisation, a tool that regulates the behaviour of community stakeholders rather than corporations. [3] Again, it's business as usual, rebranded as ethics.

Liberal feminism

In a globalised, misogynist, consumer culture, criticism of the industrialisation of women's oppression is needed more than ever. However, liberal feminism not only fails to provide this criticism but instead offers justification of such practices. The liberal feminist defence of the sex trade has crept into politics, policy, and research. Rather than reporting on the large proportion of girls and women forced into the trade, liberal feminism focuses on the few who, with some 'choice', feel 'empowered'. Such an approach makes invisible the systemic inequality, exploitation and coercion that forces millions of girls and women into the trade.

This endorsement of exploitative industry by liberal feminism further marginalises the women most harmed in the trade. In this context, we can understand how liberal feminism is analogous to CSR. CSR promotes the concept of a 'benevolent' corporation that can serve both social justice and capitalist growth, while liberal feminism argues for benevolent industries that can serve women's rights and capitalism. By using liberal feminist rhetoric, women are silenced from criticising the industries that exploit them. As a consequence, like CSR, liberal feminism makes social injustices invisible by rebranding them as 'choices'. Hence, liberal feminism bolsters the inequality it claims to resolve.

While liberal feminism is not a corporate movement per se, it is comparable to CSR on several levels. First, on a theoretical level, liberal feminist theory relies on the same problematic assumptions as CSR theory. These assumptions are based upon conventional economics and classical liberalism. These include the assumed separation of the private and public spheres and the assumed intact power of nation-state regulation. Both of these assumptions are challenged under advanced globalisation. Second, on an analytical level, liberal feminism avoids structural or critical analysis of power. Liberal feminism often discusses power as an individual negotiation rather than a structural, contextual reality. While this may help some women to feel 'empowered' on an individual level, it only makes invisible the broader systemic forces that undergird oppression. Third, on a practical level, liberal feminism evades empirical data on the realities of women's oppression under globalised capitalism. For instance, high levels of sexual violence and sex trafficking are largely dismissed by liberal feminism. Rather than these trends being interrogated as urgent symptoms of growing global male supremacy, they are increasingly replaced with discussions on 'whorephobia', or the need to support 'underage sex work'.

Liberal feminism envisions that equality of the sexes can be achieved by equal participation in global capitalism. This bypasses any critique of the structures inherent to a global free market system and its effects on women. A critical, or more radical, approach means interrogating patriarchy and the global institutions that sustain it. The liberal vision seeks only to make patriarchy more equitable by branding it as 'choice'. This is not so much feminism as it is a Westernised corporate strategy. 'Choice' is only relevant if you are a wealthy and powerful enough consumer, as the following examples demonstrate. As we will see, this is rarely applicable to marginalised women.

Globalised sexual objectification

Liberal feminism applies a contradictory approach to its analysis of sexist practice. On the one hand, it fights for female bodily autonomy, often in the form of 'reproductive rights'. On the other hand, it simultaneously promotes the industries that objectify and commoditise the female body. This is epitomised by pornography and pornographic objectification of the female body, which, for instance, has given rise to alarming rates of labiaplasty. While liberal feminism may be critical of cultural practices in the global South, such as female genital mutilation, some maintain that Western cultural 'beauty' practices that brutalise female bodies are an edifice of agency and choice.

The 2013 documentary, *Vagina Diaries*, [4] explored the trend of labiaplasty: 'a surgical procedure that will reduce and/or reshape the labia minora'. [5] In the documentary, viewers saw a scene where a woman who had barely reached adulthood was laid across a surgeon's table, legs splayed. The male practitioner worked quickly and coolly with a set of metal tools; there was a hissing noise and the young woman squinted in pain. She was clearly distressed, yet there was no one to comfort her in this sterile cosmetic surgery environment. Several weeks later the young woman reported that she was still not entirely comfortable with what happened.

The documentary considers the role of media, pornography and relationships in shaping the perceptions of young women. However, liberal feminist analysis looks to situate the woman's story within the narrative of 'personal agency' and 'my body, my choice' rhetoric. Liberal feminism tends to disregard the interrelationships between sex industry standards of female appearance and increasing pressure on women to conform. Under liberal feminism these actions can be constituted as a result of women's individual empowerment as consumers.

Globalised sexual exploitation

Girls are increasingly surrounded by the influence of the sex industry, with much of the visual culture of the West saturated with pornographic imagery. This is coupled with a dangerous, global epidemic of male entitlement. Thai reports show around 40 per cent of the sex industry is made up of underage girls. [6] Male sexual entitlement is colonising the third world with the vigour of a transnational corporation. This local–global industrialising of sexual exploitation is constraining the rights and choices of girls globally. Working to legitimise this exploitation only solidifies the *lack of choice* for girls and women.

Another 2013 documentary film entitled, *I am a Girl*, [7] explored the stories of a number of girls living in different countries. One girl in particular had an all-too-familiar story in Cambodia. Kimsey was just 13 years old when she was first forced to have sex for money. She didn't know what sex was. She didn't know what to expect. All she knew was that it would hurt and she was scared, but she had no choice. Now at age 15, she is embroiled in a complex, deeply collectivist, yet abusive set of circumstances that she is trying desperately to escape. At the time of airing, Kimsey was still living in Cambodia and fighting to flee her poverty and abuse. Despite this, the production did not frame what had happened to this girl – at age 13 – as rape, but instead suggested that she had 'chosen' to become an 'underage sex worker'. [8]

Liberal feminism fails to criticise the industry that exploits girls like Kimsey. Liberal feminism more often wholly defends the industry and instead frames any criticism of the sex trade as 'sex negative' or even 'whorephobic'. In liberal feminist rhetoric, the notion of child sex abuse is obscured with an all-encompassing defence of the sex trade. Indeed, the rebranding of child sex abuse as 'underage sex work' is now a tenet of the more extreme elements of liberal feminism. Like CSR, liberal feminism uses discursive strategies to disguise systemic oppression and even brand it as a type of freedom. These strategies not only support exploitative industries, but the sex traffickers too. As Lydia Cacho found in her investigations of the child sex trade, traffickers increasingly capitalise on the liberal feminist language of 'choice' to justify their actions. [9]

Liberal feminism envisions that full and equal participation in a capitalist consumer culture is equivalent to women's liberation, even if that participation hinges upon child sex abuse and exploitation. The very language of women's liberation is now replaced with depoliticised and individualistic terms such as 'empowerment' and 'agency'. Such terms make systemic constraints against women invisible under global capitalism.

Both liberal feminism and CSR, in effect, promote capitalism as a kind of solution, rather than a cause of systemic injustice. CSR looks to recruit marginalised workers into the capitalist system, often by offering necessary funds in exchange for their exploitation. Similarly, liberal feminism looks to recruit marginalised girls and women into the patriarchal system by arguing that money or 'choice' can justify or void exploitation. Yet no amount of compensation can turn sexual exploitation into a 'choice'.

The liberal feminist approach reframes the economic disadvantage that may force girls and women into the sex trade as 'choice'. To defend an industry that hinges upon impoverished girls and women's lack of choice, and instead frame it as being primarily about 'women's choices', shows that liberal feminism is reserved for women with the economic power required to have such choice. 'Choice' for middle-class women in the first world is entirely incomparable to those living in poverty, especially those who are children. Yet, the few (first world) women with 'choice' come to represent all girls and women globally for liberal feminism. As a result, liberal feminism poses to further silence and exploit women already on the margins of society.

Conclusion

Social responsibility is being capitalised upon as a new market opportunity. Feminism is being replaced by the corporatisation of women's oppression. The slave trade is fast expanding. Girls and women are dying as a result of male violence, sexual violence, femicide and violence against the female body in so many forms. In such a context, women need activism that is urgent, deliberate and challenging. A liberal feminism that seeks only to negotiate with existing forms of 'agency' will merely ensure women remain on the boundaries of patriarchy.

Feminism must be resolute in interrogating injustices that are more global, political and interconnected than ever before. There is nothing to be gained from framing sexist practices as 'choice', 'agency' or 'empowerment'. There is nothing to be gained from a feminism that makes concessions and deliberates over whether 'agency' is involved while girls and women continue to die. We will never find female agency within patriarchy, consumer choice will never replace liberation, and sexualising feminism will only ever reinforce the sexist status quo. As Audré Lorde famously said, 'the master's tools will never dismantle the master's house'. [10]

PART III:
SEXUALITY

A fine line between pleasure and pain?
On the issue of 'choosing' sexual violence

Laura Tarzia

Whatever choice a woman is making and she is the one deciding to do ... even if it is a degrading sexual act ... is absolutely feminism. [1] — Belle Knox

Sexual violence perpetrated by men against women remains a major feminist concern in the 21st century. Despite the many advances women have made in other spheres, sexual violence is still globally prevalent and continues to impact upon the health and wellbeing of women and girls. Sexual violence against women is often perpetrated by intimate partners, as well as by strangers, and takes many forms, including rape, sexual assault, unwanted sexual advances or comments, trafficking, and sexually coercive behaviour. [2] Globally, one in three women have experienced either physical or sexual violence, [3] while in Australia, it is estimated that almost one in five women has experienced sexual assault since the age of 15. [4] The impact of sexual violence is known to be severe and long lasting, and it would be fairly uncontroversial to suggest that both liberal and radical feminists are committed to its eradication. I argue, however, that liberal feminists who advocate 'choice' and 'sex positivism' cannot hope to eliminate sexual violence against women while remaining uncritical of sexual practices that eroticise dominance and subordination. I contend that an overemphasis on 'consent' as the criteria for differentiation between sexual violence and so-called 'kinky' sex is problematic, and provides a deceptively easy solution to the contradictions inherent in the politics of desire, while failing to acknowledge the impact of patriarchal society on women's choices. The aim of this chapter is not to criticise individual women who engage in bondage and discipline, sadism and masochism ('BDSM'), but rather, to highlight the contradictions present in the response of liberal and 'sex positive' feminism.

The last few decades have seen an entire industry grow up around sexual practices involving elements of BDSM, and other forms of sexual play characterised by exchanges of power between a dominant and submissive partner. These are generally known collectively by the term BDSM, although there are a variety of subcultures within the community. In BDSM, both physical and emotional pain may be inflicted on the submissive by the dominant as part of the 'scene' or 'play'. Common BDSM activities include, but are not limited to, spanking, flogging, caning, role-playing, fetishes, and the use of restraints or gags. [5] The submissive may be the recipient of the dominant's attentions, or they may be required to service the dominant in a master/slave type relationship. Thanks to the bestselling erotic novel, *Fifty Shades of Grey*, BDSM – once viewed as a deviant subculture – has reached a mainstream audience and increasingly become the subject of attention and debate. [6] *Fifty Shades of Grey* and its two sequels have been enormously successful, with a classical music album, a clothing range, a line of sex toys, and a film adaptation released in 2015. [7] Marketed primarily to women, the phenomenal success of this series, in which the virginal and naïve protagonist, Anastasia Steele, enters into a BDSM relationship with billionaire Christian Grey, has largely been attributed to the fact that it supposedly taps into women's secret erotic desires, particularly the desire to be sexually submissive. [8] Although the BDSM community has been quick to distance itself from the books, arguing that the controlling, manipulative, and stalker-ish behaviour of Christian Grey is at odds with the ethics of BDSM, it has nonetheless reignited the debate between radical feminists and liberal feminists regarding the relationship between sex and violence.

The liberal feminist response to BDSM

Since the mid-1990s, the so-called third wave of feminism has gained traction, partly in response to the perceived rigidity of radical feminism and partly due to divisions within the feminist movement that arose during the second wave. Third wave feminism emphasises the individual agency of women, and argues that women should be supported in their choices no matter what those choices are. In this way, third wave feminism shares much in common with liberal feminism, and certainly adheres to its central tenets regarding 'choice' and individualism. In this chapter, I use the terms interchangeably and generally refer simply to 'liberal feminism' as encompassing 'sex positive feminism', 'sex radicalism', 'raunch feminism' and 'choice feminism'. These variations each assert that all sexual choices made by women are inherently feminist ones. For example, liberal feminists refuse to problematise prostitution, stripping, pornography, or sexual objectification, providing these activities are a woman's choice. Similarly, BDSM is viewed completely uncritically, as just another item on the sexual menu that women actively consent to take part in and gain pleasure from. 'Sex positive' writer and therapist, Kath Albury, asks disbelievingly of her readers: 'Do women *really* need to be protected from "male violence" in the form of BDSM pornography?' [9] It is evidently incomprehensible, to liberal feminists, that something that produces orgasms could possibly be anti-feminist or problematic. As Jessica Wakeman writes in an online essay for *The Frisky*: 'Getting spanked and dominated in bed by an enthusiastic partner was the most sexually liberating feeling of my entire life.' [10]

In short, the freedom to express one's 'liberated' sexual choices through BDSM is understood by liberal feminists as empowering and transgressive. To liberal feminists, BDSM is an alternative to the norm of compulsory heterosexuality, offering an opportunity for women and men to negotiate and share the power within a sexual encounter.

Since within the BDSM community there are dominant women and submissive men, as well as same-sex BDSM couples, this is taken to mean that BDSM is inherently more egalitarian than traditional heterosexuality, and that it has the power to subvert gender norms by parodying and even 'queering' them, highlighting their performative nature.

While a 'liberated' sexuality, where we subvert the patriarchy through orgasms, may sound like a good idea, by examining some of the key arguments of the liberal feminist approach to BDSM, it becomes clear that their position is simplistic and naïve, and cannot seriously address the issue of sexual violence against women. I advocate instead, for a radical feminist approach, despite the recent emergence of 'sex critical' positions that attempt to straddle the middle-ground between 'sex positive' and 'sex negative' feminisms.

BDSM and consent

Liberal feminists and practitioners of BDSM highlight a critical point of difference between sexual violence and BDSM, namely, consent. The BDSM community operates, in theory, by a strict set of rules including 'SSC' (safe, sane and consensual), and 'RACK' (risk aware consensual kink), which are intended to ensure that nobody comes to harm. BDSM practitioners argue that all partners carefully negotiate and renegotiate the boundaries of their sexual encounters beforehand, including the use of 'safewords' to stop proceedings in case 'no' is not recognised (for example in a rape or forced sex scene). Miriam Weeks, otherwise known as porn star Belle Knox, argues that: 'BDSM is all about consent. Abuse is all about a lack thereof.' [11] There are a number of issues, however, with this reliance on consent as the delineator between BDSM and sexual violence against women.

First, the notion that women can consent to violent sex in a patriarchal rape culture needs careful critique. Women are socialised from birth to be pleasing to men; they internalise the idea that they owe men sex, and that they should enjoy it. [12] Whether 'consent' is understood as an enthusiastic 'yes' or simply not saying 'no' makes little difference when we consider how women and men are guided into contrasting masculine and feminine roles with very different relationships to power and autonomy. This does not mean that women who engage in BDSM do not genuinely feel aroused or excited by it. As radical feminist theorist, Sheila Jeffreys, points out, being subordinated can feel sexy. [13] Neither does it mean that women do not have the *capacity* to consent. Rather, it suggests that consent on its own is not enough to set BDSM apart from sexual violence.

Second, some liberal feminists suggested there is a double standard. That if athletes such as boxers can acceptably consent to the harm they inflict on each other, then women should be able to acceptably consent to violence that occurs in the bedroom (or the dungeon). Setting aside the fact that we quite happily draw the line with regards to consent in other areas (for example, that minors cannot consent to sexual activity or that one cannot consent to being murdered), the answer lies in the wider implications that sexual violence has and sport does not. For example, from a legal perspective, Cheryl Hanna has argued that using consent to determine whether a crime had occurred would allow 'people, mostly men, to use violence to satiate their sexual desires'. [14] She points out that if consent were allowed as a defence it would create a dangerous precedent in sexual assault cases where the victim is physically injured, whereby the perpetrator could simply argue that the victim 'consented' to being hurt. In other words it would become impossible to tell if the victim had really consented, or, like many abused women, felt coerced into saying that she did.

Third, the assertion that consent guidelines prevent abuse from occurring within the BDSM community is seriously misleading. Many BDSM bloggers write about experiences of rape, abuse, and harm, when their consent was ignored and their bodily integrity violated. [15] These accounts suggest that such violation is not a rare occurrence.

A recent survey by the National Coalition for Sexual Freedom, a United States-based BDSM organisation, found that 30.1 per cent of respondents had had a pre-negotiated limit violated and 14.9 per cent had experienced having a 'safeword' or safe sign ignored. [16]

BDSM and choice

Similar to the idea that women can freely consent to violent BDSM in a patriarchal system is the idea that they 'choose' to participate in it in order to satisfy their own desires and needs. The concept of choice is central to liberal feminist politics, and it is common to hear the claim that being able to choose is the *point* of feminism and that women should not judge each other for the content of their 'choices'. This rhetoric of choice-as-liberation focuses on the individual, thus ignoring the ways in which our choices are constrained by our environment. It also avoids the challenges of making the personal political, and of taking a position that may be perceived as unpopular, unsexy, or exclusionary.

Choice, however, is also deprived of meaning if the options from which a woman is choosing are limited or the choice is made under coercion. People often wonder, for example, why women in abusive domestic relationships choose to stay. However, if we consider that these women are often financially and emotionally dependent on their partners, it becomes clear that although they may have 'chosen' to stay – in the most hollow sense of the term – that 'choice' is not a free one. Likewise, not all women in the world have the social capital or financial stability to be able to 'choose' what they will and will not do, a fact that liberal feminism, as a primarily white, middle-class movement, tends to conveniently ignore. This is not to say that a woman who chooses to engage in BDSM is necessarily in the same position as a victim of domestic violence or someone living in poverty, however, in a society where sexual desire is defined primarily as *male* desire, what kind of sexual choices can women actually make? Under patriarchy, a woman is taught that her desires are to please men sexually – that making him happy should make her happy. I do not question that individual women really do want to engage in BDSM, but I do question these as 'authentic choices' when what is constructed as sexual pleasure – what is erotic, sexy, fun – is ultimately something we are taught by a male-dominated society in which violence against women and girls is at epidemic levels.

BDSM and liberated desire

The idea that we all possess an 'authentic' sexual desire that needs to be 'liberated' from political constraints is a common theme in liberal feminist writings about BDSM. Wakeman, describing her personal sexual journey which culminated in her embracing her desire to be spanked, writes: 'It took me far too many years to realise that it wasn't very feminist of me to police my own sexuality, to label it "good for feminism" or "bad for feminism". It is what it is!' [17] This rhetoric epitomises the liberal feminist position, where desire exists in a vacuum untouched by the influences of culture or society. Although the intention of liberal feminists is to disassociate female desire from the shame associated within patriarchal culture – an admirable goal – it is impossible to know what 'natural' or 'liberated' female desire looks like until such time as we no longer live under a system of entrenched inequality. Furthermore, as Jeffreys points out, this is essentially putting the cart before the horse and it misdirects feminist energies that could be better spent combating sexual violence against women:

> The pursuit of the orgasm … diverts our energies from the struggles that are needed now against sexual violence … Questioning how those orgasms feel, what they mean politically … is not easy, but it is also not impossible. A sexuality of equality suited to our pursuit of freedom has still to be forged and fought for if we are to release women from sexual subjugation. [18]

The pursuit of the orgasm is simply not enough to fuel an effective movement for women's liberation.

BDSM and gender equality

Liberal feminists and BDSM activists argue that rather than being misogynist, BDSM is inherently transgressive and empowering because women can be either dominant or submissive in the sexual encounter. The existence of lesbian sadomasochism and gay BDSM are also cited in support of this argument. However, former BDSM insiders have argued that the apparent 'equality' of BDSM is an illusion. Blogger antiplodon, for example, describes her experience as a female dominant in the BDSM scene:

> As a female dominant, many of the acts I was made to perform on men were acts of verbal degradation, humiliation, and emotional abuse. This included such things as verbal humiliation with words like bitch, slut, whore, and pussy ... Because the most humiliating thing they could imagine was being treated like a woman. [19]

This suggests that the sexual excitement gained from playing with dominance and submission in BDSM only makes sense because it emulates the real situation of male dominance and female submission that exists in patriarchal models of sex. The idea that a woman belongs at the bottom of the sexual hierarchy, whether she takes on the role of the submissive, or the dominant, is what gives BDSM its meaning. Even when non-heterosexual partners engage in BDSM, they are still, in the end, replicating the power dynamics laid out in compulsory heterosexuality. It is difficult to see how this is transgressive, or particularly useful to the feminist cause. Furthermore, as various radical feminists have pointed out, once the 'scene' is over, a submissive man can return to the position of power, whereas women must confront social and sexual subordination in their everyday lives.

Conclusion

In this chapter I have argued that liberal feminism does not provide us with the necessary tools to truly combat sexual violence against women. By refusing to critique BDSM and other sexual practices that eroticise male dominance and female subordination, liberal feminists fail to acknowledge the ways in which sexual violence is entrenched within society and impacts on the ways in which we understand sexuality in general. As I have argued, BDSM should not escape critique simply because women consent to it, choose to participate in it, or because they can play the dominant role. Each of these elements, it can be argued, is rendered meaningless in the context of patriarchal culture. It is therefore inconsistent for liberal feminists, on the one hand, to advocate for a world free from sexual violence against women, while simultaneously supporting sexual practices in which that same violence is enacted. In order to effectively combat sexual violence against women, feminists need to continue to fight to eradicate patriarchal culture in all its forms, and continue the important but often unpopular task of problematising the notion that sexual desire is undeniably and inherently 'good'.

A human right to prostitute others?: Amnesty International and the privileging of the male orgasm

Caroline Norma

Sexual desire and activity are a fundamental human need. To criminalise those who are unable or unwilling to fulfil that need through more traditionally recognised means and thus purchase sex, may amount to a violation of the right to privacy and undermine the rights to free expression and health. [1] — Amnesty International

Since 1999, a number of countries have legislated against the buying of people for prostitution. Sweden, South Korea, Norway, Iceland, Canada, Ireland and Northern Ireland have all criminalised the activities of prostitution buyers. The policy to criminalise the sex industry and its customers (but decriminalise people in prostitution) is supported by the European Union and Council of Europe, and is advocated for by Equality Now and the European Women's Lobby. It is an unprecedented way of making policy on prostitution, and is known internationally as the 'Nordic Model'.

The spread of the Nordic Model represents nothing less than the withdrawal, from men, of their longstanding legal right to buy women for sexual use. Unsurprisingly, this attracts opposition from sex industry businesspeople and their supporters. Some have argued, for example, that the Nordic Model actually exacerbates the harms of sex work. [2] In such a view, sex industry 'customers' are benign parties to prostitution transactions. It is their absence, rather than their presence, that is seen as a threat to women in prostitution. Australian academic Barbara Sullivan, for instance, downplays the threat of men's violence against women in prostitution when she states that 'clients value the work of sex workers because they often pay a significant amount of money for these services'. [3] Yet we know that prostitution buyers represent a significant violence risk for women both within and outside of the sex industry. [4] A frequent claim of liberal feminists is that prostitution may be justified on the basis of its monetary worth to women.

Typical is JaneMaree Maher, Sharon Pickering and Alison Gerard's 2013 observation that 'a number of workers from Southeast Asia [in a brothel in Australia] were remitting money to support family members back home' and the women saw 'this type of work ... as both necessary for family support and acceptable on that basis'. [5] In the liberal feminist view, female freedom derives from the 'right' to receive financial compensation for sexual exploitation, and struggle for public acceptance of this right characterises the liberal approach to prostitution. In this approach the prostitution buyer becomes virtually invisible.

This liberal defence of prostitution, on the side of an individual woman's 'human right' to 'sell herself' for monetary gain, has popularly circulated in Western countries for more than three decades. In recent years it has spawned a further defence of prostitution, this time on the side of the buyer. A new, mirror-image defence of prostitution buyers has emerged to construct men as legitimate sexual consumers, and as rational choice decision-makers who buy women for prostitution to facilitate their individual 'free expression and health'. This chapter describes the recent involvement of Amnesty International ('AI') in the construction of such a defence of prostitution buyers, and shows the defence to have arisen specifically in opposition to the Nordic Model.

The 'autonomy and health' of the prostitution buyer

In April 2012, AI commenced a review of its policy platform on prostitution. For more than 10 years before this, AI had taken a sexually liberal position on prostitution that 'criminalising consensual sex between adults is a breach of human rights'. [6] The United Kingdom ('UK') branch was particularly active in seeking a revision of this stance towards a more proactive endorsement of the 'rights' of sex industry participants, including buyers. After undertaking a review in 2013, AI's London-based secretariat released a number of policy background documents in which prostituting others is described as an exercise of 'personal autonomy', and government policy criminalising the purchase of sexual services (the centrepiece of the Nordic Model) is condemned as state suppression of individual autonomy and health, as follows:

> Men and women who buy sex from consenting adults are also exercising personal autonomy ... Some develop a stronger sense of self in their relationships with sex workers, improving their life enjoyment and dignity. At a very basic level, expressions of sexuality and sex are a primary component of the human experience, which is directly linked to individuals' physical and mental health. The state's interference with an adult's strategy to have sex with another consenting adult is, therefore, a deliberate interference with those individuals' autonomy and health. [7]

The AI secretariat retrospectively explained that it released the documents to initiate a 'global consultation process' on the issue of 'prostitution and human rights', but the documents pre-emptively put beyond question the possibility AI members might support the criminalisation of prostitution buyers. The documents cite, for instance, the recent UNAIDS assertion that 'end demand' initiatives that decriminalise workers, while penalising 'clients', do not reduce the incidence of prostitution nor improve the lives of 'sex workers'. AI goes even further to defend the activities of buyers on the basis that 'some individuals buy sex from sex workers as an exercise of personal autonomy'. [8] This claim is supported with declarations about the negative consequences of criminalising buyers, including a purported resultant increase in the incidence of HIV transmission, and greater extortion of prostituted people by buyers and police. The documents provide no source for these assertions, and their bases in empirical research are likely to be weak. [9]

It has been suggested that the proposal by the AI secretariat to change the organisation's official platform was potentially influenced by the activism of Amnesty UK member Douglas Fox, a founder of, and business partner in, one of the UK's largest escort agencies. [10] Fox has publicly boasted about playing such a role, but Amnesty UK published a rebuttal of the claim in 2013. [11] An impetus to the AI proposal might alternatively have come from actions by the organisation's UK Paisley branch in 2012. This branch made a submission to a public consultation held by a Scottish parliamentarian that endorsed a proposal to introduce the Nordic Model. [12] Amnesty UK was alerted to the existence of this endorsing submission, and called for the Paisley branch to withdraw it. Branch members refused to do so and since that incident, Amnesty UK seems to have felt compelled to publicly insist on an opposing stance against the criminalisation of buyers. From this series of events, a defence of prostitution buyers appears to have been constructed out of an opposition to the demands of the Nordic Model.

The global consultation process on 'prostitution and human rights' undertaken by AI appears similarly to have been designed on the basis of opposition to the Nordic Model. Individuals charged with undertaking consultation in a number of countries are connected to organisations that actively campaign against radical feminist approaches to prostitution. The consultation process in Australia, for example, was carried out by an executive member of the Women's Electoral Lobby ('WEL'), which has a long history advocating for the decriminalisation of the sex industry in Australia. WEL's national conference in 1974 voted in favour of decriminalising all aspects of prostitution. [13] Similarly, in Canada, the consultation process was led by a well-known advocate of full sex industry decriminalisation. [14] It appears, at the international level as well, that pro-decriminalisation groups were asked about their views on the issue prior to the public consultation. The Global Network of Sex Work Projects, for example, is mentioned in one of the initial policy background documents. [15] The International Union of Sex Workers also indicated on its website that AI sought its input about the decriminalisation of 'sex work', [16] in response to which it published a document on the topic of 'Sex Work and Human Rights'. [17]

Radical feminist critique of the buyer defence

A number of radical feminists responded to the AI defence of prostitution buyers. Julie Bindel writes that: 'By definition, men who are willing to pay for sex already have a contemptuous attitude towards women – they are not interested in an equal relationship, or a meaningful exchange with a partner.' [18] Kathleen Barry further comments on AI's inconsistency in recognising the irrelevance of female consent in its well-known violence against women campaigns addressing problems such as domestic violence, but insisting on consent as the arbiter of the harm (or lack thereof) in relation to the actions of prostitution buyers. Barry alternatively recommends a more fundamental 'human rights' approach to prostitution that recognises the buying of human beings for sexual use as a form of violence, irrespective of considerations of victim 'consent' to the behaviour. She writes: 'for once and for all, let us remove the issue of the victim's consent in every case of sexual crimes. In calling for new human rights law to make prostitution a violation of human rights, we are displacing the misogynist paradigm with a human rights one.' [19]

Further critique of Amnesty's defence of buyers came from prostitution survivor organisations in the United States, Canada and the UK, which have mobilised in recent years to campaign against

the sex industry and advocate for worldwide adoption of the Nordic
Model. These organisations comprise publicly declared victims of sex
industry exploitation, and have become a significant force opposing the
'sex worker rights' organisations that formed in the 1990s to support
sex industry decriminalisation. They include SPACE International
(Survivors of Prostitution-Abuse Calling for Enlightenment) and
Sex Trafficking Survivors United, which together co-ordinated an
online petition against the Amnesty proposal. The mobilisation of
survivors internationally from the turn of the 21st century had already
brought a quantum shift to campaigning for the Nordic Model, and
the movement responded swiftly and effectively to the Amnesty
proposal. As a result, AI attracted notable condemnation on social
media for making the protection of the male orgasm a greater priority
than the protection of women's rights.

Conclusion

The defence of prostitution buyers as 'consumers' of sexual services
rests on a liberal view of prostitution as an activity of individually
consenting adults who rationally choose to enter into a commercial
sexual transaction, free of outside forces and constraints. In this
formulation, prostitution buyers are socially equal to the people they
buy, and pose no particular threat or risk to women individually or
collectively. Just as an individual woman's right to choose to enter
prostitution must be defended in the liberal feminist view, so too must
an individual man's 'right' to buy a person for prostitution be upheld.
This equalising of prostituted people and sex industry customers
excludes any notion of economic or sexual inequality and places
beyond view any consideration of the abolition of prostitution.
The Nordic Model, on the other hand, poses a genuine threat to the
longstanding 'right' of men to exercise sexual dominion over women
through prostitution, and to profit from this dominion. It represents
a legislative vehicle for abolitionists to reckon over the question of

male sexual rights, and to confront men's prostitution behaviour as a historically enshrined human rights entitlement. The insistence of the Nordic Model on the decriminalisation of prostituted people has forced the hand of sex industry businesspeople and their supporters; in addition to the sex industry's usual defence of women's 'right' to 'sell themselves', they have been newly forced to construct a defence of *prostitution buyers* in order to protect the sex trade from moves towards abolition. AI has recently contributed to the construction of this new defence, specifically through steps it took in opposition to the Nordic Model. But the world's largest human rights organisation was able to make this contribution only because of the significant 'human rights' discourse that already exists in the form of liberal feminist claims to women's 'right' to profit from sexual exploitation. The liberal feminist defence of prostitution continues to underpin efforts against the Nordic Model and persists as an obstacle to the realisation of radically feminist egalitarian social relations.

If pornography is sex education, what does it teach?

Meghan Donevan

Consider just one of the dilemmas of inexperienced women. We all hear about oral sex, but what is it? ... Although how-to sex manuals may give descriptions of oral sex, the most accessible and graphic source of information is pornography. By watching videos, you can vicariously experience the techniques of dozens – even hundreds – of women. Pornography is one of the most benevolent ways a woman can experience who she is sexually. [1] — Wendy McElroy

This chapter refutes the liberal feminist claim that pornography is a useful form of education. By comparing a working definition of sexual health to the realities of pornography, it demonstrates that pornography fails to meet the basic requirements for sexual education. In particular, mainstream pornography does not promote safer sexual experiences, sex that is free from coercion, discrimination and violence, and sex that encourages a positive and respectful approach to sexuality and sexual relationships.

Many young people view pornography before or during the stage in which they receive sex education in school. Indeed, pornography has arguably become a substitute for sexual education. In Australia's 2012 'Let's Talk About Sex' survey, for instance, 64 per cent of Australian young people said they relied on pornography for learning about sex. [2] But early exposure to pornography and use of pornography as sexual education is a worldwide phenomenon, is not limited to the wealthy nations of the global North. As Amee Wurzburg's research in Kenya shows, for example, Kenyan children are increasingly accessing

pornography, to the extent that most children's first introduction
to sexuality is, in fact, via pornographic content, and it is through
pornography that these children 'gain their ideas about sexual
contraception, sexual positions, and sexual consent'. [3]

One of the reasons for this reliance on pornography is a
general lack of sexual education within schools. Inadequate sexual
education may be due to cultural, religious, or political reasons,
but this lack consequently results in young people being educated
at a later age than they should be, or important topics failing to
be addressed, such as pornography, for fear of parental reproach.
This failure to provide effective sexual education is all the more
prominent in developing countries, [4] which is especially problematic
given the severity of HIV/AIDS, rape, and gender-based violence.
Significant taboos around the discussion of sexuality are common,
which means that even if sexual education programmes exist,
by and large parents and teachers do not feel able to discuss
sexuality with children in the home and school. As liberal feminist
Wendy McElroy and other pro-pornography scholars [5] suggest,
then, pornography could potentially be seen as a substitute or
complement to sexual education, particularly when other forms of
education are lacking or nonexistent. However, contrary to these
arguments, and to the liberal feminist notion that pornography can
provide particularly useful sex education for women, this chapter
will demonstrate that pornography fails, quite drastically, to meet
the requirements of an education that promotes sexual health when
it comes to contraceptives, consent, discrimination, and violence,
hardly providing the basis for sexual liberation and equality.

Sexual health, contraception and sexually transmitted infections

If pornography is to be considered a positive or useful form of sexual
education, its messages and content should support an appropriate
definition of sexual health. Here, I will use the working definition of

sexual health adopted by the World Health Organisation ('WHO'), which is stated as follows:

> Sexual health is a state of physical, emotional, mental and social wellbeing in relation to sexuality ... Sexual health requires a positive and respectful approach to sexuality and sexual relationships, as well as the possibility of having pleasurable and safe sexual experiences, free of coercion, discrimination and violence. For sexual health to be attained and maintained, the sexual rights of all persons must be respected, protected and fulfilled. [6]

The following examples will highlight, however, that pornography does not promote positive sexual health messages. Instead, in a variety of ways, it undermines the WHO's emphasis on respect and developing a safe kind of sex, 'free of coercion, discrimination and violence'. This is most obvious in mainstream pornography through the lack of safe, visible contraceptive use and the prevention of sexually transmitted infections ('STIs'), as well as the frequent depiction and eroticising of sexual violence and racism.

With regard to basic safe sexual experiences, an initial requirement is often seen as the promotion and use of condoms, both as a form of contraception and to assist in the prevention of STI transmission. An analysis of the top eight pornography websites on Google investigated whether this was the case. [7] It was found that condoms were never used for oral–genital sexual activity, and were only mentioned in a very small portion of written material on the websites. There were no verbal or written warnings about the risk of HIV/AIDS and other STIs, or the advisability of safer sex. Likewise, a recent content analysis of mainstream pornography found that only one of the 304 scenes analysed, contained any discussion about pregnancy concerns or the risk of STIs, while only 10.9 per cent of scenes contained condom usage. Rather than being the exception, unprotected sex is the norm in the pornography industry.

Sexual violence

If pornography does indeed provide positive sex education, as is claimed by some, it should also exclusively endorse sexual experiences that are free from coercion, discrimination, and violence. Whether pornography is linked to violence against women is an ongoing debate within academia. [8] Some see a significant association between exposure to pornography and attitudes supporting sexual aggression. [9] Others argue that violence in pornography is the exception and, that at worst, pornography has a neutral effect on viewers. For instance, Australian academic, Alan McKee, estimates that the frequency of physical aggression in mainstream pornography is uncommon – only occurring in about 1.9 per cent of scenes in X-rated pornography available in Australia. Yet the problem with McKee, and many other researchers' methods when analysing violence in pornography, is that violence is only identified when an act was clearly intended to cause harm and, at the same time, is met by obvious resistance from the target of aggression.

In contrast, when the definition of aggression is broadened to all violent acts, regardless of how the target responds to the aggression, approximately 90 per cent of mainstream pornography scenes contain physical aggression and 50 per cent of scenes contain verbal aggression. [10] Psychology professor, Ana Bridges and colleagues, for example, also recognise that certain acts such as 'ass-to-mouth' ('ATM') can be categorised as harmful. The practice of ATM, where a man removes his genitals or an object from one woman's anus, straight to another woman's mouth, is highly correlated with the presence of verbal and physical aggression in pornography scenes, which, according to Bridges and colleagues, 'provides criterion validity to ATM as an inherently degrading practice'. [11] It is also worth noting that less than 10 per cent of scenes contained positive behaviours, including kissing, laughing, embracing, caressing, and verbal compliments. [12] Based on a less restricted (and unrealistic) definition of violence, aggressive acts are shown to be the norm, while acts that communicate positive, healthy relationships are the exception.

The fact that targets of aggression in pornography have been found to 'nearly always' respond either positively or neutrally to acts of aggression is also worrying when considering the 'education' provided to viewers. Social learning theory posits that observing others directly or via the media influences people's perceptions of what behaviours are acceptable or inacceptable. [13] When the viewer observes that an action is 'rewarded', they may internalise that behaviour as positive, and vice-versa. In the context of pornography, children may perceive that certain sexual behaviours commonly thought to inflict discomfort, such as ATM, double penetration, or physical aggression, will yield pleasurable consequences. [14] Indeed, it appears that the message portrayed in mainstream pornography is that aggression during a sexual experience can be pleasure enhancing for both men and women. Consequently, young viewers may develop unrealistic expectations about the nature of sexual encounters. [15]

When it comes to discrimination based on sex in pornography, there are various arguments about whether pornography is harmful or potentially 'empowering' for women. Pro-pornography scholars, including many liberal feminists, argue that pornography is empowering because actresses themselves have *chosen* to have sex on film and consequently, they have access to a job that need not be differentiated from other jobs, of which female viewers can further explore their sexuality. One female pornography producer referred to in Chyng Sun et al's study stated: 'you could do a porn where a girl is getting choked and hit and spit on, the guy's calling her a dirty slut and stuff and that's okay. That can still be feminist as long as everybody there is in control of what they're doing.' [16] Following this line of argument, as long as actors in pornography are consenting, the overwhelming (94.4 per cent) majority of aggressive acts directed towards women found in Bridges et al's study (and countless others) should be accepted as 'empowerment'.

Yet it is important to understand the social contexts in which people make 'free', consenting choices. Although an act may superficially appear to be a voluntary choice, the conditions under which many women make these decisions do not provide an adequate range of opportunities. When a woman's range of choices all entail physical, mental, and emotional risks, then she is still choosing from limited and undesirable options. Assuming the opposite – that women in pornography are fully consenting and do feel empowered being targets of aggression – viewers of pornography are not necessarily aware of behind the scenes issues of consent. Or, if young girls experiment with replicating what they see on film when exploring their sexuality, would they, as targets of aggression, become empowered? With the widespread nature of violence against women and girls, it is very risky to associate being a target of aggression with empowerment.

Indeed, the case for an alternative kind of pornography, which is more 'woman-friendly', is frequently raised in pro-pornography arguments, often by liberal feminists and 'third wavers', or by others supportive of the idea that pornography provides positive sex education. However, there are two issues that should be raised. First, gender-equal, non-violent pornography is extremely difficult to find. Secondly, the films that are held up as meeting these criteria generally fail to escape constrictive notions of gender, whereby aggression and the themes of domination and submission remain. [17] While it is believed that women who are placed in decision-making positions can affect the constrictive representations of gender roles, a study of 250 of the most rented pornography titles, shows that there is hardly any difference in content when comparing female and male pornography producers. [18] Although the female producers tend to show more female performers in scenes, and include more female-to-female sex acts, an equal number of aggressive acts were present compared with mainstream, male-produced pornography. In addition, in parallel with male producers, the overwhelming targets of aggression in productions created by women, were still women. Finally, coinciding with other findings, 97.5 per cent of women displayed pleasure or responded neutrally to the acts of aggression. In effect, the only significant difference between female and male producers in mainstream pornography is that the female directors portray significantly more woman-to-woman violence. Again, suggesting that pornography cannot provide a useful platform for positive sex education that promotes gender equality.

Sexual equality and racism

Sexism and racism are systems of oppression that often coexist, and so it is not surprising that we find racist material in pornography. Yet according to media studies expert Daniel Bernardi, who in fact agrees with many aspects of the liberal feminist sex position on pornography, pro-pornography scholars fail to address the facts of racism, and instead focus on the aesthetic or educational aspects of pornography. [19] He considers this highly problematic, since 'watching pornography ... might lead to the perpetuation – or ignorance – of violent ideologies such as racism' especially when considering the 'volumes and volumes of pornographic texts [that] draw upon and perpetuate volumes and volumes of racist attractions'. [20]

Pornography reinforces both racial and sexual stereotypes. In one study, for instance, it was found that in the 'interracial' subgenre of pornography, black men were 'marketed by a racialised economy of scale', being described as 'big' or 'long' or 'huge' or 'gigantic'. [21] When shown in a group, black men were also presented as a pack of sexual predators and were associated with 'deviant' and 'perverse' forms of sexuality. Gloria Cowan and colleagues' analysis of pornography likewise showed that black actors were portrayed as having lower

status than white actors, [22] defined by the size of their penises, scoring
the lowest on intimacy measures, and appearing as 'sex machines
lacking humanity'. [23] When it comes to black women, Vednita Carter
contends that pornography perpetuates the myth that all black
women are whores, often being called names like 'black ghetto ho'.
[24] Black cultural studies expert, Mireille Miller-Young, argues that the
experiences of black female performers in the pornography industry
are 'shaped by a racialised and gendered sexual commerce where
stereotypes, structural inequalities, and social biases are the norm'.
[25] She notes that the 'construction of white beauty and desirability is
precisely defined by what this beauty is not – the deviant and repulsive
black women's body'. [26] While this is a prevalent part of mainstream
media, pornography heightens this inequality by portraying black
women in a seriously degrading way, with an excessive appetite for
rougher sex and 'animal-like' tendencies, often in contrast to white
women. The stereotype of Latina women as 'all ass' is also common
in mainstream pornography. Bernardi says that Latina women are
'systematically and persistently reduced to a hyperbolic ass, overflowing
and always ready for public penetration'. [27] Finally, paralleling Edward
Said's understanding of Orientalism, Asians in pornography are
constructed as exotic, feminine, servile and childlike pleasure sources
for white colonial consumption. [28]

Bernardi concludes that pornography engages in overt and implicit,
complex if not always explicit, forms of racism: 'Indeed, when it
comes to the representation of race – black, brown, red, white, yellow;
gay, straight; transsexual – pornography today is very much about
yesterday's ideology of hate.' [29] Liberal feminists therefore mistakenly
defend pornography's educational benefits while overlooking both
the inherent sexism and racism. By not challenging the institution
of racism, pornography certainly fails as positive education that
promotes respect.

Greater effects

Consumers are not the only ones affected by pornography, those who are in a relationship with consumers, whether those relationships are intimate, family-based, or just friendships, are also affected. [30] Pornography plays a role in shaping the identity and sexuality of young people, in particular, as discussed in the documentary titled *Porn Damaged* (*'Porrskadat'* in Swedish). The filmmakers and interviewees regard pornography as a medium defining what sexuality is and what it should look like. It portrays sex as an encounter predicated on submission and domination, even when it is made for a female audience. It is a fantasy world where women are always ready for sex and enjoy all types of sexual activity, including aggressive and degrading acts. Consequently, pornography may create unrealistic and potentially harmful expectations about sexual experiences and relationships. This, of course, affects real-life sexual relationships. For instance, various studies have noted that pornography consumers tend to lose sexual interest in their partners and that sexual intimacy within the relationship is damaged. [31] Women whose partners view pornography may feel inadequate, objectified, or unable to 'compete' with women in pornography. They may experience direct or indirect pressure by their partners to act out what is seen in pornography. Or, body image ideals may be perpetuated even more so than by normal advertising and media, since all parts of a woman are displayed, and are desired and objectified by both male actors and men viewing pornography. Thus, pornography shapes views, expectations, and behaviours about sexuality in ways that are likely to be damaging for relationships and social norms in general and, in this way, should not be considered useful education.

When thinking about developing countries, the failure of the concept of pornography as positive education is all the more clear. In previous research on this topic, I have used South Africa as a case study since it is emblematic of other nations in the global South with growing access to a range of media and the proliferation of the internet. Given the prevalence of HIV/AIDS, rape, sexual exploitation, and gender-based violence in South Africa, it is difficult to see how further, uncritical representations of sexual violence and unsafe sex, are helpful. Pornography is a form of media that an increasing number of South African youth are accessing, and it certainly does not challenge the norms of sexism and racism, nor combat the risk for HIV/AIDS. If South African youth are increasingly exposed to media that depicts women always submitting to men's sexual advances and enjoying pain and brutalisation, then the argument that pornography does not exacerbate sexual violence is not convincing. Rather, pornography is likely to undermine the fight against an array of oppressions, including the fight against HIV/AIDS, sexism and racism.

Ways forward

Pornography fails to promote, and actively works against, appropriate sexual health standards, and simply cannot be considered a sufficient complement or substitute for positive sexual education, as some scholars and liberal feminists suggest. What, then, should be done to minimise the harms of pornography and to provide young people the thorough sex education they need? From the supply side, pornography producers should be forced to provide warnings about the harms of their products. Green compares the pornography industry to the tobacco industry, noting that cigarette packets now have warnings about the negative consequences of smoking. [32] This argument is especially valid in countries where there is little access to sex education due to cultural taboos surrounding the open discussion of sex.

Of course, various sexual education standards are found across different countries, as alluded to previously, and are affected by culture, politics, and religion. Yet even in the global North we find that discussions about pornography in secondary school sexual education classes are often absent, anecdotally this seems to be, by and large, due to parents thinking that by avoiding the topic their children will less likely begin watching pornography. On the contrary, by avoiding this topic, young people will continue to watch pornography while lacking alternative and informed narratives about respectful sex, as well as being exposed to depictions of eroticised discrimination and violence.

Sexual education, then, should begin at an early age and continue throughout secondary school, focusing on sex equality and 'providing positive messages about sex as something "pleasurable and intimate" in the context of a relationship'. [33] Alongside promoting gender-equal sexuality throughout primary school and secondary school, sex education curriculums and teaching strategies should be updated to address pornography exposure. Rather ironically, given that those critical of pornography are often labelled 'anti-sex', this is anything but an 'anti-sex' argument. It is a call for to engage more with ideas about sex, and to have public discussions about sex, so that sex education is not seen as something to be left to a multibillion dollar industry that makes its profits from a model of sex underpinned by sexism, racism and violence.

If sexual health programmes should promote a sexuality that is non-discriminatory, and non-violent, then pornography is most definitely not the answer. Pornography ultimately promotes higher-risk behaviours through the prevalence of violent acts, discrimination, and unsafe sexual practices. Thus, it is deeply flawed to understand pornography as a useful substitute or complement to any form of sex education.

The oppression that dare not speak its name? Silences around heterosexuality in contemporary feminism

Julia Long

So what do we do? Vow never to fall in love with a man? ... Let's face facts: heterosexual women are attracted to, and fall in love with, men. So we're stuck with them if we want love, sex and babies. [1] — Jennifer Keishin Armstrong and Heather Wood Rudúlph

Given the unrelenting levels of violence, misogyny and labour exploitation to which men subject women, and in view of the much-vaunted 'resurgent' feminist movement within the United Kingdom ('UK'), an obvious but seldom-asked question arises: why aren't women abandoning heterosexuality in droves, and forging new lives and communities with women at the centre?

In order to answer this question, we need to look at what is happening within contemporary feminism in the UK context. In some respects at least, mainstream British feminism appears to have moved on from the liberal preoccupation with individual 'choice' and 'agency' that dominated debates over the 1990s. While such liberal elements *are* still in evidence – particularly within academic feminism – many feminist groups demonstrate some recognition of the pervasive and structural nature of male domination, and the inadequacy of liberal notions of individual 'choice' and 'agency' in theorising, understanding and addressing these structural issues.

It is difficult to talk in general terms about contemporary British feminism, as it is too diffuse and its elements often too contradictory to form a coherent movement. In many ways it is the result of the third wave notion that feminism *itself* is a matter of individual choice and preferences, rather than collective political action with the shared goal of women's liberation from patriarchy. However, if we look at feminist activity over the first decade or so of the 2000s, it is clear that a number of groups and campaigns – some of which have received considerable media attention – have contributed to shaping the direction and priorities of current UK feminism. [2] Broadly speaking, these groups mobilise against male violence, with differing emphases on sexual objectification, sexual harassment, and other forms of male violence, some explicitly recognising pornography and prostitution in their understanding of male violence against women. Groups such as Million Women Rise and the London Feminist Network organise annual marches against male violence which attract thousands of women, and feminists in many towns and cities across the UK also organise similar Reclaim the Night marches.

Daughters of Eve and FORWARD have raised awareness of female genital mutilation as a human rights abuse; Everyday Sexism has provided a platform for women to document experiences of harassment and discrimination. OBJECT has been instrumental in putting sexual objectification on the feminist agenda, leading successful campaigns to reform licensing laws for lap dancing clubs, curtail the sale of 'lads' mags' from supermarkets and to address male demand for prostitution. Large-scale activist events such as the UK Feminista and Feminism in London conferences have covered issues including pornography and prostitution from an understanding of both as forms of male violence. Latterly, misogyny has become the focus not only of feminist outrage but also of more general media attention, in the context of online social media threats and harassment of feminists; music videos and lyrics that promote rape and sexual violence; and the growth of 'lad culture' corresponding to increasingly prevalent and accessible internet pornography.

However, given this focus on male violence, sexual objectification and misogyny, a simple, observable fact is conspicuous by its absence from the debates: the fact that, as women, we are expected to form primary, and preferably lifelong, attachments to members of the group that oppresses, abuses and kills us. Why is acknowledgement of compulsory heterosexuality so glaringly absent from mainstream feminist discourse?

An understanding of heterosexuality as instrumental to male domination is crucial to radical feminist analysis. As Adrienne Rich outlined several decades ago, heterosexuality cannot simply be understood as a matter of sexual preference or an innate orientation, but rather as a patriarchal institution and set of practices via which men exert power and maintain control over women. [3] In the early years of second wave feminism, groups such as The Furies and Radicalesbians developed devastating critiques of heterosexuality as intrinsic to women's oppression, and asserting the need for lesbian feminism in order to realise women's liberation. In the words of Ginny Berson, a member of The Furies Collective: 'Lesbianism is not a matter of sexual preference, but rather one of political choice which every woman must make if she is to become woman-identified and thereby end male supremacy.' [4]

From the late 1960s through the 1980s, the rejection of heterosexuality and embracing of lesbian feminism was an exhilarating, if often painful and besieged, personal and political journey made by many women. Anti-lesbian social attitudes meant that lesbian mothers leaving male partners were at serious risk of violence, discrimination and loss of custody of their children. Within this hostile and inhospitable context, lesbians poured a huge amount of energy into the development of lesbian feminist and woman-centred politics, culture and community, for the benefit of all women. Lesbian feminists, with their commitment to loving women and understanding of the personal as political, were central to the wider feminist movement. Crucially, the creation of a lesbian feminist community highlighted the structurally-enforced nature of heterosexuality, and meant that for abused, disenchanted and disaffected heterosexual women, there was a visible alternative: somewhere to go.

Why, then, is there so little evidence of a similar trajectory among a new generation of UK feminists? And why has lesbian feminism been so marginalised? There is certainly no evidence that heterosexuality has become, in any way, a more benign arrangement for women: in the UK, one in four women experiences domestic violence, and men continue to kill their female partners or ex-partners at a rate of two every week. [5] Studies repeatedly show little willingness on the part of men to carry out their fair share of domestic labour and childcare; women testify as to how men repeatedly 'mansplain', interrupt and fail to listen to them. [6] Within activist groups, women also testify to their male partners' sense of sexual entitlement, consumption of pornography and frequenting of lap dancing clubs as part of male-bonding activities.

On this basis, heterosexuality looks a decidedly unappealing prospect for women. So why is there so little rejection or even discussion of it among mainstream feminists? Obviously, women are subjected to feminisation processes and heterosexist imperatives from infancy, in the form of toys, clothes, magazines, stories, songs, education, family practices and traditions, beauty practices, media narratives, systems of social approval and peer pressure. These feminising and heterosexualising practices function to produce an obedient and compliant feminine subject, who is encouraged to experience, for example, painful, expensive and tedious beauty practices as pleasurable, and male attention as desirable, no matter her direct experience to the contrary.

While there may have been critiques of some of these practices, the twin tyrannies of femininity and heterosexuality remain largely unexamined within mainstream feminist groups. There seem to be a number of reasons for this. Firstly, and most importantly, is the lack of valuing of women-only organising, which means that women's spaces are not being created, and consciousness-raising among women has become almost impossible. Consciousness-raising was central to women's politicisation during the second wave, forming the basis for developing theory and action. Consciousness-raising and women-only discussions were the route via which the personal became understood as political; the context within which femininity and heterosexuality were analysed, critiqued and, by many women, rejected. The preoccupation of many activist groups and many student feminist societies with involving, engaging and 'educating' men precludes a critical examination of heterosexuality: how can this oppressive institution be examined and rejected if women's boyfriends and husbands are present?

The lack of consciousness-raising means that many UK feminist groups currently tend to construct patriarchal oppression as somehow 'over there' – in Parliament, in pornography, in 'lads' mags', in *The Sun* newspaper – rather than 'right here', in one's personal life and relationships. In this construction, the words 'patriarchy' and 'misogyny' themselves come to stand in as convenient abstractions that facilitate the avoidance of naming men directly as oppressors. This tendency in turn means that mainstream UK feminism is currently limited to a predominantly liberal, reformist agenda, which in the case of groups such as OBJECT and No More Page 3, means single-issue campaigning. Feminist organising is reduced to a reformist tactical repertoire of petitions, placards, Twitter hashtags, marches and demonstrations, rather than revolutionary acts of refusing to accommodate men, rejecting femininity, forging primary bonds and relationships with women, setting up all-female collectives, and creating lesbian feminist communities and culture.

The construction of patriarchal oppression as 'over there' means that heterosexuality stands out as one of the last bastions of patriarchy where the notion of individual choice remains thoroughly unexamined.

This leads to curious scenarios such as the phenomenon of feminists who might be critical of the notion of 'choice' and 'agency' in relation to oppressive systems such as pornography and prostitution, posting pictures of themselves in wedding dresses on social media, and defending their 'choices' in relation to marriage – even to the extent of taking their husband's surname – as a purely private affair. In an article for *The Guardian* titled 'How to have a feminist wedding', [7] Laura Bates of the Everyday Sexism Project defends her choices to marry, to wear an engagement ring and to wear white a white wedding dress during a ceremony held in a church. Featuring a picture of Bates in a long white wedding gown, standing on a pile of feminist books and wielding a bouquet in the shape of women's symbol, the article seems to be an exercise in insulting superficiality, eliding serious questions of heterosexuality and its institutions. Heterosexuality and the institution of marriage itself thus go unexamined and unquestioned.

Alongside the taboo of questioning women's 'choices' in relation to heterosexuality and marriage, another reason for the general lack of critique around heterosexuality lies in the co-option of many lesbians within queer and lesbian, gay, bisexual and transgender ('LGBT') political agendas. Lesbians who centre their lives and identities within LGBT communities tend not to see their sexuality within the context of patriarchal oppression of women, but instead, experience it either as an innate orientation or a sexual identity. Few lesbians in these contexts even call themselves lesbians, more frequently adopting male terms such as 'gay' or 'queer'. The influence of gay male culture and queer politics has been instrumental in undermining feminist analyses of pornography, prostitution and sadomasochistic sexual practices within such communities. [8] The influence of transgenderism has resulted in lesbian spaces and boundaries being disrespected, as exemplified by the 'Overcoming the Cotton Ceiling' workshop held by American reproductive rights group Planned Parenthood in Toronto in 2012, the purpose of which was to 'explore the sexual barriers queer trans women face within the broader queer women's communities' and to 'strategise ways to overcome them'. In the context of the influence of queer and transgender politics, the location and identification of lesbians as the depoliticised (at least in a feminist context) 'L' within LGBT communities has correspondingly contributed to the erasure of lesbian feminism within feminist politics, to the detriment of all women, both lesbian and heterosexual alike.

Finally, the construction of lesbianism as a recreational sexual practice available to heterosexual women has served to disarticulate and defang the revolutionary potential of women loving other women, through reframing lesbianism as simply part of the sexual repertoire of the sophisticated, modern woman. [9] This phenomenon is probably best understood in relation to the fetishisation of lesbianism within pornography, where a representation of sexual activity between women is rendered a spectacle for male consumption and pleasure. This fetishisation and the increasing numbers of same-sex experiences among women who do not consider themselves to be lesbian mean that, for example, references to 'girl crushes' replace the serious threat to heterosexuality presented by lesbian feminism.

The consequences of a lack of critique of heterosexuality and the erasure of lesbian feminism from feminist politics are extremely serious in terms of the future of a feminist movement and ultimately, the future of women generally. As long as mainstream feminism is preoccupied with including men, it is obstructing the very thing that most needs to happen: the building of a mobilised, enraged and woman-loving women's liberation movement. It seems extraordinary that at the moment, a woman seeking support after experiencing violence from her male partner is unlikely to encounter a lesbian feminist support worker in a women's refuge or rape crisis centre. It seems equally extraordinary that among all the support that she will be offered, the insight that heterosexuality is not inevitable is unlikely to be forthcoming. It is even more extraordinary that such observations are seldom made at all within the women's sector, and within feminist activist circles.

Nonetheless, in the face of the lack of feminist politics around heterosexuality, there have been some crucial departures in recent years. The first has been the flourishing of a number of radical feminist blogs critiquing heterosexuality and showing a renewed interest in lesbian feminism. [10] These blogs, and the presence of radical lesbian feminist individuals and groups on social media, are currently producing pioneering lesbian feminist work in the face of relative silence from academic and mainstream activist feminists. Other important UK-specific developments include a number of women-only, radical feminist conferences, two of which – RadFem 2012 and RadFem 2013 – foregrounded lesbian feminism, generating huge interest among younger women who previously had little chance to discuss these topics within other groups. [11] Finally, in the wake of these conferences, the task of rebuilding lesbian feminist politics and community has begun, in the form of online networks, artistic output and small local, intergenerational groups. It is the commitment and vision of those involved in these projects that is helping to create a space where the tyranny of compulsory heterosexuality can at last dare to speak its name.

PART IV:
ACTIVISM AND CHANGE

Political not generational:
getting real about the second wave

Finn Mackay

Thus, third wave feminism seeks to develop a more individualised form of feminism, which can respond to diversity and ambiguity. By advocating an analytical move away from understanding gender in collective terms, third wave feminism often promotes instead a 'politics of difference', starting from the specificity of women's experience. The aim is not to develop a feminism that makes representational claims on behalf of women, but to advance a politics based upon self-definition and a concern with how women define their personal relationship with feminism. [1] —

Shelley Budgeon

In the 1990s you could not move for stories about the death of feminism, the lack of politics in younger women and indeed the political disengagement of youth as a whole. Now though, the media are busy suggesting that our social movement is in fact enjoying a third (or even fourth) wave. When it is commented on, this new visible resurgence of feminist activism is often attached to younger women, furthering a generational narrative that tends to position older and younger women as opponents on a battlefield of feminist theory. This linear and simplistic explanation of the progress of feminism as a social movement suggests that across the Western world at least, feminism has moved from a recognisable first wave in the 1800s and 1900s, through to a second wave from the late 1960s into the 1980s and a third wave appearing since the 1990s and arising 'out of a critique of the second wave'. [2]

Emerging in very different socioeconomic and cultural environments, each successive wave has been attached to successive generations and often been viewed as their product and possession, considered to reflect the unique circumstances of that generation, as well as the feminism which went before. This generational attachment has led to the lazy assumption that all modern, contemporary feminist activism must be third wave if it involves young women or a new generation of activists. For example, in her book on the future of feminism, feminist academic and policy activist Sylvia Walby asserts that: 'Third wave feminism is a label attached to the contemporary feminism of young women, which defines itself as different from previous forms.' [3] Foundational proponents of third wave feminism such as Jennifer Baumgardner and Amy Richards [4] have encouraged the association of third wave with younger women, declaring that anyone born after the early 1960s inherited a world already transformed by feminism, the success of which obscured the struggles that went before, necessitating a new style of engagement with feminism. This is quite a common usage of the term, it is used as a simple chronological reference point to specify a particular point in feminism, shorthand for contemporary or young feminism and it is also used ideologically to refer to a certain type of feminism and standpoint.

In this chapter, I shall bring in the voices of feminist activists involved in the British women's liberation movement ('WLM') and outline how they themselves understand the third wave. In 2012 I interviewed and surveyed over 100 activists of many different backgrounds, based all over England. [5] The research was cross-generational, the respondents were from all different age groups, from teens to sixties. For many of these activists, the term 'third wave' freights particular political ideologies, and is not used simply as a generational referent or chronological marker point. Radical feminists, in particular, voice strong opposition to the term, and refuse deterministic classification as third wave merely because of their age or because they are currently active in this latest resurgence of feminism. Several of the radical feminists I spoke to were aged in their twenties and thirties, technically they could be viewed as a 'new generation' of activists, (as a third or fourth wave of feminists) yet their feminism had more in common with the theory and activism associated with the second wave. For these women, their feminism was nothing to do with their age, and everything to do with their politics.

I shall argue here that the label of third wave, in particular, should not be casually and simplistically applied to contemporary or young feminists, that the label is distinctly ideological and often wedded to several features which are antithetical to radical feminism, namely: the erasure of women-only space and a pro-sex industry and pro-pornography stance.

What is radical feminism?

Radical feminism is one strand of feminism, usually identified as beginning in the United States ('US') and being a product of the second wave of feminism. Like feminism more broadly, there is no single definition of radical feminism; and there are probably as many definitions as there are people who identify as feminists. Likewise, my own understanding of radical feminism is just that, my own; and there will be sisters who disagree with my standpoint on various issues, though we may share some core fundamentals in common.

My own definition of radical feminism contains four criteria which arguably set it apart from other schools, types or tendencies of feminism: a focus on patriarchy/male supremacy; recognition of male violence against women as a keystone of women's oppression; extension of the term 'violence against women' to include pornography and prostitution; and the use and promotion of autonomous women-only political organising. Radical feminist theory has also contributed political critiques of compulsory heterosexuality and of the nuclear family as well as much more. Like all strands of feminism, it is also concerned with and has been active around social justice issues more generally, on social class, poverty, racism, homophobia, environmentalism, anti-militarism and the masculinisation of wealth and power, for example.

There are many critiques of radical feminism, some of which have in turn influenced some elements of contemporary third wave feminism, which then attempts to define itself in relation to these critiques. Not all these critiques of radical feminism are valid, indeed, some are based on a received wisdom about radical feminism which is blatantly incorrect and fuelled by misogynistic and homophobic caricatures. There is the recurrent assertion that radical feminism is essentialist; this is the suggestion that it posits a priori, natural differences between women and men, and simplistically aggrandises femaleness and femininity. Several famous radical feminists have been accused of essentialism or biological determinism over the years, such as Mary Daly, Adrienne Rich and Andrea Dworkin; though the latter once described biological determinism as 'the most pernicious ideology on the face of the earth'. [6]

Returning to early radical feminist texts and attempting to untangle the received wisdom about their position from their actual body of work, it is clear that this theory was in fact far from essentialist. Early works emphasised that gender is a social construct; therefore, that male violence is not a biological fact and that it can be reduced and even ended. As one radical feminist humorously summarised in the British *Rev/Rad Newsletter,* back in 1981:

> The fact that I don't myself believe all men are absolute pigs makes me even more enraged and disgusted with the overwhelming majority who are, precisely because I know men could be so different. Women who regard all men as implacable enemies because they are biologically male are simply giving men an excuse for their male supremacist behaviour. [7]

The charge of essentialism is just one of the many common stereotypes used to attack radical feminism, however, and it shows itself in one of the most popular accusations, that of so-called 'man-hating'. Radical feminism often seems the vessel for popular images and imaginings of a feminism gone too far, an extreme, evangelical or fundamental version, referred to by some opponents as, 'feminist fundamentalism'. [8]

What is third wave feminism?

Third wave feminism appears to have emerged from the US in the 1990s, although some sources suggest the term was coined there much earlier, in the mid-1980s, in an unpublished collection on feminism and racism influenced by the identity politics of the 1980s that characterised the Western WLM at that time. [9] The term 'third wave' is usually attributed to Rebecca Walker, founder of the Third Wave Foundation in America in 1993 and editor of a third wave collection in 1995. [10] Walker's work to encourage political participation and leadership among younger women is perhaps why the term then came to be linked to young women.

Third wave feminism has become associated with cultural forms of activism, often articulated in virtual spaces and often autobiographical, focused on identity projects and experiences of personhood in contemporary society. Since the late 1990s, the internet has provided a conducive space for such personal expressions in the form of art, poetry, music, political commentary, and autobiographical blogs. This defining autobiographical element has led to criticism that the third wave is individualistic rather than collective, that it has an unhealthy dependence on consumerism as a medium through which to define itself, and that it focuses too much on the notion of choice. [11]

Self-defined third wave activism and theory often delineates itself through a focus on intersectionality [12] and a questioning or disavowal of 'woman' as a universal category, having been influenced by queer theory and recent transgender and transexual liberation movements. Third wave feminism, broadly speaking, appears more likely to include men and less likely to take a clear critical stance against pornography, prostitution and the wider sex industry.

Radical feminists rap the third wave

United Kingdom ('UK') activists in my research had several similar understandings of the term 'third wave'. They often connected third wave ideology with 'postfeminism', for example, and were opposed to what one 34-year-old radical feminist 'Charlotte' termed 'glib, depoliticised, postfeminist claptrap'.

Charlotte was a local government officer living in Yorkshire in the North of England; she had been involved in the WLM for around three years. Kira, the youngest self-identified radical feminist, at 27 years old, was a full-time journalist and resident in the South West of England; she linked third wave feminism with liberalism and neoliberal narratives regarding the reification of choice:

> I think the third wave in particular are perhaps related to a liberal, libertarian idea of feminism that's very pro-porn; and about, this is my choice, you know, if a woman does it, it's a feminist choice, you know, even if it's just a choice to have a glass of white wine. So I don't identify as third wave myself.

Helen, in her late fifties, gave a very similar account of this perceived brand of contemporary feminism, a version that the scholar Michaele L. Ferguson [13] has labelled, 'choice feminism'. The radical feminists in my study often conflated this choice feminism with third wave feminism, viewing the two as synonymous: 'I think there is a misunderstanding that whatever a woman "chooses" is feminist simply by virtue of the fact a woman "chose" it.'

The activists did see a link between third wave feminism and a pro-porn and pro-prostitution stance. They said that third wavers, as they called them, liked to describe themselves as 'pro-sex' but that really they were just 'pro-sex industry'. Often this pro-sex industry stance is defended on the grounds of 'choice', which seems to have almost a religious status in many third wave narratives and claims. While the activists I spoke to felt that there has been an increasing expansion and normalisation of the sex industry since the 1990s, in particular, they were frustrated that third wave feminism, with its frequent opportunity for platforms in the media and culture, was not offering any critique or even any troubling of this phenomenon. Not only is it presented as a matter of personal choice whether people earn an income through this industry, but also a matter of personal choice as to whether others decide to buy and access it. The former decision is often portrayed as some kind of empowerment for women and for all people earning money through the industry of prostitution. Many activists mentioned that it was almost taboo to question such portrayals, because this was seen as questioning the individual choices of women and men; this meant that such issues therefore seemed out of bounds within third wave feminist spaces.

The influence of neoliberalism, plus the ramifications of an ongoing backlash against the gains of the WLM were also seen to have contributed to the development of this current version of feminism. 'Choice feminism' was seen by the activists I met as a weak and depoliticised version of feminism which asserts that power for women lies in their capacity to make choices, regardless of what those choices are, what influences may lie behind them, what environment they are made in or what consequences they may have. The activists I spoke to complained that practices they viewed as anti-feminist could be defended in the current climate as a woman's choice, thus silencing any critique. This choice feminism does nothing to undermine a patriarchal status quo in which women, and younger women in particular, are called upon to define themselves as empowered neoliberal subjects through their consumer practices, or 'choices', in every sphere of life. These consumer practices too often, perhaps inevitably, maintain hegemonic heterosexualised femininity, even when they are practised by those identifying with alternative spaces and subcultures, such as those of third wave feminism.

Mary, a 44-year-old charity director in London and an activist for over 20 years, articulated this suspicion, emphasising that choices are made in certain circumstances and should not be off the debating table for challenge or critique:

> Far be it for me to talk about such old fashioned ideas as false consciousness, but if you find that your voices are what the patriarchy would like you to say and do anyway, then surely that is up for debate. I'm not saying you shouldn't do it, I'm just saying, surely, it's up for challenge.

All the radical feminist participants in my study voiced opinions against pornography, prostitution and the wider sex industry, and saw this as an important part of their radical feminist politics. This is perhaps unsurprising, given that radical feminist theory is uniquely placed to tackle these subjects, producing pioneering feminist analyses of pornography from the late 1970s and into the 1980s. [14] Efra, an activist in her early twenties illustrated this stance:

> I identify as a radical feminist and by this I mean that I want to end the patriarchy and capitalism which both work together to oppress and exploit women. My feminism regards prostitution, pornography, lap dancing etc, as forms of violence against women and definitely *not* work.

Third wave: ideological not generational?

The surfacing of a self-defined and recognisable new wave of feminism could suggest the demise and/or rejection of the previous wave. As claims to a third wave are occurring alongside a continuing feminist movement, which contains feminists whose activism began in previous decades, as well as younger feminists aligned to the second wave; the waves would appear to be overlapping. What is arguably occurring, with *some* articulations of third wave feminism, therefore, is a *rejection* of the previous wave, rather than a *replacement* following a death by natural causes. As mentioned earlier, some third wave commentary and theory does set up a caricatured portrayal of second wave feminism, which it can then use as some sort of 'straw feminist' to knock down and define itself clearly against. This defining process depends on presenting second wave feminism and radical feminism in particular as man-hating, humourless, 'anti-sex', prudish, racist, homophobic and transphobic; these common refrains continue and are so embedded in the public consciousness around feminism and feminists we hardly even need to spell them out. Such stereotypes enjoy huge popularity despite the archives full of evidence which arguably exposes them as false. In addition, by making a caricature out of such politics, these positions are also defused of power, in an attempt to render ridiculous, fictional and laughable the valid and very real politics of separatism, the sexuality of lesbianism, and the principle of autonomous women-only organising, for example.

Many of the radical feminists I met in my research, and who I also work alongside every day, are younger feminists, or a new generation of feminists, they are often aged in their twenties and thirties, yet they reject the 'new and improved' version of feminism that they see attached to the term third wave, and instead position themselves very strongly with second wave feminism. These feminists did not want to be branded as 'third wave feminists' simply because of their age; they vehemently disagreed with the political ideology that they associated with third wave feminism as they saw it. They were anti-porn and prostitution, and they believed in the importance of women-only space and women-only organising.

Conclusion

In conclusion, it could be seen as simply semantics, whether one refers to the current phase of feminism as third (or fourth) wave or not, as, either way, an exciting resurgence of diverse feminism and feminist activism certainly appears to be taking place in the UK and across the world. Within it are feminist activists of a variety of definitions or none, and while some may attach negative ideologies to what they perceive as third wave feminism, some may be unaware of such debates or identify as third wave in a purely chronological sense. Likewise, others may consciously identify as third wave for ideological reasons, and proudly associate that label with a pro-porn stance, or with a commitment to mixed organising and the involvement of men.

However, this current phase of the WLM also includes feminists, such as those activists I met, who explicitly do not wish to be identified as third wave feminists, because of the politics they associate with this term. In order to respect the full variety of feminist self-definitions then, I suggest that media commentators, and indeed scholars, should underline that the term third wave carries not only chronological meaning, but, for many feminists, holds ideologies that they care not to be associated with in any way. Lazy categorisations of all contemporary feminism or the feminism of younger women as somehow by default part of a so-called new wave, third or fourth wave, are simplistic assumptions imposed upon political standpoints that are as complex and varied as they always were.

* * * * *

Some of the content of this chapter has been developed from an earlier work published in the journal *Social Movement Studies* (2014) and is reproduced here with permission from Taylor & Francis.

Abuse masked as a 'cultural practice': speaking out against female genital mutilation

Naela Rose

We believe it is our duty to bring to the attention of our readers the dangers that any attempt to pass off the practice of excision as intrinsically criminal would cause ... Demanding a penal sentence for a custom that does not threaten the republican order and which nothing prevents from being considered as a matter of private choice ... would be tantamount to demonstrating an intolerance which can only create more human dramas than it claims to avoid. [1] — Martine Lefeuvre

The last few years have seen renewed public interest in activism against female genital mutilation ('FGM'). In the United Kingdom ('UK'), many would now be familiar with the work of Integrate Bristol and schoolgirl Fahma Mohamed, the 17-year-old junior trustee of the charity, who made international headlines after meeting the secretary-general of the United Nations. This chapter first outlines why the term 'female genital mutilation' is so important and how FGM relates to the UK context, before moving on to detail the way in which the current Integrate Bristol campaign against FGM has taken shape and succeeded. The chapter finishes by reflecting on why taking a human rights approach is more useful than understanding harmful cultural practices against girls as simply 'choices'. Throughout, I offer some first-hand insights into what it has been like to be counted among those women speaking out against FGM in my work with Integrate Bristol.

Why 'female genital mutilation'?

In the last two decades there has been an increasing move in popular reporting to refer to FGM as 'female circumcision'. This has occurred at much the same time as some opposition to criminalising FGM, particularly in academic circles. At Integrate Bristol, however, we believe it is important that people use the correct terminology when discussing FGM in order to avoid ambiguity and to remember that FGM must be seen as firmly embedded in the context of violence against women and girls. The problems associated with discussing FGM openly have been further complicated by the distortion and popularisation of terms such as 'female circumcision'. FGM refers to the excision of certain parts of female genitalia and it covers four types of mutilation. Type four is the most extreme form of genital excision/mutilation and includes the removal of both the outer and inner labia and the *closing up* of the entire vaginal area. To compare FGM to any form of 'circumcision' is to diminish the violent and traumatic nature and practice of FGM. The detrimental health implications of this mutilation include (but are not limited to) extreme physical and emotional trauma, inability to have sexual intercourse, a lack of sexual pleasure, hindrance to normal bodily functions such as menstruation and urination, and serious infections. In order for us to work together as an international community to serve and protect women and girls who have been subjected to FGM, we must discuss and name it for what it is – an unacceptable and cruel form of gender-based child abuse.

Female genital mutilation in the UK

Integrate Bristol has sought to emphasise the significant risk of girls, aged 11 to 12 years of age, falling victim to FGM during the summer holiday period in which family members take their daughters abroad to have them cut. This method of practising FGM outside the UK has grown in popularity in recent years as it enables parents and carers to continue carrying out FGM on their daughters, despite it being illegal to take girls abroad with the intention of having them cut. The National Society for the Prevention of Cruelty to Children describes girls from affected communities as at 'imminent risk of being subjected to FGM' when they are taken out of the UK over the summer holidays. Their website warns that 'teachers should be alert to a girl talking about a planned visit to her family's country of origin, especially if she mentions a special occasion when she will "become a woman"'. [2] Yet girls in the UK remain at risk of undergoing FGM during the summer holidays, between leaving primary school and entering secondary school. As the Integrate Bristol campaign puts forward, many teachers remain ignorant of the risks to their female students; the majority of educational professionals still do not receive the necessary training that would enable them to better understand and protect many of the children in their care.

The campaign begins

Rather unexpectedly, it was a horse riding trip in 2007 that signified the start of what would become one of the most influential and successful anti-FGM charities in UK history. When Bristol schoolteacher Lisa Zimmermann took 12 of her female students on an equestrian outing, she became aware of an epidemic of abuse that prevented the girls from enjoying the simple pleasure of riding through the British countryside. Frustrated by the lack of opportunity provided to girls in schools to discuss and ask questions about FGM, Lisa decided something else had to be done. As many found it difficult to speak openly about FGM initially, she encouraged her female students to express themselves through poetry.

Over time, the girls involved in the impromptu writing project, many who came from FGM-affected communities, grew in confidence. The anonymity of writing provided them with a safe space to vocalise their feelings; as with many other forms of abuse, attempting to articulate the impact of a traumatic event can prove as difficult as remaining silent. Zimmermann formed Integrate Bristol and began to apply for funding in order to facilitate the ever-growing numbers of girls wanting to join what was affectionately referred to by the girls involved as 'the fanny club'.

Today, over 150 people have worked with Integrate Bristol and, since its inception, many of those who belonged to the original 12 have gone on to become junior trustees of the charity. Furthermore, in recent years, talking openly about FGM has not only become an acceptable debate to have among activists and human rights organisations, it has also become woven into political discourse. FGM is now one of the most discussed forms of child abuse in the UK and members of the thriving charity are calling for change from the very top. They have been hard at work since the charity formed and have continued to fight for an end to FGM once and for all. For the first time, young people's voices are leading the debate on FGM. Their voices are not just being heard, but bringing about meaningful change in the political arena in the UK. In fact, the voices of the people of Integrate Bristol are not only reaching the ears of average British citizens – thanks to significant press coverage of their anti-FGM campaign work – they are also influencing and forming UK government policy on FGM and violence against women and girls in the context of education, as well as contributing to the broader political discourse surrounding this harmful cultural practice.

The campaign takes off

In 2014, the people of Integrate Bristol took the UK campaigning world by storm. Led by Fahma Mohamed, and working together with *The Guardian* newspaper, it launched one of the fastest growing petitions change.org had ever seen. John Coventry of change.org said at the time that: 'This has become the biggest thing we have ever done. We had no idea it would get this big.' Over the following weeks, Fahma's petition to then-education secretary Michael Gove gained over 230 000 signatures of support. The people's request of Gove was simple, but effective; they asked him to write a letter about the risks of FGM to all British schools before the summer holidays.

In a world where young people are often perceived as politically disengaged, Fahma's insistence, and passion for the cause to bring FGM education into British schools made headlines around the nation. The success of the campaign in rallying such a high quantity of signatures is particularly impressive in light of the recent local UK elections, which were reported to have mustered only a measly 35 per cent turnout.

On 6 February 2014, Fahma travelled to London with four other young women from Integrate Bristol to meet with Gove and discuss educational reform regarding teaching about FGM in schools. The Department of Education did not substantiate these rumours, but perhaps the reason the international press left before the meeting had ended was because the Department of Education had planned to congratulate the women on a successful campaign and send them back to Bristol, with a hearty handshake. Perhaps Gove underestimated the impact of four feisty, brown women in headscarves, talking to him about vaginas. As Fahma put it: 'He didn't stand a chance!' After the meeting, Gove, not only agreed to send the letter to all head teachers in the UK, but also promised to visit the young women at their school in Bristol to observe how best practice is being implemented. Three days later, Gove was in Bristol, and 230 000 signatures later, Gove signed the petition himself and sent a 'back to school' letter to every school in England warning them to be alert to the dangers of FGM, as requested.

The unusual nature of the campaigning strategy of Fahma and Integrate Bristol may have helped to garner such political clout around the world. In the case of Fahma's petition to Gove, the very image of a Muslim teenage girl writing to a male politician about vaginas, asking him to contact all head teachers before the summer holidays, warning them of the dangers of the approaching 'cutting season', certainly subverts the expectations of a politically disengaged, younger generation. Fahma's bold action fascinated the media and poignantly highlighted the systematic lack of government leadership in relation to FGM awareness and education in the UK. That's not to say that any person from Integrate Bristol could have been put forward. Fahma was the right woman for the job but it had been a long road getting there.

The campaign goes global

Fahma's role in leading the campaign calling for revision of the UK government's approach to the enforcement of FGM safeguarding policies drew international attention. Most notably UN secretary-general Ban Ki-moon who met with Fahma and reinforced her call to use education as the tool for change: 'It has been deeply inspiring for me to hear that a 17-year-old, Fahma Mohamed, supported by *The Guardian*, has attracted well over 200 000 signatures to her petition demanding action to end female genital mutilation.'[3] Indeed, Fahma's actions have also been commended in Parliament and attracted support from ministers and elected representatives from all sides of politics. Fahma's online campaign has come to hold significance worldwide, particularly for other survivors of FGM, and she rapidly became the face of change surrounding education on FGM in the UK and beyond.

Fellow women's rights campaigner, and Nobel Peace Prize winner, Malala Yousafzai, has even publicly declared her unwavering support for Fahma's campaign. Malala said recently that:

> When we talk about education, we talk about quality education and the world should be told [about] FGM ... what is it? And how can it affect the life of a girl? I think it should be a part of education and if we remain silent then we can never achieve our goals, we can never bring about change. The only way to fight against it is to speak. I think we should support girls like Fahma and their campaign and I think we should stand up.[4]

Malala has professed her admiration and support for the people of Integrate Bristol's bravery and dedication to the cause, expressing her outrage that today millions of women and girls around the world continue to be affected by FGM. [5] The work of Integrate Bristol on this issue also inspired 24-year-old Jaha Dukureh, who launched her own change.org campaign in the United States.

Lessons learnt

The powerful appeal of Fahma's message to Gove was more effective because her youth belied her confident delivery and articulation of the long-suppressed issues of FGM survivors. Harnessing the power of women's voices has been at the heart of the campaign. While the bravery and dedication of the women campaigning with Integrate Bristol is beginning to pay off, the road to this realisation has not been without tribulations. Many women who worked on the campaign have experienced verbal abuse, physical violence and even death threats. Lisa Zimmerman recalls how difficult the early days were and the opposition the women faced:

> It takes passion and determination, and above all, resilience. We faced a lot of resistance in the early days, sometimes quite brutal. Carrying out this invaluable work on a highly controversial and secretive subject like FGM poses dangers to those leading it. The affected communities are not keen to have this abuse exposed.

Carrying out this invaluable work on a highly controversial and secretive subject such as FGM poses dangers to those leading it, as the affected communities are not keen to have such abuse exposed. In fact, elders in some communities opposed the anti-FGM work of Integrate Bristol and attempted to ban screenings of the charity's 2011 award-winning anti-FGM drama documentary, *Silent Scream*. It was only after mothers and other women in these communities rallied in support of the documentary that the screenings went ahead. Resistance is always to be expected when those brave enough to do so speak out and seek to change things, but this is particularly difficult with FGM, as the practice relies too heavily on secrecy and silence.

Women's voices entering the public discussion of FGM has propelled the issue into the media, and, as a result, into Parliament and the United Nations, forcing those in power to take action. Women will not accept the idea that gender-based violence can be excused merely because it is 'cultural'. The danger of labelling FGM a 'cultural' problem, of course, is that it implies that the practice is somehow inherent and therefore normal and acceptable. Indeed, the term 'cultural' has served for too long as a barrier to transparent discussion about FGM. It should be called what it is: a form of child abuse situated in a wider context of violence against women and girls. The term 'cultural' has prevented us from being able to properly and openly discuss FGM as a horrific form of child abuse that should not be tolerated under any circumstances. For too long, political discourse surrounding FGM in the UK has revolved around the need for 'cultural sensitivity'. We cannot afford to be culturally sensitive about abuse.

The people of Integrate Bristol are not interested in debating cultural differences and 'choices' when it comes to FGM. We feel that FGM should be understood primarily within the context of violence against women and girls and should be regarded as a form of abuse. By giving women a platform to take a stand against FGM, Integrate Bristol has helped to shift the public discourse on FGM in the UK away from a cultural issue into the realm of abuse.

Conclusion

What this campaign should give us all, is hope. It shows that women and girls are standing and resisting longstanding harmful cultural practices. This is, without doubt, the age of a new wave of feminism, defined by grassroots activism. Such developments are creating meaningful change in women's lives in the UK, and beyond, and give traction to the idea of a 'fourth wave' of feminism. [6] Perhaps we will see this wave of activism spread not just in the UK, where we have recently seen such progressive bounds towards ending FGM, but all over the world.

For the sake of equality: moving towards the Nordic Model of prostitution law in Canada

Teresa Edwards

Prostitution legislation has become a topic of priority for many feminist activist groups and academics around the world. With the introduction of what is now known as the 'Nordic Model', in Sweden in 1999, which criminalised the purchase of sex while decriminalising prostituted persons, there has emerged a new option for prostitution law that moves beyond the mainstream approaches of prohibition and full legalisation. While laws concerning prostitution have been hotly contested in Canada for decades, the recent *Bedford v Canada (Attorney General)* [1] (*'Bedford'*) case, and subsequent changes to legislation, represent a significant shift. Rather than an exclusive emphasis on 'choice' and the individual, the discussion has had to include a consideration of violence against women and structural inequality in terms of race, gender and class. This chapter offers an outline of the main approaches to prostitution legislation and its limitations, but then focuses on the Canadian context and the Nordic Model. The chapter explains the position of the Women's Coalition for the Abolition of Prostitution ('the Coalition') in supporting the Nordic Model and elements of the associated C-36 legislation in Canada highlighting, in particular, the concerns for Aboriginal women. The Canadian experience can provide useful lessons on how the understandings of inequality embedded in the Nordic Model have the potential to change legal approaches to prostitution around the world.

Legalisation and prohibition: mainstream legislative models of prostitution

The legalisation of prostitution refers to the regulation of prostitution through criminal law, labour law, and other legislation. Under this approach prostitution is regarded as a legal occupation subject to state regulation. Typically, governments have adopted the legalisation approach to regulate the sex industry through work permits, licensing and/or tolerance zones. [2]

The reasoning behind adopting legalisation has varied from place to place, but there is usually an element of belief that a legalised model will protect prostituted women, help make prostitution safer and decrease sex trafficking. However, systems of legalisation have proved to be poor protection. A report from the New Zealand Prostitution Law Review Committee, for instance, examined the after-effects of legalising prostitution in that country. It found that while women in prostitution had an increased likelihood to report incidents to police, after several years of the *Prostitution Reform Act 2003* (NZ) ('PRA') being in place, women felt there were still no real gains to their safety:

> Opinion among CJRC (Crime and Justice Research Centre) informants differed on the impact of the PRA on adverse incidents, including violence, being experienced in the sex industry. The majority felt that the PRA could do little about the violence that occurred. [3]

When looking at the increase in reporting of crimes against prostituted persons, there was actually no significant change in the pursuit of conviction against offenders: 'While sex workers are more likely to report adverse incidents to police, including violence, willingness to carry the process through to court was less common.' [4]

Unfortunately, the New Zealand study did not attempt to explore reasons for the reluctance of women in prostitution to report incidents if it would lead to pursuing charges in court. Instead, it offers a comparative look at earlier studies, with the theory that stigmatisation of those being prostituted is the main reason for their not reporting incidents. However, other research has suggested the willingness (and ability) of prostituted women to participate in court cases may be significantly more complicated than social stigma alone. Some elements that discourage women participating in court proceedings include: threats of violence against them from a pimp, or a pimp who uses a 'boyfriend' approach to recruit victims and protect himself, or issues with substance abuse as a coping mechanism for prostitution that make it difficult to participate in a drawn-out court process and also increase concern of detainment by police for possession of illegal substances.

The same report also acknowledges that the right to refuse a john was found to be problematic. In the circumstances of brothels, women needed to have a 'good reason' in order to refuse clients, and even then there was no guarantee that her right would be respected. Thirty-five per cent of the women in the study reported that in the previous 12 months they had to have sex with someone they did not want to. [5] All of this suggests that full decriminalisation or legalisation does not deliver the positive outcomes that are promised.

Legalisation is also intended to limit the spread of prostitution and sex trafficking. The idea being that if prostitution can be brought out into the open and regulated that the industry can be suitably controlled. Again, this has not been the case. This situation in Holland, where legalisation was given the go-ahead, is illustrative of the problem:

> [Legalising prostitution], rather than afford better protection
> for the women ... has simply increased the market. Rather
> than confine the brothels to a discrete (and avoidable) part
> of the city, the sex industry has spilt out all over Amsterdam
> – including on-street. Rather than be given rights in the
> 'workplace', the prostitutes have found the pimps are as

brutal as ever. The government-funded union set up to protect them has been shunned by the vast majority of prostitutes, who remain too scared to complain. [6]

In response to some of the failures of legalising prostitution, Amsterdam has moved to limit some of the bounds of legalisation. There is increasing acknowledgement that legalisation has, at best, changed how things appear on the surface without limiting exploitation and trafficking. As one reporter described the situation in Amsterdam:

> It may be well policed and eye-poppingly unusual, but the city's central red light district still feels like a place where women's hopes go to die. Around 75 per cent of the 5000 to 8000 of those working in prostitution, in the city, are from abroad, and many are believed to have been trafficked. [7]

Indeed, issues with trafficking can be seen as intimately connected to the legalisation of prostitution. Both Holland and Germany have seen an explosion in the business of prostitution and human trafficking since undertaking legalised approaches. In a recent paper that provided an analysis of 150 countries in an effort to examine the impact of legalising prostitution on rates of human trafficking, economists Seo-Young Cho, Axel Dreher, and Eric Neumayer found that, 'countries with legalised prostitution have a statistically significantly larger reported incidence of human trafficking'. [8] Sex trafficking remains popular in areas where prostitution has been legalised because there is more money to be made from trafficking women and the normative effect of legalisation means there is greater demand for prostituted persons. It is also popular because women do not generally want to enter prostitution; taking advantage of the poor, with the least options available, helps provide unwilling bodies to johns in a format that, with a little intimidation and threat of violence, can seem willing to the disinterested or uncaring.

Once prostitution is regarded as legal 'work' it is more difficult for women to escape it,[9] and the scale of the industry grows. For example, in Denmark (where there are no legal prohibitions against the purchase of persons in prostitution) the scale of street prostitution is three times higher than in Sweden (where purchasing sex is criminalised) despite Denmark's significant smaller population (roughly 5.5 million to Sweden's nine million). [10] The traditional prohibition approach to prostitution, which seeks to eliminate prostitution by criminalising all aspects of the prostitution trade, is also problematic. The criminalisation of prostituted persons is incompatible with recognition of the exploitative nature of prostitution; it also fails to provide exit support and services. [11] The Coalition argues that jail is not a women's centre or transition house and 'the police are not equipped to provide frontline support and advocacy to women in prostitution and they cannot expect women to report to police exploitation by johns and pimps if they are also subject to criminalisation'. [12]

The justifications used for both legalisation and for the complete criminalisation of prostitution often include worthwhile aspirations – including, 'suppressing the organised crime surrounding prostitution, protecting the integrity of the family, protecting non-participants from unwelcome solicitations, protecting prostitutes, and protecting minors who are coerced into a life of prostitution'. [13] But there is very little evidence available to suggest that such laws actually achieve any of these objectives. [14]

The Canadian context and the Women's Coalition for the Abolition of Prostitution

Although laws concerning prostitution have been hotly contested in Canada for decades, the recent *Bedford* case represents a new chapter to this debate. While some forms of prostitution had been understood as legal in Canada, there were laws against specific aspects of prostitution, including brothel-keeping and pimping. In *Bedford,* the Supreme

Court of Canada ruled that the *Criminal Code of Canada* provisions
– namely ss 210, 212(1)(*j*), 213(1)(*c*) – that criminalised aspects of
prostitution undermined the right to security guaranteed in s 7 of
Canada's *Charter of Rights and Freedoms*. The Supreme Court further
stated that the impacts of these provisions were disproportionate to
the law's objective of preventing public nuisance and were therefore
unconstitutional. [15] A suspended declaration of invalidity was issued
for one year, during which the government of Canada was expected
to modify its proposed legislation. [16]

During the parliamentary debate to determine the new laws
concerning prostitution, the Women's Coalition for the Abolition of
Prostitution – made up of member organisations: Canadian Association of Sexual Assault Centres, Canadian Association of Elizabeth
Fry Societies, Native Women's Association of Canada, Concertation
des luttes contre l'exploitation sexuelle, Action ontarienne contre la
violence faite aux femmes, Regroupement québécois des centres
d'aide et de lutte – advocated for the Nordic Model, for a variety of
evidence-based reasons. The Nordic Model decriminalises prostituted
women but still criminalises the individuals who prostitute them. This
model also encourages support services, including public education
and alternatives to prostitution for women. The Coalition believes the
Nordic Model is the only available approach to prostitution legislation
that is rooted in gender equality, as well as being consistent with the
Charter of Rights and Freedoms and international rights of women. [17]

This perspective is informed by the research and experiences of the
Coalition's members. These organisations provide frontline crisis and
anti-violence services, in addition to representation and advocacy for
women and girls who are at risk of being prostituted, who are or have
been prostituted, and/or who have been criminalised and incarcerated
in relation to prostitution. Based on research, their frontline efforts,
and the first-hand accounts of women in prostitution, the Coalition
maintains that the Nordic Model is the most effective option

for abolishing the gender, racial, and socioeconomic inequalities perpetrated by prostitution in Canada.

Many of these concerns were addressed in the drafting of Bill C-36, which came into law on 6 December 2014. The new law takes an approach to prostitution that could significantly reduce sexual exploitation and trafficking in Canada although, unfortunately, it falls short of a full Nordic Model, as there are some aspects of the law which continue to enable the criminalising of women in prostitution. This is an issue that still needs to be addressed and the Native Women's Association of Canada will continue to lobby the government to change this aspect of the law.

Understanding the Nordic Model: prostitution as an act of violence

What has become known as the Nordic Model of prostitution legislation originated in Sweden. In the original Swedish law, the idea was that the sale of 'sexual services' would be decriminalised but the purchase of 'sexual services' would become illegal. [18] The Nordic Model approaches prostitution from a perspective that prostitution is 'on a continuum of male violence against women' [19] and should not be regarded as any different from other forms of abuse. Prostitution is inherently dangerous to women. The majority of prostituted women state that they have suffered physical violence, sexual violence and threats during prostitution. Moreover, it has been shown that the mortality rate for women in prostitution is 40 times higher than for other women. [20]

The Coalition believes that it is impossible to dissociate prostitution from the violence it generates. Rather than having a goal to simply *reduce* violence, it should be the goal of policy makers to *reject* violence altogether. The Nordic Model embraces this approach. It characterises 'prostitution as a form of violence against women – in the same category as domestic violence and rape – and affirms the principle that women's bodies are not for sale'. [21] When prostitution is viewed from this perspective it becomes clear why criminalising the women in prostitution is the wrong approach. As Janine Benedet explains, 'in no other context of violence against women do the police arrest the woman who is subjected to violence in order to help her out'. [22] Instead, laws that decriminalise those who are prostituted, and empower them to contact police while also providing exit supports, would work long-term to end violence against women.

Prostituting women does not make them equal

It is also crucial to change the perception that prostitution is somehow a 'liberating' force for women. Instead the opposite is the case. Prostitution increases gender inequality. Indeed, it can be seen as a practice of sex inequality. Prostitution does not entail a relationship of equality; in fact, it is part of, 'a relationship of domination by one person who pays for sex over another who needs the money to survive'. [23] The relationship is patriarchal and exploitative. The problems inherent in this inequality cannot simply be disappeared by emphasising commerce: 'consent to otherwise unwanted sexual activity cannot be purchased'. [24]

Framing the legalisation of prostitution as potentially liberating, as some liberal and libertarian feminists have done, has enormous societal impacts, especially with respect to dynamics of healthy relationships between women and men:

> In countries where prostitution has been legalised, numerous women have testified that this choice has adversely affected their intimate relationships and the climate in which they work. Legalising prostitution turns it into a legitimate entertainment that entices more and more men to enjoy paid sex and concurrently encourages a view of all women as 'potential prostitutes'. Thus the prostitution model that reduces women to sex objects available to satisfy every male fantasy becomes the norm. [25]

These negative impacts extend to race. The majority of women in prostitution are poor women from minority groups. The drastic overrepresentation of poor, minority women promotes a category of women where their vulnerabilities 'select them for the most exploitative forms of prostitution'. [26] This is particularly true for Aboriginal women in Canada. In many cases, the model of sex trafficking that is dominant in a country is that of importing poor women with few economic options from other countries and forcing them into trafficking and sexual exploitation. In Canada, the dominant model is domestic trafficking, where the primary targets are those already in Canada, specifically Aboriginal women. Released in 2012 by Public Safety, Canada's National Action Plan to Combat Human Trafficking notes that of the human trafficking cases waiting to be processed, 90 per cent were considered domestic human trafficking. The report also identifies factors increasing vulnerabilities to sex trafficking as extreme poverty, unemployment, lack of education, inadequate programming, gender-based inequality, corruption, war, conflict situations, and political unrest. [27]

Not all of these factors apply to domestic trafficking in Canada; however, several are extremely relevant for Aboriginal women and girls. In fact, in an extensive review of the literature on human trafficking in Canada, Nicole Barrett found that Aboriginal women and girls made up the majority of those being sex trafficked in Canada. [28] Countries with large Aboriginal populations who have faced similar circumstances of colonisation, forced boarding school programmes, discriminatory legislation, and ongoing racism may face similar instances of drastic overrepresentation of their minority population pushed into sex trafficking if the government chooses to legalise prostitution. In a case such as this, a Nordic Model, which decreases sex trafficking and lowers the numbers of those in prostitution, can work not only as a force for gender equality but also as a force for racial equality.

Women deserve better than this 'choice'

The Coalition believes that women deserve better than what prostitution offers them and the Nordic Model embodies this belief. The vast majority of women 'are driven by poverty and violence into a life of sexual exploitation that exposes them to severe physical and psychological harm'. [29] Overwhelmingly, it has been the closing of doors and the lack of opportunities that push women into being prostituted. To regard prostitution simply as a choice is to deny the deeply troubling social factors and discrimination that play a critical role in trapping women in prostitution and sexual exploitation.

The Nordic Model provides support for those transitioning out of prostitution and has the premise that women and girls deserve better opportunities and experiences. This is why the Nordic Model, in addition to criminalising pimps and johns, 'includes programmes to prevent the purchase of sex and resources for women who want to exit prostitution'. [30] In order to change societal perceptions of prostitution, it is essential that social support for women be introduced, such as alternative sources of income. The Model goes beyond simply reducing stereotypes and misconceptions; it also seeks to address the underlying factors that push women to prostitution in the first place.

Aboriginal women and girls deserve to live free from poverty and violence

As recognised in the *United Nations Declaration on the Rights of Indigenous Peoples*, endorsed by the Canadian government in 2010, Aboriginal peoples have the collective right to 'live in freedom, peace and security as distinct peoples' and not be subjected to any act of violence (Article 7). In support of these rights, the state must take measures, in conjunction with the Indigenous peoples, 'to ensure that Indigenous women and children enjoy the full protection and guarantees against all forms of violence and discrimination' (Article 22). The state must also, 'take effective measures to ensure that programmes for monitoring, maintaining and restoring the health of Indigenous peoples, as developed and implemented by the peoples affected by such materials, are duly implemented' (Article 29).

In no way does the legalisation of prostitution or the criminalisation of women afford Aboriginal women the ability to achieve fulfilment and prosperity. Instead these models punish women for their poverty either by sanctioning their exploitation or by imprisoning them for circumstances beyond their control. Allowing Aboriginal women to be subject to the systematic violence associated with prostitution does not protect them. Previously in Canada, for Aboriginal women:

> the state has pushed [them] from one institution to another – residential schools, foster homes, group homes, and prisons, to name a few. The Native Women's Association of Canada refuses to accept brothels as the new official institution for Aboriginal women and girls. [31]

The exploitation women face in the sex trade is in no way a replacement for the obligations contained in the *United Nations Declaration on the Rights of Indigenous Peoples*. The sex trade will not improve the social conditions of Aboriginal women. Had Canada adopted a legal model that encouraged prostitution to continue, it would have been an abrogation of the duties owed by the state to Aboriginal women.

Some have claimed this new legislation reproduces colonial state violence against Aboriginal women and girls by increasing police power. What this analysis fails to recognise is that prostitution is not a traditional activity for Aboriginal women and, in fact, is 'the world's oldest oppression'. It is a system, like Canada's residential school system, that has been imposed on our Aboriginal communities. Prostitution is part of the continuum of colonial male violence against Aboriginal women and girls, telling women – incorrectly – that they are disposable in life and that predators can harm them without recourse. [32]

The Coalition therefore advocates for the state to respect the treaty rights and international human rights of Aboriginal peoples so they may meet their physical, cultural and spiritual needs free from violence and poverty. Adopting the Nordic Model, in its entirety, would have been a very meaningful step towards the government upholding these obligations and helping to establish a legal system premised more fully on achieving substantive equality for Aboriginal women. Through the provision of exit services and alternatives to prostitution a Nordic Model would ensure that Aboriginal women trapped in prostitution do not need prostitution to survive, thus allowing them to exit for real opportunities for them and their communities.

Conclusion

In response to the ruling in *Bedford* the federal government put together Bill C-36, the *Protection of Communities and Exploited Persons Act, SC 2014, c 25*. This Act came into effect on 6 December 2014. While the main ideas behind the Act borrow some elements from the Nordic Model, including stricter penalties for johns and pimps, a focus on public awareness campaigns, and training for police officers, 'as it stands, the new laws still criminalise both the buying and selling of prostitution in certain circumstances, such as when it takes place near schools, day care centres and playgrounds'. [33] Moreover, although Bill C-36 will provide funding for exit programmes, the $20 million spread over five years is likely to be insufficient. Thus while the Act is laudable in the strides it has taken from previous prostitution legislation, it nevertheless falls short of implementing the Nordic Model.

The review of the evidence on legalising and criminalising prostitution suggests that the Nordic Model is ideal if one's goal is to decrease prostitution, sex trafficking, and violence against women while also providing for support to exit prostitution for the many who are trapped within it. The Nordic Model provides both for the protection of women and, because it helps take away the demand for prostitution and sex trafficking, helps end discrimination against minority women as well. Women are the victims of prostitution. It is only by fully criminalising the pimps and buyers, while completely decriminalising those prostituted, that we can pave the way through legislation to appropriate protections for prostituted women and providing a path out of exploitation. Such a legal stance will also help achieve a significant change in the social perceptions around the commodification of women.

Saying 'I don't': moving beyond marriage

Meagan Tyler

The only opinion that matters when it comes to our marriage is ours. [1] —
Jessica Valenti

The institution of marriage, and the wedding industry that surrounds it, provide highly influential social norms. Despite rising divorce rates, and changing understandings of intimate relationships and family types, marriage has retained a significant cultural hold. The bridal industry, in Australia alone, is worth more than $4 billion, [2] and most women still abandon their maiden names at the altar. But public discussion about these trends tends to simply focus on celebrating the individual choice of participants to enter into matrimony rather than seeing that choice as largely culturally constrained and part of the ongoing prominence of marriage *as an institution*. In this climate, challenges to marriage have largely faded from public view and, with them, the feminist aims of abandoning marriage in order to achieve equal personhood, sexual autonomy and a fair division of household labour. It is argued here, that critiques of marriage need to be revived in order to counter narratives about the 'equal partnership' of marriage and to end the reliance on the state as the ultimate arbiter of intimate relationships. It is put forward that opting out of marriage, and challenging its position as a crucial social institution, offers greater potential for a meaningful sense of equality.

'Feminist weddings' and (in)equality

There has been a recent revival of interest in the battlelines between feminism, marriage and (in)equality. From women publicly lamenting their female friends changing their names after getting hitched, to prominent liberal feminists providing 'how-to' guides for having 'feminist weddings', it appears as though the concept of eschewing marriage altogether has somehow fallen off the list of options. Even relatively mild criticisms of matrimony and its associated traditions are seen as attacks on individual women's 'choices'; choices that are seemingly made in a cultural and political vacuum, according to some commentators, who represent the issue as one of purely personal significance:

> It is not the role of the feminist movement to prescribe the way women live their lives. The role of the movement is to empower women to make their own choices – even if other feminists don't agree with them ... People make these decisions within the context of their own lives, their own family and their own relationship. [3]

As this excerpt neatly demonstrates, in a culture of individualised 'choice', feminist concerns about marriage and its links to women's inequality become recast as feminists judging other women and trying to 'prescribe the way women live their lives'. Rather than acknowledging the patriarchal underpinnings of marriage, and the ways in which these may inhibit all women's freedom and equality, there have instead been attempts to reclaim marriage as a positive, and even potentially feminist, enterprise for individual women. Prominent liberal feminists Laura Bates (founder of the Everyday Sexism Project) and Jessica Valenti (founder of *Feministing*), for example, have both written about their interpretations of incorporating feminism into their weddings, [4] and how marriage itself can represent an equal partnership. Indeed, in a recent edition of *Ms. Magazine* in the United States, Audrey Bilger claimed that it is a 'feminist principle' that marriage should be a 'union of two equals'. She asks:

> What does it matter if we bring feminism into our discussions of marriage equality? For one thing, it means that this struggle

is not just about the rights of lesbians and gay men – as big a deal as that is. Whether you're straight or gay, if you're committed to the feminist principle that marriage is a union of two equals, then you need to take this fight personally. [5]

The concept of marriage as a site of (potential) equality, however, largely ignores the way in which marriage in the West, and in many other areas of the world, fundamentally relies on and reinforces, inequality. Indeed, sexual inequality lies at the very heart of marriage as an institution. Western marriage contracts are, as Carole Pateman has argued, founded upon the union of two *unequal* partners. [6] In addition, the valorisation of marriage creates a hierarchy of legitimacy among various types of intimate relationships, with those that are sanctioned as 'marriage' being more culturally valued than others. If these problems with marriage are not even confronted there can be little hope of reappropriating the institution for more equitable outcomes.

To be fair, both Bates and Valenti have acknowledged the patriarchal foundations of marriage in public discussions of their own weddings, but they seem to subsequently wish them away rather than acknowledging the virtual impossibility of overcoming them. We must recognise that it is not possible to live completely outside of the social norms that surround us, however much we may resist them. Social change cannot be brought about by simply reimaging marriage as a 'union of two equals', although things would be much easier if this were really the case. Nor is it possible for an individual couple to simultaneously participate in, and undermine, the entire social meaning of the larger tradition of marriage as, individually, we do not get to determine the meaning of that tradition. Weddings (like all traditions) and the institution of marriage carry such cultural weight, at least in part, because of the shared social meanings surrounding them.

'Marriage equality' and same-sex marriage

While the possibility of equality within marriage has been touted
in mainstream, liberal feminism, mixing notions of equality with
nuptials has become most noticeable in the increasing popularity
of the term 'marriage equality', used in support of a push towards
legalising same-sex marriage. Given the decades of critique from
radical lesbian and gay scholars, that have highlighted the inequalities
of marriage, this seems a rather odd turn of phrase to have gained
currency. But the change in terminology reflects a change in the
terrain of the debates around marriage and also in understandings of
what constitutes feminism; in particular, notions of individual choice
and empowerment over collective liberation.

In some ways, the rallying cry of 'marriage equality' can be
understood as a practical response to reactionary social mores. In
the Australian context, a potent mix of homophobia, religion and
conservative politics have largely necessitated a position that is
celebratory of marriage, in order to create a platform for same-sex
marriage which is not overly threatening. That is, it can be easier to
try and join existing institutions, however flawed, rather than demand
serious reform or social change. The support for same-sex marriage
has therefore has resulted in some strange contradictions. Marriage,
which feminists and gay rights activists alike derided and decried
in the 1970s, is now being held up by some gay rights activists and
liberal feminists, as a hallowed social institution. Even self-proclaimed
libertarians, who would normally baulk at any state intervention in
private matters, are talking about the right of individuals to invite the
state into their most intimate affairs.

To be clear, this is, in no way, an argument against same-sex
marriage, specifically. Rather, it is an argument against marriage,
generally. As Claudia Card argues:

> Although the exclusion of LGBTs from the rites and rights

of marriage is arbitrary and unjust, the legal institution of marriage is itself so riddled with injustice that it would be better to create alternative forms of durable intimate partnership that do not invoke the power of the state. [7]

However, she also astutely points out that: 'excluding us is hardly a step toward the abolition of marriage'. [8] The case for same-sex marriage, in a context where heterosexual marriage is still of significant social, political, economic, legal and religious importance, is completely understandable. The problem, from a radical feminist perspective, has arisen with the creeping characterisation of marriage as something to be revered rather than something to be criticised.

The emphasis on the importance of participating in marriage has also created strange bedfellows, with those normally aligned to the progressive side of politics finding common ground with conservatives. Many politically conservative pundits are quite comfortable with the idea of same-sex unions as they see them shoring up marriage as an institution. Essentially, the more people that join, the better. The Australian Marriage Equality website, prominently displays the following quote from Chris Berg, a fellow at the Institute of Public Affairs (a neoliberal think tank with notably conservative political affiliations): 'Extending the marital franchise to gay and lesbian couples would multiply the number of Australians who can join this crucial social institution, spreading the positive impact of marriage on society.' [9] The 'positive impact', whatever this is presumed to be (as discussed further below), is certainly not experienced by women.

In the United States, a number of prominent social conservatives have also come out in support of same-sex marriage, including Jonathan Rauch, author of the terribly titled: *Gay Marriage: Why it is Good for Gays, Good for Straights, and Good for America.* [10] Rauch has argued that same-sex unions should not only be made legal, but also be encouraged because marriage helps rein in men's immutable sex drives (how lesbian women fit into this plan is a mystery) and makes them more responsible citizens. [11] Accepting this position requires buying into the kind of reductionist arguments about sex and sexuality that have been used in the past to justify rape on the grounds of biological necessity. [12]

Marriage and sexual inequality

Indeed, it is this understanding of men's natural sexual 'needs' that has often been used to support the idea of sexual access in heterosexual marriage. Historically, it was seen as impossible for a man to rape his wife as she legally abdicated her sexual autonomy when she signed the marriage certificate. Her consent was implied for the rest of her married life. While there is a popular perception that times have changed in the West, legal protection against rape in marriage is only a relatively recent phenomenon. In the Australian state of Queensland, new laws providing legal protection from marital rape did not take effect until 1989, and the change took even longer in England, with the marital exemption to laws regarding sexual assault and rape only removed in the early 1990s. [13]

Furthermore, such legal changes seem to have had only a minimal effect on attitudes. There is an entire genre of marital self-help books, backed by the authority of sex therapy, which reinforce the idea that marriage requires a husband's unfettered sexual access to his wife. [14] In the bestselling, and widely recommended self-help text, *Passionate Marriage*, Dr David Schnarch recounts various case studies with patients. In his own account, Schnarch – as a therapist – advises a patient, 'Audrey', that it is her own fault she feels pressured to have sex with her husband. He explains to her: 'You may have to choose between having sex and not being married ... Yes, you feel "pressured" to have sex. But the pressure is part of your choice. You agreed to monogamy – not celibacy.' [15] Such 'advice' highlights just how integral sexual access to wives is still deemed to be in modern marriage.

This belief in men's sexual rights to wives persists, at least in part, because the history of marriage in the West is one of sexual oppression. European marriage was, historically, a contract endorsed by the state in which a man gained control and rights over a woman and their children, who were seen as little more than goods and chattels. In fact, the institution of marriage was built upon the contractual 'partners' being unequal. In the 1800s, John Stuart Mill maintained that wives were the only slaves left permitted by law. In *The Subjection of Women*, he described a wife's position as that of a 'personal body-servant' required to service her husband; in Mill's terms, a kind of domestic dictator. [16] He argued not that all husbands were inevitably prone to violence and despotism, but that marriage, as a legal and social institution, created such a role for men and granted them permission to inhabit it at will.

Mill did not argue that all marriages were bad or that all husbands were oppressive thugs. The issue is not whether or not an *individual* marriage is a 'good marriage' or whether or not some individuals are happy inhabiting the roles of wife and husband. The issue is that the very roles of wife and husband exist in the first place. Simply stating that there are 'good marriages' does not undo the historical burden that modern marriage still carries with it today. As Card argues:

> pointing out that many marriages are very loving, not at all violent, and proclaim to the world two people's honourable commitment to each other, seems to me analogous to pointing out, as many slave-owners did, that many slave-owners were truly emotionally bonded with their slaves, that they did not whip them, and that even the slaves were proud and honoured to be the slaves of such masters. [17]

Such instances, whether they truly exist or not, do not prove that slavery is an institution which causes no harm. This is precisely why many 20th century feminists continued to argue along similar lines as Mill. Iris Marion Young, for instance, claimed marriage was the 'cornerstone' of patriarchal power. [18] Christine Delphy has long maintained that marriage is the primary way that women's labour is exploited by men, [19] and Carole Pateman, in *The Sexual Contract*, famously likened marriage to prostitution and sexual servitude. [20]

The ever-present history of marriage (in)equality

Almost all of those involved in current 'marriage equality' campaigns, and the rebranding of marriage as compatible with feminism, seem to think such critiques are outdated. Yet, in Australia, the vast majority of women take their husband's name after marriage, [21] so labels of male ownership are definitely still alive and well. It seems quite extraordinary that this practice should still be so prevalent in the 21st century, but the tradition of women giving up their own, premarital identity to take their husband's names has, like marriage itself, been repackaged as just one of many 'choices' available. Except there was no great period in Australia when women *did* keep their names as a matter of course, and this is not one or two women changing their names after the wedding, but a sizeable majority. It takes impressive twists of mental gymnastics to pretend that it is merely coincidence that leads thousands of women to prefer their husband's names over their own, rather than a complex interplay of cultural conditioning and social pressure. The fact that it is seen as less hassle to go the trouble of changing a name, rather than keeping it, speaks volumes about the expectation that women will give up part of their premarriage identities.

The appropriation of a married women's labour is also a tradition that is still going strong. Several studies [22] have shown that married couples, regardless of their period of prior cohabitation, experience an exaggerated sexual division of labour after the wedding day that results in women undertaking an even more disproportionate burden of household chores. Simply by getting married, women increase, on average, their unpaid work by around 60 per cent. [23] Sociologist Janeen Baxter argues that this may be explained by understanding de facto relationships as providing 'a period of relative freedom in which to negotiate more equal roles' which the social expectations of marriage might otherwise inhibit. [24]

These contemporary examples of ownership and appropriation suggest that marriage relies on, and perpetuates, gender inequality between men and women. It may be tempting to believe that because, in the context of same-sex marriage, two men or two women marry, that these issues of inequality will be irrelevant. However, as the activists of previous decades attempted to expose, the dominant construction of heterosexuality is incredibly powerful and insidious. The overlay of heterosexual norms that sexualise the unequal power relations of dominance and submission do not magically disappear in all gay and lesbian relationships. [25] This is why simply asking for access to an existing institution is not the same as demanding fundamental changes to that institution or the relations it is built upon. If the request is to join under the existing terms, then it must be recognised that those existing terms cannot create real equality.

There is also hope, in some quarters, that the entry of feminists into marriage and the acceptance of same-sex marriage, might actually help to reform the institution itself. That is, some argue that 'feminist weddings' and the extension of marriage rights (and rites) to gay men and lesbian women is, in effect, demanding a fundamental change to marriage that may force a rethinking of its very meaning and purpose. While this may be possible in theory, given the admiring terms currently used to describe marriage, even by those groups which, in the past, would have been highly critical of the institution, it seems unlikely. If the difficulties of overcoming the dark past of marriage are not, at the very least, acknowledged, then it will remain impossible to revolutionise its future.

Finally, aside from connections to heteronormativity and gender inequality, the valorisation of marriage reinforces inequality between those who marry and those who do not. This hierarchy already exists in heterosexual relationships, and in many places around the globe, means not only that non-married couples are seen as less legitimate but that they may also be denied a variety of legal, social and economic benefits bestowed upon married couples. Given the way in which the norm of marriage perpetuates this form of inequality, it surely makes more sense to work towards unravelling the importance of marriage as an institution, or better still, to work towards its abolition, rather than its extension.

When the very real issues of marriage *inequality* are emphasised over the rhetoric of 'equal partnerships', it is difficult to understand why there is such a desire to buy into marriage at all. The real problem is, of course, that marriage remains constructed as an essential social, political, economic, legal and religious institution. To be sure, there are many people, even some feminists, who wish to enter marriage, but these examples do not offer evidence of the worthiness of the institution or prove that it can be a vehicle for social justice. Ultimately, opting out of marriage altogether would provide a quicker path to progress, as only the death of marriage can bring about the hope of more genuine equality for all.

Building feminism, resisting porn culture: where to from here?

Rebecca Whisnant

In chapter one, I wrote about some of the fundamental differences between radical feminism and liberal or third wave feminism and, in particular, how these branches of feminism approach pornography. I also wrote about the importance of radical feminism for recognising and resisting oppression. In this chapter, I pick up these threads again and discuss the key elements that radical feminism can contribute to the rebuilding of a powerful movement for women's liberation in the era of porn culture.

First things first, we need more people, more of the time, out there presenting radical feminist critique. I happen to know, for instance, that many bright and well-intentioned young people are toeing the third wave, sexual libertarian line because it's *all they've been taught* in their women's studies classes. And, of course, many people outside the academy have very little exposure to feminist critiques of virtually anything. So part of this is a sheer labour problem. We need more bodies and more voices. But not only do we need more people doing and saying the same things, I think that we also need to do and say some different things, or at least some additional things. As porn culture becomes ever more pervasive and soul-destroying, and as it starts to directly affect more people's lives in ways they're aware of, many people are looking for a way out. The problem is that they don't see any alternative, and much of what they're told is different and alternative really isn't.

For instance, the most obvious cultural and political force that presents itself as an alternative – indeed, is often seen as the only alternative – to porn culture is a religious, predominantly Christian, social conservatism. Now that's no good for women, and part of the appeal of third wave, pro-porn politics resides in its apparent rebellion against such conservatism. This leads me to my first suggestion about how to frame our critique of porn culture: namely by showing that – contrary to popular belief – conservative and pornographic ideologies of sex and gender are very nearly synonymous, the surface differences between the two obscuring their fundamental unity. As radical feminists have long observed, male sexual ownership and control of women is a matter of fundamental *agreement* between the male-defined political right and the almost equally male-defined political left. The right typically supports the private male ownership of women one at a time, as wives and daughters, localised in the home and the 'traditional family'; whereas the left too often defends men's collective sexual ownership of women outside the home, in the 'public domain', including in pornography and prostitution. To reject *both* forms of male sexual ownership, as radical feminists do, is thus to commit the ultimate heresy.

Yet only such principled rejection can effectively challenge the sexual abuse and commodification of women and girls both inside and outside the 'traditional family'. Until we find ways to communicate the linked dangers of *both* forms of male control, the fear of one form will continue to send women and girls directly into the lap of the other. The conservatives say to us:

> Hey, ladies, don't like what you see in pornography? Ugly, isn't it? You say you don't want that to happen to you, or for men to think of you like that? Well, then, be good girls and keep your legs closed. Be abstinent until marriage, and then God says your husband has to honour and value you and protect you from other men. (You just have to obey him).

Meanwhile, women and girls who recognise the patriarchal trap of 'traditional family values' are urged to demonstrate their independence and rebellion against said values by buying a stripper pole and learning to lap dance. 'What? You say that doesn't seem like authentic female sexuality or sexual liberation to you? What are you, a right-wing, "anti-sex" prude?'

This surface conflict in sexual ideology between right and left serves male power by masking a deeper agreement. For both camps, after all, it is an article of faith that sex makes women dirty, cheap, less valuable, that being fucked literally degrades women and girls. Furthermore, in both camps, women and girls are systematically made to suffer for having sex. In the world of pornography, the sex itself – aggressive, hostile, humiliating – is the punishment, the mechanism by which men viscerally experience their manhood by putting women in our place. In the world of 'traditional family values' the suffering of shame, stigma, unwanted pregnancy (or at least the fear of it), and forced childbirth is a woman's just punishment for having had sex that she shouldn't have had. And in both worlds we hear the constant refrain – sometimes whispered, sometimes shouted – 'Bitch. Slut. Dirty whore. You're getting what you deserve.' As Andrea Dworkin once put it: 'Pretending to argue, they collude. And if one don't get you, the other will.' [1]

As daunting as this convergence is, it also suggests a certain hermeneutic of feminist resistance, one that, happily, is pretty easy to communicate. People who care about justice and who want a way out of porn culture need to act and think in ways that won't make *either* bunch of woman-haters happy. If you're doing and saying things that the religious right and the libertarian left *both* really hate, then you're on the right track! So that's my first suggestion.

My second suggestion is that we connect our critique of pornography and porn culture to a broader critique of the commodification of everyday life and, in so doing, promote a non-marketised conception of freedom. Now that's a mouthful, I know. To start illustrating it, I want to share with you a couple of anecdotes from my recent trip to a college which shall remain nameless, but which is known both for its stellar academics and for its progressive politics. I'll call it 'Alt. College'.

Overall, my visit to Alt. College was wonderful: I visited some classes and gave an anti-pornography slideshow in the evening to a large and receptive audience. During the question and answer period that followed, a young woman raised her hand. Clearly troubled by what she had heard and seen, she asked: 'Well, what if we all just get together and tell the porn industry that this isn't what we want – that we want something more complex, more diverse, less hateful and one-dimensional? Wouldn't they have to change their ways and give us what we want?'

There are many assumptions lurking in this query that we would do well to challenge, but what I want to highlight is the faith that's being shown in the wonders of the capitalist marketplace. To this very bright, progressive, feminist young woman, here in this bastion of liberal-to-radical politics, it seemed plausible to think that – in this connection at least – the market will solve all of our problems. Now in making this assumption, there is something important that she fails to understand, namely that the cultural products of mega-corporations are much more like advertising than they are like art. When powerful and profit-hungry entities go hunting for market share at any cost, what those entities will produce and sell is whatever gets the *most* people in the gut the *fastest* and makes them want *more* of *that now*. This will never be equality. It will never be complexity. It will never be anything thoughtful or meaningful or reflective. Not ever.

Let me share one more anecdote from Alt. College that will help me go a bit deeper with this idea. That afternoon, I had visited the gender studies senior seminar course to talk with the students about feminist politics and pornography. At one point in the discussion, a young woman raised her hand, and said: 'Well, these days things are different. People in my generation want sexuality to be an important part of their lives; they want to be free and open with their sexuality. So that's why they want to make and use pornography.' There's a sweet kind of humour here: every generation thinks it invented sex. But more relevant, for our purposes, there are two massive assumptions underlying this young woman's comment, both of which we need to challenge whenever we see an opening to do so.

The first assumption is that, for some experience or activity to be important, real, and considerable, it must be made into an image: take a picture, roll video, turn on the webcam. As Gail Dines is fond of pointing out, we live in an image-based culture. Everything has to be made into an image, and we derive our conception of who and what we are largely from the images that surround us. But here is a question: when you are doing something – virtually anything – are you more or less free in doing it when you know someone is watching? What if they're taking pictures? What if they're going to show those pictures to a whole bunch of people you don't even know? (Are you feeling free yet?) For instance, do you dance crazier and more freely when you're by yourself in your bedroom, or out at the nightclub when your image is being projected on the big screen?

The second assumption underlying this young woman's comment is that, for some experience or activity to be important, real, and considerable, it must be made into a commodity. But here is another question: when you put some activity into the marketplace – that is, you decide to sell it instead of just doing it – does that make you more or less free in doing it? For instance, suppose you like to make music. Up until now it's been a hobby, something you do in your spare time, but now you've decided that you want to get signed with a major label. All of a sudden you're not free to make any old kind of music you want, are you? Now it's: 'What do they think they can sell? What's in vogue this week, and are you it, and if not, can they make you into it?'

So we face a bizarre phenomenon in many discussions of pornography, in that it's only with respect to sex that many otherwise progressive and leftist people assume that putting something into the capitalist marketplace makes it *more* free (or is evidence that one is free in doing it). We need to find ways to challenge the naïve and regressive conceptions of freedom as the freedom to enter the marketplace and/or to choose among the options that the marketplace offers us. We need to suggest to people that – in many everyday contexts, but perhaps especially for the most intimate and potentially creative activities of our lives, like sex and sexuality – *real* freedom in that activity means neither selling it nor letting somebody with a profit motive tell us what it is supposed to look and feel like.

My final suggestion is one that's been made before, and that is that we need a vision of alternatives. The makers of ostensibly-feminist porn claim to be providing such a vision, and that's why their message is appealing to many: we sense a need for alternatives, and that need is real, but more commodified images isn't it. But it is true that our side needs to be more than just, as Dworkin once aptly put it: 'the morbid side of the women's movement'. [2] There's something to that, inevitably, and rightly so: there is no way to face down the industries of sexual exploitation without confronting some very ugly realities. We must not flinch from that task, and we must continue to find ways to help others face those realities without dying inside. But we can't *just* be 'Atrocities"R"Us'. We also have to give people (including ourselves) some inspiration and some room to move. This is a tall order but I'm going to provide here three quick ideas for moving in this direction.

First, note the connection to my point about withdrawing from the market. To open up the space for new thinking and experimentation, we need to detox, to get out of the path of porn culture's cynical, manipulative, and hateful messages. To start thinking our own thoughts and dreaming our own dreams, first we have to get away from the bastards who are shouting at us through megaphones. Second, we need to draw on our own experiences of love and sex as joy and communion (and encourage others to draw on theirs). As radical feminists have long emphasised, patriarchy constructs our sexuality very profoundly, and even the most enlightened among us are not immune to that construction. But the construction, for most people at least, does not go 'all the way down'. Despite everything, many people do have experiences of mutual and egalitarian sexuality – or at least hints or glimmers of it – and that's really good news. We need to encourage people to tap into these experiences, hints, and glimmers, to remember what they know from their own lives: that no pimp or corporation sold to them or ever could, and to want more of it.

Third and finally, as we continue to tell people what sexual freedom isn't, we should also encourage them to think deeply and creatively about what it is. What would *real* sexual freedom look and feel like, the kind that *everyone* can have, instead of the kind that amounts to freedom for some at others' expense? We need to richly imagine, and encourage others to richly imagine, another world: one in which no woman or girl is ever called 'slut', 'prude', 'bitch', 'cunt', or 'dyke'; in which no woman, man, or child ever has to fear rape or suffer its damage to their spirits; in which men do not control their own and other men's behaviour by the threat of being seen and treated as women; and in which lesbian love and connection is not reduced to a pornographic fetish for men. In this world, every woman and girl sees her own body as beautiful, no man or boy is made to see his as a weapon, and people take part in sexual activity only when (and only because) they expect to enjoy it and to be honoured and fulfilled therein. It can be painful to think in this way, because we become more acutely aware of just how far away we are from this better world. But the third wave has one thing right: desire can be, or can become, a form of power. We need to use the power of our desire for this world – our desire to bring it into being for ourselves and for our children and our grandchildren – to unite us and to animate our thinking and strategising about how to take our culture back from the pornographers.

ENDNOTES

Introduction
Miranda Kiraly and Meagan Tyler

[1] Catharine MacKinnon, 'Liberalism and the Death of Feminism' in D Leidholdt and J Raymond (eds), *The Sexual Liberals and the Attack on Feminism* (Teacher's College Press, 1990) 12.

[2] Emily Gosden, 'Germaine Greer: online trolling shows men now even less tolerant of women', *The Telegraph* (London), 27 April 2014.

[3] The concept of women as class is generally traced back to Kate Millett's foundational text *Sexual Politics*. In *Sexual Politics* (Granada, 1971) Millett posits that men and women are socialised into 'basic patriarchal polities' where men as group are bestowed with superior status and power over women as a group (p. 26), an idea which has since been employed by a number of prominent radical feminists including Kathleen Barry, Andrea Dworkin, Alison Jaggar, Catharine MacKinnon, and Monique Wittig. This is not to suggest that women are a totally homogenous group, that all women experience oppression in exactly the same way, or that there are no divisions among women. It is simply to highlight that it is still important to understand women's inequality – as women – vis-à-vis men.

[4] Catharine MacKinnon, 'Feminism, Marxism, Method, and the State: An Agenda for Theory' (1982) 7 *Signs: Journal of Women in Culture and Society* 515, 515.

[5] Katharine Viner, 'She never hated men', *The Guardian* (London), 13 April 2005.

Not your father's *Playboy*, not your mother's feminist movement: feminism in porn culture
Rebecca Whisnant

[1] Jenny Kutner, '"Feminism is just owning your s*** and feeling good about your decisions": Salon talks with the hosts of "Guys We F**ked"', *Salon* (online), 29 December 2014, <http://www.salon.com/2014/12/28/feminism_is_just_owning_your_s_and_feeling_good_about_your_decisions_salon_talks_with_the_hosts_of_guys_we_fked/>.

[2] Robin Morgan, 'Theory and Practice: Pornography and Rape' in *The Word of a Woman: Feminist Dispatches 1968–1992* (Norton, 1992).

[3] Susan Brownmiller, *Against Our Will: Men, Women, and Rape* (Simon & Schuster, 1975).

[4] For a full explanation of the ordinance and a defence of its constitutionality, see Dworkin and MacKinnon, *Pornography and Civil Rights: A New Day for Women's Equality* (Organising Against Pornography, 1988). The book is out of print, but the full text is available from: <http://www.nostatusquo.com/ACLU/dworkin/other/ordinance/newday/TOC.htm/>.

[5] M Karp and D Stoller (eds), *The Bust Guide to the New Girl Order* (Penguin, 1999).

[6] See, eg, Jon Elster, *Sour Grapes: Studies in the Subversion of Rationality* (Cambridge University Press, 1983). For a specifically feminist discussion, see also Martha Nussbaum, 'Adaptive Preferences and Women's Options' (2001) 17 *Economics and Philosophy* 67. Ann Cudd discusses adaptive preferences (or, as she calls them, 'deformed desires') in chapter 6 of her *Analysing Oppression* (Oxford University Press, 2006).

[7] Like virtually any political movement or school of thought, 'third wave feminism' is not a monolithic entity, and not everyone who identifies as a third wave feminist will agree with all (or any) of the views described herein as prototypically third wave. Furthermore, many third wave feminists (including some whose writings I cite here) have done valuable political work on a number of fronts.

[8] Andrea Dworkin, *Right Wing Women* (Perigee Books, 1983) 220.

[9] Jennifer Gilley, 'Writings of the Third Wave: Young Feminists in Conversation' (2005) 44 *Reference & User Services Quarterly* 187, 189.

[10] J Baumgardner and A Richards, *Manifesta: Young Women, Feminism, and the Future* (Farrar, Straus and Giroux, 2000).

[11] See, eg, Marilyn Frye, 'Oppression' in *The Politics of Reality: Essays in Feminist Theory* (Crossing Press, 1983).

[12] R Whisnant and K Mantilla, 'Backlash and a Feminism that is Contrary to Feminism' (2007) 37 *Off Our Backs* 58, 60.

'I do what I want, fuck yeah!': moving beyond 'a woman's choice'

Meghan Murphy

[1] Lauren Barbato, 'Scenes from SlutWalk LA 2012', *Ms. Magazine* (online), 8 August 2012, <http://msmagazine.com/blog/2012/08/08/scenes-from-slutwalk-la-2012>.

[2] Meghan Murphy, 'Feeling uncomfortable: a response to SlutWalk DC's defence around holding a fundraiser as a "gentlemen's club"' on *Feminist Current* (13 May 2011) <http://feministcurrent.com/2703/feeling-uncomfortable-a-response-to-slutwalk-dcs-fundraiser-at-a-gentlemens-club/>.

[3] Claire Provost, 'UN Women justice report: get the data', *The Guardian* (online), 6 July 2011, <http://www.theguardian.com/global-development/poverty-matters/2011/jul/06/un-women-legal-rights-data>.

[4] Hannah Betts, 'Psychology of stripping. Interview with Dita Von Teese', *The Times* (London), 25 February 2006.

Depoliticising the personal: individualising body image and disordered eating in *The Beauty Myth*

Natalie Jovanovski

[1] Naomi Wolf, *The Beauty Myth: How Images of Beauty are Used Against Women* (Vintage Books, 1990) 272.

[2] M Love and B Helmbrecht, 'Teaching the Conflicts: (Re)Engaging Students with Feminism in a Postfeminist World' (2007) 18 *Feminist Teacher* 41.

[3] Wolf, above n 1, 10.

[4] Ibid 11.

[5] Andrea Dworkin, *Woman Hating* (Dutton Press, 1974).

[6] Wolf, above n 1, 208.

[7] Ruth Groenhout, 'Essentialist Challenges to Liberal Feminism' (2002) 28 *Social Theory and Practice* 51.

[8] Wolf, above n 1, 277.

[9] Groenhout, above n 7, 61.

[10] Wolf, above n 1, 273–4.

[11] Ibid 18.

[12] Sheila Jeffreys, *Beauty and Misogyny: Harmful Cultural Practices in the West* (Routledge, 2005) 7–8.

[13] Wolf, above n 1, 272.

[14] Lucy Serpell et al, 'Anorexia Nervosa: Friend or Foe?' (1999) 25 *International Journal of Eating Disorders* 177.

[15] Michelle Lazar, 'Entitled to Consume: Postfeminist Femininity and a Culture of Post-Critique' (2009) 3 *Discourse and Communication* 371.

[16] E Papies and K Nicolaije, 'Inspiration or Deflation? Feeling Similar or Dissimilar to Slim and Plus-Size Models Affects Self-Evaluation of Restrained Eaters' (2012) 9 *Body Image* 76.

Questioning 'choice' and 'agency' in the mail-order bride industry

Kaye Quek

[1] Nicole Constable, *Romance on a Global Stage* (University of California Press, 2003) 90.

[2] Ibid; Nicole Constable, 'International Marriage Brokers, Cross-Border Marriages and the US Anti-Trafficking Campaign' (2012) 38 *Journal of Ethnic and Migration Studies* 1137; Nora Demleitner, 'In Good Times and in Bad: The Obligation to Protect "Mail Order Brides"' in K Askin and D Koenig (eds), *Women and International Human Rights Law* (Transnational Publishers, 2000).

[3] Constable, *Romance on a Global Stage*, above n 1.

[4] L. E. Orloff and H Sarangapani, 'Governmental and Industry Roles and Responsibilities with Regard to International Marriage Brokers: Equalising the Balance of Power Between Foreign Fiancés and Spouses' (2007) 13 *Violence Against Women* 469, 471.

[5] Vanessa Brocato, 'Profitable Proposals: Explaining and Addressing the Mail-Order Bride Industry Through International Human Rights Law' (2004) 5 *San Diego International Law Journal* 225, 233; Jackie Jones, 'Trafficking Internet Brides' (2011) 20 *Information & Communication Technology Law* 19, 23.

[6] Brocato, above n 5, 232.

[7] Ibid 231.

[8] Testimony to United States Senate Committee on Foreign Relations, 'Mail-Order Brides: Exploited Dreams', United States Senate, Washington, DC, 13 July 2004 (Michele A. Clark).

[9] Constable, *Romance on a Global Stage*, above n 1; Constable, 'International Marriage Brokers, Cross-Border Marriages and the US Anti-Trafficking Campaign', above n 2.

[10] Constable, *Romance on a Global Stage*, above n 1, 89–90.

[11] Ibid 63.

[12] Ibid 88–9.

[13] Demleitner, above n 2, 626.

[14] Ibid 625.

[15] Testimony to United States Senate Committee on Foreign Relations, 'Mail-Order Brides: Exploited Dreams', United States Senate, Washington, DC, 13 July 2004 (Michele A. Clark).

[16] *Russian Women Asian Women and Latin Women Dating Service – Mail Order Brides* (2010) A Foreign Affair <http://www.loveme.com>.

[17] *Heart of Asia Personals* (2010) Heart of Asia <http://www.heart-of-asia.com/>.

[18] *Meet Brazilian Girls Meet Single Brazilian Girls and Ladies* (2010) Brazilian Women–Brazilian Girls <http://www.brazilianwomen-braziliangirls.com/>.

[19] M O'Connor and G Healy, *The Links Between Prostitution and Sex Trafficking: A Briefing Handbook* (EWL and CATW-I, 2006) 26.

[20] *Beautiful and Educated Mail Order Brides from the Philippines* (2010) Manila Beauty <http://www.manilabeauty.com>.

[21] *Russian Brides – Single Russian Women Dating – Russian Girls* (2010) Chance for Love <http://www.chanceforlove.com/>.

[22] Testimony to United States Senate Committee on Foreign Relations, 'Human Trafficking: Mail Order Bride Abuses', United States Senate, Washington, DC, 13 July 2004, 40 (Suzanne H. Jackson).

[23] See, eg, Demleitner, above n 2, 625.

[24] *AnastasiaDate Offers a Thrilling Companionship with Romantic and Caring Women*

From Abroad (2010) Anastasia International <http://www.anastasiadate.com/>.

[25] See, eg, *Russian Women Asian Women and Latin Women Dating Service*, above n 16; Constable, *Romance on a Global Stage*, above n 1.

[26] *Russian Women Asian Women and Latin Women Dating Service*, above n 16.

[27] *Meet Brazilian Girls Meet Single Brazilian Girls and Ladies*, above n 18.

[28] Abigail Stepnitz, *Male-Ordered: The Mail-Order Bride Industry and Trafficking in Women for Sexual and Labour Exploitation* (Poppy Project, 2009).

Feminism and the neoliberal state

Margaret Thornton

[1] Wendy Brown, *States of Injury: Power and Freedom in Late Modernity* (Princeton University Press, 1995) 170.

[2] E. P. Thompson, *Whigs and Hunters: The Origin of the Black Acts* (Pantheon Books, 1975) 184.

[3] Karl Marx, 'The Civil War in France' in David McLellan (ed), *Karl Marx: Selected Writings* (Oxford University Press, 1977) 539.

[4] Michel Foucault, 'Governmentality' in Graham Burchell et al (eds), *The Foucault Effect: Studies in Governmentality* (University of Chicago Press, 1991).

[5] See, eg, Clare Burton, *Subordination: Feminism and Social Theory* (Allen & Unwin, 1985); Suzanne Franzway et al, *Staking a Claim: Feminism, Bureaucracy and the State* (Allen & Unwin, 1989); R Pringle and S Watson, '"Women's Interests" and the Post-Structuralist State' in M Barrett and A Phillips (eds), *Destabilising Theory: Contemporary Feminist Debates* (Polity Press, 1992).

[6] S Tombs and D Whyte, 'Unmasking the Crimes of the Powerful: Establishing Some Rules of Engagement' in S Tombs and D Whyte (eds), *Unmasking the Crimes of the Powerful: Scrutinizing States and Corporations* (Peter Lang, 2003) 264.

[7] Anne Summers, *The End of Equality: Work, Babies and Women's Choices in 21st Century Australia* (Random House, 2003) 21.

[8] Gayatri Chakravorty Spivak, *In Other Worlds: Essays in Cultural Politics* (Methuen, 1987).

[9] Judith Butler, *Bodies that Matter: On the Discursive Limits of 'Sex'* (Routledge, 1993).

[10] See, eg, Jane S. Jaquette, 'Feminism and the Challenges of the "Post-Cold War" World' (2003) 5 *International Feminist Journal of Politics* 331, 339.

[11] Catharine MacKinnon, *Towards a Feminist Theory of the State* (Harvard University Press, 1989) 157.

[12] Franzway et al, above n 5, 161.

[13] Brown, above n 1, 67.

[14] Michel Foucault, *The Archaeology of Knowledge* (A. M. Sheridan Smith trans, Tavistock, 1972) 31.

[15] See, eg, Genevieve Lloyd, *The Man of Reason: 'Male' and 'Female' in Western Philosophy* (Methuen, 1984).

[16] Marian Sawer, *The Ethical State? Social Liberalism in Australia* (Melbourne University Press, 2003) 87.

[17] Damien Cahill, 'New-Class Discourse and the Construction of Left-Wing Elites' in M Sawer and B Hindess (eds), *Us and Them: Anti-Elitism in Australia* (API Network, Australia Research Institute, Curtin University of Technology, 2004) 89.

[18] Sawer, *The Ethical State?,* above n 16, 91–4.

[19] Marion Maddox, *God Under Howard: The Rise of the Religious Right in Australian Politics* (Allen & Unwin, 2005).

[20] See, eg, Brown, above n 1, 185.

[21] Catherine Hakim, *Key Issues in Women's Work: Female Diversity and the Polarisation of Women's Employment* (Glasshouse Press, 2nd ed, 2004).

[22] Jenny Chalmers et al, 'Part-time Work and Caring Responsibilities in Australia: Towards an Assessment of Job Quality' (2005) 15 *Labour & Industry* 41, 43.

[23] D Brennan and E Adamson, 'Child Care and Australian Social Policy' in J Bowes and R Grace (eds), *Children, Families and Communities* (Oxford, 2012); PayScale Human Capital, *Child Care / Day Care Worker Salary (Australia)* (2014) <http://www.payscale.com/research/AU/Job=Child_Care_%2f_Day_Care_Worker/Hourly_Rate>.

[24] Iris Marion Young, 'Polity and Group Difference: A Critique of the Ideal of Universal Citizenship' (1989) 99 *Ethics* 250, 253.

[25] Summers, above n 7.

[26] Barbara Pocock, *The Work/Life Collision* (Federation Press, 2003).

[27] Rosemary Whip, 'The 1996 Australian Federal Election and its Aftermath: A Case for Equal Gender Representation' (2003) 18 *Australian Feminist Studies* 73.

[28] Marian Sawer, 'Constructing Democracy' (2003) 5 *International Feminist Journal of Politics* 361, 365.

[29] Jane Mansbridge, 'Anti-Statism and Difference Feminism in International Social Movements' (2003) 5 *International Feminist Journal of Politics* 355, 356.

The illusion of progress: a betrayal of women from both ends of the political spectrum

Miranda Kiraly

[1] Dorchen Leidholdt, 'Introduction' in D Leidholdt and J Raymond (eds), *The Sexual Liberals and the Attack on Feminism* (Teachers College Press, 1990) xiv.

[2] See, eg, Keith Burgess-Jackson, 'John Stuart Mill, Radical Feminist' (1995) 21 *Social Theory and Practice* 369.

[3] Denise Schaeffer, 'Feminism and Liberalism Considered: The Case of Catharine MacKinnon' (2001) 95 *American Political Science Review* 699, 700.

[4] See, eg, *Criminal Code, Evidence Act and Other Acts Amendment Act 1989* (Qld) s 31; Kate Painter, 'Wife Rape in the United Kingdom' (Paper presented at the American Society of Criminology 50th Anniversary Meeting, San Francisco, 20–23 November 1991) 3–4.

[5] Catharine MacKinnon, 'Liberalism and the Death of Feminism', above n 1, 6.

[6] Miriam Robin, '"Political feminists" and compulsory voting on Mark Latham's hit list', *Crikey* (online), 1 August 2014, <http://www.crikey.com.au/2014/08/01/political-feminists-and-compulsory-voting-on-mark-lathams-hit-list/>.

[7] MacKinnon, 'Liberalism and the Death of Feminism', above n 1, 4.

[8] Ibid.

[9] Iris Marion Young, *Justice and the Politics of Difference* (Princeton University Press, 1990) 193–215.

[10] Jenny Turner, 'As Many Pairs of Shoes as She Likes' (2011) 33 *London Review of Books* 11, 11–15.

[11] Ibid.

[12] 'Tony Abbott unveils new ministry', *ABC News* (online), 16 September 2013, <http://www.abc.net.au/news/2013-09-16/abbott-unveils-new-ministry/4960186>.

[13] Leidholdt, above n 1, ix.

[14] Schaeffer, above n 3, 706.

[15] Meghan Murphy, 'Who gets a say? The sex work lobby & the silencing of feminism' on *Feminist Current* (8 December 2011) <http://feministcurrent.com/4024/who-gets-a-say-the-sex-work-lobby-the-silencing-of-feminist-voices/>.

[16] Leidholdt, above n 1, xv.

[17] Ibid.

[18] *Roe v Wade*, 410 US 113 (1973).

[19] Catharine MacKinnon, 'Reflections on Sex Equality Under Law' (1991) 100 *The Yale Law Journal* 1281, 1311.

[20] MacKinnon, 'Liberalism and the Death of Feminism', above n 1, 7.

[21] Ibid.

[22] Leidholdt, above n 1, xi.

[23] Chilla Bulbeck, *Living Feminism: The Impact of the Women's Movement on Three Generations of Australian Women* (Cambridge University Press, 1997) 224.

[24] Catharine MacKinnon, *Feminism Unmodified: Discourses on Life and Law* (Harvard University Press, 1987).

[25] Leidholdt, 'When Women Defend Pornography', above n 1, 129.

[26] MacKinnon, 'Liberalism and the Death of Feminism', above n 1, 11.

[27] Michaele L. Ferguson, 'Taming of the Shrew? Choice Feminism and the Fear of Politics' (2010) 8 *Perspectives on Politics* 247, 262.

[28] Andrea Dworkin, 'Woman-Hating Right and Left', above n 1, 31.

[29] Ibid 30.

[30] Linda Barclay, 'Liberal Daddy Quotas: Why Men Should Take Care of the Children, and How Liberals Can Get Them to Do It' (2013) 28 *Hypatia* 163, 168.

[31] Schaeffer, above n 3, 706.

The making of women's unfreedom:
sexual harassment as harm
Helen Pringle

[1] Bettina Arndt, 'Don't let the prudes deprive us of the spice of sexual banter', *The Sydney Morning Herald* (Sydney), 18 July 2012.

[2] Australian Human Rights Commission, *Working Without Fear: Results of the Sexual Harassment National Telephone Survey 2012* (2012).

[3] John Stuart Mill, 'On Liberty (1859)' in John M. Robson (ed), *Collected Works of John Stuart Mill vol. xviii* (University of Toronto Press, 1977) 223–4.

[4] *Sex Discrimination Act 1984* (Cth) s 28A. Similar provisions against harassment can be found at state and territory levels, with the principal anti-discrimination statutes being the *Anti-Discrimination Act 1977* (NSW) pt 2A; *Equal Opportunity Act 1984* (SA) s 87; *Equal Opportunity Act 1984* (WA) div 4, *Anti-Discrimination Act 1991* (Qld) ch 3; *Discrimination Act 1991* (ACT) pt 5; *Anti-Discrimination Act 1996* (NT) s 22; *Anti-Discrimination Act 1998* (Tas) s 17; and *Equal Opportunity Act 2010* (Vic) ss 92–102. Depending on the circumstances, a victim of harassing conduct may also call on a range of other remedies, such as civil or criminal proceedings for assault, breach of the employment contract or of occupational health and safety laws.

[5] Lawrence J. Epstein, *At the Edge of a Dream: The Story of Jewish Immigrants on New York's Lower East Side 1880–1920* (Wiley Publishing, 2007) 67–8; Daniel E. Bender, '"Too Much of Distasteful Masculinity": Historicising Sexual Harassment in the Garment Sweatshop and Factory' (2004) 15 *Journal of Women's History* 91, 100. See also Reva B. Siegel, 'A Short History of Sexual Harassment' in C MacKinnon and R Siegel (eds), *Directions in Sexual Harassment Law* (Yale University Press, 2003).

[6] Kathrin S. Zippel, *The Politics of Sexual Harassment: A Comparative Study of the United States, the European Union and Germany* (Cambridge University Press, 2006) 1–2.

[7] Jeffrey Minson, 'Second Principles of Social Justice' (1992) 10 *Law in Context* 1, 12–13. See the discussion in G Mason and A Chapman, 'Defining Sexual Harassment: A History of the Commonwealth Legislation and its Critiques' (2003) 31 *Federal Law Review* 195, 221.

[8] *Meritor Savings Bank v Vinson* 477 US 57 (1986).

[9] *Declaration on the Elimination of Violence Against Women*, UN General Assembly, UN Doc A/RES/48/104 (20 December 1993) art 2(b).

[10] Catharine MacKinnon, 'Beyond Moralism: Directions in Sexual Harassment Law' in *Women's Lives, Men's Laws* (Harvard University Press, 2005) 186.

[11] Helen Garner, *The First Stone: Some Questions About Sex and Power* (Picador, 1995).

[12] See *Fraser-Kirk v David Jones Ltd* [2010] FCA 1060 (29 September 2010). Fraser-Kirk's claim did not involve harassment *as discrimination* under the *Sex Discrimination Act 1984* (Cth), but was made under the *Trade Practices Act 1974* (Cth) and the *Fair Trading Act 1987* (NSW), and in contract, tort and equity.

[13] See Wendy Frew, 'Finally, someone calls halt to the game', *The Sydney Morning Herald* (Sydney), 6 August 2010, 15; Sarrah Le Marquand, 'It's not a good look when even women don't get it', *The Daily Telegraph* (Sydney), 7 August 2010, 29; Patricia Easteal et al, 'Sexual Harassment on Trial: The DJs Case' (2011) 36 *Alternative Law Journal* 230.

[14] 'Hill's DJs Comments Fall Flat', *AAP*, 3 August 2010. See also Emily Bourke, 'Designer sorry for sexual harassment gaffe', *ABC Transcripts*, 4 August 2010 (Hill says that her inner 'silly person had taken over') and Jackie Frank, 'Frankly Speaking, with Alannah Hill' (2013) 211 *Marie Claire* (Australia) 50, 50–2 (in which Hill claims, 'I just wanted to lighten the vibe').

[15] The Canadian sexual assault case of *R v Ewanchuk* [1999] 1 SCR 330, 372 (L'Heureux-Dubé J) dissenting in part, identifying as a central rape myth that women are presumptively sexually accessible until they resist.

[16] Bellinda Kontominas, 'David Jones sex harassment case: publicist sues for $37 million', *The Sydney Morning Herald* (Sydney), 2 August 2010.

[17] *Horne & McIntosh v Press Clough Joint Venture* [1994] EOC 92–556.

[18] *Henson v Dundee*, 682 F2d 897, 902 (11th Cir, 1982) (Vance J), quoted in *Meritor Savings Bank v Vinson* 477 US 57, 67 (1986).

[19] Katherine M. Franke, 'What's Wrong with Sexual Harassment?' (1997) 49 *Stanford Law Review* 691.

[20] Sandra Lee Bartky, *Femininity and Domination: Studies in the Phenomenology of Oppression* (Routledge, 1990) 27.

Entitled to be free: exposing the limits of choice
Shakira Hussein and Camille Nurka

[1] Christina Scharff, *Repudiating Feminism: Young Women in a Neoliberal World* (Ashgate, 2012).

[2] Ibid 45.

[3] Clare Midgley, *Women Against Slavery: The British Campaigns, 1780–1870* (Routledge, 1992); Antoinette Burton, *Burdens of History: British Feminists, Indian Women and Imperial Culture, 1865–1915* (University of North Carolina Press, 1994); Louise Newman, *White Women's Rights: The Racial Origins of Feminism in the United States* (Oxford University Press, 1999).

[4] Edward Said, *Orientalism* (Vintage Books, 1994) 6.

[5] Gustave Flaubert, *Flaubert in Egypt: A Sensibility on Tour* (Francis Steegmuller trans, Penguin, 1972) 220.

[6] Rebecca Watson, 'About Mythbusters, Robot Eyes, Feminism, and Jokes' on *Skepchick* (20 June 2011) <http://skepchick.org/2011/06/about-mythbusters-robot-eyes-feminism-and-jokes/>.

[7] Ibid.

[8] Rebecca Watson, 'The Privilege Delusion' on *Skepchick* (5 July 2011) <http://skepchick.org/2011/07/the-privilege-delusion/>.

[9] Anne McClintock, 'The Angel of Progress: Pitfalls of the Term "Post-Colonialism"' (1992) 31–32 *Social Text* 84.

[10] Ibid 88.

[11] 'Ban Welcomes UN General Assembly Resolutions Eliminating Female Genital Mutilation' (2014) UN News Centre <http://www.un.org/apps/news/story.asp?NewsID=43839#.U7eOJZSSyn8>.

[12] *Intensifying Global Efforts for the Elimination of Female Genital Mutilations*, GA Res, 67/146, UN GAOR, 67th sess, 60th plen mtg, UN Doc A/RES/67/146 (5 March 2013) 2 <http://www.un.org/en/ga/search/view_doc.asp?symbol=A/RES/67/146>.

[13] Ibid.

[14] World Health Organisation, 'Female Genital Mutilation', fact sheet no. 241 (February 2014) <http://www.who.int/mediacentre/factsheets/fs241/en/>.

[15] World Health Organisation, *Global Strategy to Stop Health-Care Providers from Performing Female Genital Mutilation UNAIDS, UNDP, UNFPA, UNICEF, UNHCR, UNIFEM, WHO, FIGO, ICN, IOM, WCPT, WMA, MWIA* (WHO Press, 2010) 1.

[16] *Crimes Act 1900* (NSW) s 45.

[17] Nikki Sullivan, '"The Price to Pay for Our Common Good": Genital Modification and the Somatechnologies of Cultural (In)Difference' (2007) 17 *Social Semiotics* 395, 398.

[18] Australian Government, Department of Human Services, 'Requested Medicare Items Processed from January 2002 to December 2002', Medicare Australia Statistics, item 35533 (2014) <https://www.medicareaustralia.gov.au/statistics/mbs_item.shtml>; Australian Government, Department of Human Services, 'Requested Medicare Items Processed from January 2012 to December 2012', Medicare Australia Statistics, item 35533 (2014) <https://www.medicareaustralia.gov.au/statistics/mbs_item.shtml>.

[19] HealthConsult, *MBS Reviews. Vulvoplasty Protocol*, report prepared for the Department of Health and Ageing (HealthConsult, 2013) 6.

[20] Ibid 4.

[21] D Veale and J Daniels, 'Cosmetic Clitoridectomy in a 33-Year-Old Woman' (2012) 41 *Archives of Sexual Behaviour* 725.

[22] World Health Organisation, 'Female Genital Mutilation', above n 14.

[23] R Bramwell at al, 'Expectations and Experience of Labial Reduction: A Qualitative Study' (2007) 114 *BJOG: An International Journal of Obstetrics & Gynaecology* 1493, 1495.

[24] Sullivan, above n 17, 400.

[25] Ibid 396.

[26] Susie O'Brien, 'Our laws are not negotiable', *The Herald Sun* (online), 5 March 2013, <http://www.heraldsun.com.au/news/opinion/our-laws-are-not-negotiable/story-e6frfhqf-1226590281341>.

[27] Lara Prendergast, 'The campaign against FGM must ignore intersectionality', *The Spectator* (online), 25 February 2014, <http://blogs.spectator.co.uk/coffeehouse/2014/02/the-campaign-against-fgm-must-not-become-clouded-by-intersectionality/>.

[28] Stephanie Peatling, 'Abortion will lead to Muslim nation: MP', *The*

Sydney Morning Herald (online), 14 February 2006, <http://www. smh.com.au/news/national/abortion-will-lead-to-muslim-nation-mp/2006/02/13/1139679540920.html>.

29 Kate Gleeson, 'The "Political Plaything of Men": Tony Abbott and the Enduring Significance of Abortion to the Christian Right' in Nick Walker (ed), *Essays 2014, Politics* (Australian Scholarly Publishing, 2014) 5.

30 Ibid 11.

31 Michelle Goldberg, 'Europe's birth strike', *The American Prospect* (online), 7 April 2009, <http://www.prospect.org/article/europe8217s-birth-strike>; Ross Douthat, 'Is feminism the new natalism?', *The Atlantic* (online), 8 April 2009, <http://www.theatlantic.com/personal/archive/2009/04/is-feminism-the-new-natalism/56084/>.

32 Sara Ahmed, *The Promise of Happiness* (Duke University Press, 2010).

33 Ibid 65.

'We love make-up, romance, high heels and men, of course': the contradictions of 'pop feminism'

Kate Farhall

1 'Interview: Helen Gurley Brown: Bad Girl' (1994) 27 *Psychology Today* 22.

2 See, eg, Kristen Harrison, 'Television Viewers' Ideal Body Proportions: The Case of the Curvaceously Thin Woman' (2003) 48 *Sex Roles* 255; K Harrison and J Cantor, 'The Relationship Between Media Consumption and Eating Disorders' (1997) 47 *Journal of Communication* 40; Robin Nabi, 'Cosmetic Surgery Makeover Programmes and Intentions to Undergo Cosmetic Enhancements: A Consideration of Three Models of Media Effects' (2009) 35 *Human Communication Research* 1.

3 See, eg, J Kim and L. Ward, 'Pleasure reading: Associations Between Young Women's Sexual Attitudes and Their Reading of Contemporary Women's Magazines' (2004) 28 *Psychology of Women Quarterly* 48; J Kim and L. Ward, 'Striving for Pleasure Without Fear: Short-Term Effects of Reading a Women's Magazine on Women's Sexual Attitudes' (2012) 36 *Psychology of Women Quarterly* 326; Alyssa Robillard, 'Music Videos and Sexual Risk in African American Adolescent Girls: Gender, Power and the Need for Media Literacy' (2012) 43 *American Journal of Health Education* 93; L. Ward,

'Understanding The Role of Entertainment Media in the Sexual Socialisation of American Youth: A Review of Empirical Research' (2003) 23 *Developmental Review* 347; Eileen Zurbriggen et al, *Report of the APA Taskforce on the Sexualisation of Girls* (American Psychological Association, 2010) <http://www.apa.org/pi/women/programs/girls/report.aspx>.

[4] Bauer Media Group, *Cosmopolitan* (2014) <http://www.bauer-media.com.au/brands/cosmopolitan/>.

[5] Rosa Silverman, 'Miley Cyrus: I'm one of the world's biggest feminists', *The Telegraph* (online), 13 November 2013, <http://www.telegraph.co.uk/culture/music/rockandpopmusic/10445850/Miley-Cyrus-Im-one-of-the-worlds-biggest-feminists.html>.

[6] Lily Rothman, 'A Sobering Look at Beyoncé and Jay Z's Sexy Song "Drunk in Love"', *Time Magazine* (online), 30 January 2014, <http://time.com/3090/drunk-in-love-controversy/>.

[7] P Farvid and V Braun, '"Most of us Guys are Raring to go Anytime, Anyplace, Anywhere': Male and Female Sexuality in *Cleo* and *Cosmo*' (2006) 55 *Sex Roles* 295; Kathryn McMahon, 'The Cosmopolitan Ideology and the Management of Desire' (1990) 27 *Journal of Sex Research* 381; Gloria Steinem, 'Sex, Lies and Advertising' in R McChesney and B Scott (eds), *Our Unfree Press: 100 Years of Radical Media Criticism* (New Press, 2004) 160; Naomi Wolf, *The Beauty Myth* (Random House, 1991).

[8] Farvid and Braun, above n 7; Kim and Ward, '*Striving for Pleasure Without Fear*', above n 3; A Ménard and P Kleinplatz, 'Twenty-One Moves Guaranteed to Make His Thighs Go Up in Flames: Depictions of "Great Sex" in Popular Magazines' (2008) 12 *Sexuality & Culture* 1.

[9] Kim and Ward, 'Pleasure Reading', above n 3, 49.

[10] Farvid and Braun, above n 7, 296, 299.

[11] Laurie Ouellette, 'Inventing the Cosmo Girl: Class Identity and Girl-Style American Dreams' in G Dines and J Humez (eds), *Gender, Race and Class in Media* (Sage, 3rd ed, 2011) 221; C Moran and C Lee, 'On His Terms: Representations of Sexuality in Women's Magazines and the Implications for Negotiating Safe Sex' (2011) 2 *Psychology & Sexuality* 159; Ménard and Kleinplatz, above n 8; McMahon, above n 7; Gail Dines, *Pornland: How Porn has Hijacked our Sexuality* (Beacon Press, 2010).

[12] Harrison, 'Television Viewers' Ideal Body Proportions', above n 2; Harrison

and Cantor, 'The Relationship Between Media Consumption and Eating Disorders', above n 2; Nabi, above n 2; Zurbriggen et al, above n 3.

[13] Amy R. Malkin et al, 'Women and Weight: Gendered Messages on Magazine Covers' (1999) 40 *Sex Roles* 647.

[14] Ibid 653.

[15] Kim and Ward, 'Pleasure Reading', above n 3, 49.

[16] Sandra Lee Bartky, *Femininity and Domination: Studies in the Phenomenology of Oppression* (Routledge, 1990).

[17] Katherine D. Gapinski et al, 'Body Objectification and "Fat Talk": Effects on Emotion, Motivation, and Cognitive Performance' (2003) 48 *Sex Roles* 377, 377.

[18] Ibid; D Tolman and M Porche, 'The Adolescent Femininity Ideology Scale: Development and Validation of a New Measure for Girls' (2000) 24 *Psychology of Women Quarterly* 365.

[19] Gapinski et al, above n 17.

[20] Kim and Ward, 'Pleasure Reading', above n 3, 56.

[21] Paul J. Wright, 'Sexual Socialisation Messages in Mainstream Entertainment Mass Media: A Review and Synthesis' (2009) 13 *Sexuality & Culture* 181, 192.

[22] Emma Halliwell et al, 'Are Contemporary Media Images Which Seem to Display Women as Sexually Empowered Actually Harmful to Women?' (2011) 35 *Psychology of Women Quarterly* 38, 42.

Business as usual, rebranded as ethics: the whitewashing of systemic injustice

Laura McNally

[1] Emily Gosden, 'Germaine Greer: online trolling shows men now even less tolerant of women', *The Telegraph* (London), 27 April 2014.

[2] Gert Hald et al, 'Pornography and Attitudes Supporting Violence Against Women: Revisiting the Relationship in Nonexperimental Studies' (2010) 36 *Aggressive Behaviour* 14.

[3] Subhabrata Banerjee, 'Corporate Social Responsibility: The Good, the Bad and the Ugly' (2008) 34 *Critical Sociology* 51.

[4] Rebecca Deans, 'Vagina Diaries draws attention to hidden cost of labiaplasty', *The Conversation* (online), 27 November 2013, <http://theconversation.com/vagina-diaries-draws-attention-to-hidden-cost-of-labiaplasty-20341>.

[5] Sheila Jeffreys, *Beauty and Misogyny* (Routledge, 2005) 28.

[6] See, eg, Michele R. Decker et al, 'Sex Trafficking, Sexual Risk, STI and Reproductive Health Among a National Sample of FSWs in Thailand' (2011) 65 *J Epidemiol Community Health* 334.

[7] Andy Ruddock, 'I Am a Girl: 21st-century lessons from 1970s feminism', *The Conversation* (online), 5 March 2014, <http://theconversation.com/i-am-a-girl-21st-century-lessons-from-1970s-feminism-23771>.

[8] Ibid.

[9] Lydia Cacho, *Slavery Inc.: The Untold Stories of International Sex Trafficking* (Portobello Books, 2013).

[10] Audré Lorde, 'The Master's Tools Will Never Dismantle the Master's House' in *Sister Outsider: Essays and Speeches* (Crossing Press, 1984) 110–113.

A fine line between pleasure and pain?
On the issue of 'choosing' sexual violence

Laura Tarzia

[1] Belle Knox, 'In Defence of kink: my first role as the Duke porn star was on a rough sex website, and no, that doesn't make me a bad feminist', *xoJane* (online), 19 March 2014, <http://www.xojane.com/sex/belleknox-duke-porn-star-rough-sex-feminism-kink/>.

[2] World Health Organisation and London School of Hygiene and Tropical Medicine, *Preventing Intimate Partner and Sexual Violence Against Women: Taking Action and Generating Evidence* (2010) <http://apps.who.int/iris/bitstream/10665/44350/1/9789241564007_eng.pdf>.

[3] Ibid.

[4] *Personal Safety Survey, Australia, 2012* (11 December 2013) Australian Bureau of Statistics <http://www.abs.gov.au/ausstats/abs@.nsf/mf/4906.0/>.

[5] Meg Barker et al, 'Kinky Clients, Kinky Counselling? The Challenges and Potentials of BDSM' in Lyndsey Moon (ed), *Feeling Queer or Queer Feelings: Radical Approaches to Counselling Sex, Sexualities and Genders* (Routledge, 2007) 106–24.

[6] See, eg, Meg Barker, 'Consent is a Grey Area? A Comparison of Understandings of Consent in *50 Shades of Grey* and on the BDSM Blogosphere' (2013) 16 *Sexualities* 896; Dionne van Reenen, 'Is This Really What Women Want? An Analysis of *Fifty Shades of Grey* and Modern Feminist Thought' (2014) 33 *South African Journal of Philosophy* 223.

[7] Lynn Comella, 'Fifty Shades of Erotic Stimulus' (2013) 13 *Feminist Media Studies* 563.

[8] Lisa Downing, 'Safewording! Kinkphobia and Gender Normativity in *Fifty Shades of Grey*' (2013) 4 *Psychology & Sexuality* 92.

[9] Kath Albury, *Yes Means Yes: Getting Explicit About Heterosex* (Allen & Unwin, 2002).

[10] Jessica Wakeman, 'First time for everything: getting spanked', *The Frisky* (online), 1 July 2009, <http://www.thefrisky.com/2009-06-01/first-time-for-everything-spanking/>.

[11] Knox, above n 1.

[12] Barker, 'Consent is a Grey Area?', above 6.

[13] Sheila Jeffreys, *How Orgasm Politics Has Hijacked the Women's Movement* (Spring 1996) On the Issues Magazine <http://www.ontheissuesmagazine.com/1996spring/s96orgasm.php/>.

[14] Cheryl Hanna, 'Sex is Not a Sport: Consent and Violence in Criminal Law' (2001) 42 *Boston College Law Review* 239.

[15] Barker, 'Consent is a Grey Area?', above n 6.

[16] *Consent Counts Survey* (2012) National Coalition for Sexual Freedom <https://ncsfreedom.org/key-programs/consent-counts/consent-counts.html/>.

[17] Wakeman, above n 10.

[18] Jeffreys, above n 13.

[19] Hellborndaughter, 'BDSM isn't okay just because there are submissive men' on *Tumblr* (2014) <http://survivorsofkinkunite.tumblr.com/post/92861836643/bdsm-isnt-okay-just-because-there-are-submissive/>.

A human right to prostitute others?: Amnesty International and the privileging of the male orgasm

Caroline Norma

[1] Amnesty International Secretariat, *Decriminalisation of Sex Work: Policy Background Document* (2013) Amnesty International. Document available from: <https://sites.google.com/a/amnesty.org.au/aia-activist-portal/bulletin-board/consultationondraftsexworkpolicy?pli=1>.

[2] Jay Levy, *Criminalising the Purchase of Sex: Lessons from Sweden* (Routledge, 2014).

[3] Barbara Sullivan, 'Feminism and Female Prostitution' in Roberta Perkins et al (eds), *Sex Work and Sex Workers in Australia* (University of New South Wales Press, 1994) 262.

[4] Brian Heilman et al, *The Making of Sexual Violence: How Does a Boy Grow Up to Commit Rape?* (International Centre for Research on Women, 2014) 14.

[5] JaneMaree Maher et al, *Sex Work: Labour, Mobility and Sexual Services* (Routledge, 2012) 50.

[6] Amnesty International, *Have Your Say – Amnesty's Sex Work Policy* (2 April 2014) <http://www.amnesty.org.au/leader/comments/34256/>.

[7] Amnesty International Secretariat, *Decriminalisation of Sex Work*, above n 1.

[8] Amnesty International Secretariat, *Background Information for Survey Participants: Amnesty International Consultation on Proposed Policy on Decriminalisation of Sex Work*, Amnesty International. Document available from: <https://sites.google.com/a/amnesty.org.au/aia-activist-portal/bulletin-board/consultationondraftsexworkpolicy?pli=1>.

[9] Ibid.

[10] Kat Banyard, *The Equality Illusion: The Truth About Men and Women Today* (Faber & Faber, 2010) 140.

[11] Amnesty International UK, *Douglas Fox and Amnesty International*, Amnesty International (1 February 2014) <http://www.amnesty.org.uk/douglas-fox>.

[12] Melissa Gira Grant, 'Amnesty, human rights and the criminalisation of sex work', *New Statesman* (online), 12 June 2013, <http://www.newstatesman.com/lifestyle/2013/06/amnesty-human-rights-and-criminalisation-sex-work>.

[13] Barbara Sullivan, 'Prostitution Politics in Australia' in Joyce Outshoorn

(ed), *The Politics of Prostitution: Women's Movements, Democratic States and the Globalisation of Sex Commerce* (Cambridge University Press, 2004) 24.

[14] Kate Shannon et al, 'Shannon, Bruckert & Shaver: Canada must set sex workers free', *National Post* (online), 7 April 2013, <http://fullcomment. nationalpost.com/2014/04/07/shannon-bruckert-shaver-canada-must-set-sex-workers-free/>.

[15] Amnesty International Secretariat, *Background Information for Survey Participants*, above n 8.

[16] International Union of Sex Workers, *IUSW Response to the Amnesty International Consultation on Decriminalising Sex Work* (8 April 2014) <http:// www.iusw.org/2014/04/iusw-response-to-the-amnesty-international-consultation-on-decriminalising-sexwork/>.

[17] International Union of Sex Workers, *Sex Work and Human Rights* (March 2014) <http://www.iusw.org/wp-content/uploads/2014/04/ SexWorkAndHumanRightsIUSWMar14.pdf>.

[18] Julie Bindel, 'An abject inversion of its own principles', *Daily Mail* (online), 24 January 2014, < http://www.dailymail.co.uk/news/article-2544983/ JULIE-BINDEL-An-abject-inversion-principles.html >.

[19] Kathleen Barry, *Why is Prostitution a Violation of Human Rights*, Abolish Prostitution Now (2013) <http://abolishprostitutionnow.wordpress.com/ why-is-prostitution-a-violation-of-human-rights/>.

If pornography is sex education, what does it teach?

Meghan Donevan

[1] Wendy McElroy, *XXX: A Woman's Right to Pornography* (St Martin's Press, 1995).

[2] M Giordano and A Ross, *Let's Talk About Sex: Young People's Views on Sex & Sexual Health Information in Australia* (June 2012) Australian Youth Affairs Coalition <http://www.redaware.org.au/wp-content/uploads/2012/10/Lets-TalkAboutSex_AYACYEAH_FinalReport.pdf>.

[3] Amee Wurzburg, *Nairobi Youth Sexual Culture: Gaining Insight on Youth Under-standings of Sexuality Through Formal Sexual Health Education and Exposure to Pornography* (2011) Independent Study Project Collection <http:// digitalcollections.sit.edu/isp_collection/990/>.

[4] Liberty Eaton et al, 'Unsafe Sexual Behaviour in South African Youth' (2003) 56 *Social Science Medicine* 149, 151.

[5] See, eg, Osmo Kontula, 'The Role of Pornography in Media and in Sex Education' (2008) 45 *Tidsskrift for Norskpsykologforening* 739.

[6] *Sexual and Reproductive Health*, World Health Organisation <http://www.who.int/reproductivehealth/topics/gender_rights/sexual_health/en/>. Note that this definition is a contribution to ongoing discussions about sexual health, and does not represent an official WHO position.

[7] S Green, 'HIV and AIDS, the Internet Pornography Industry and Safer Sex' (2004) 15 *International Journal of STD & AIDS* 206.

[8] This chapter focuses on heterosexual pornography. However, parallel arguments are made in Christopher Kendall, *Gay Male Pornography: An Issue of Sex Discrimination* (UBC Press, 2004).

[9] Several non experimental, experimental, and meta-analysis studies (which include both laboratory and naturalistic studies) have found that pornography consumption significantly predicted sexual aggression and attitudes supporting violence against women, even when controlling for other relevant individual characteristics that have predicted aggression in other studies. See, eg, Neil Malamuth et al, 'Pornography, Individual Differences in Risk and Men's Acceptance of Violence Against Women in a Representative Sample' (2012) 66 *Sex Roles* 427; Neil Malamuth et al, 'Pornography and Sexual Aggression: Are There Reliable Effects and Can We Understand Them?' (2000) 11 *Annual Review of Sexual Research* 26; Mike Allen et al, 'A Meta-Analysis Summarising the Effects of Pornography II: Aggression After Exposure' (1995) 22 *Human Communication Research* 258; Gert Hald et al, 'Pornography and Attitudes Supporting Violence Against Women: Revisiting the Relationship in Nonexperimental Studies' (2010) 36 *Aggressive Behaviour* 14; Neil Malamuth et al, 'Pornography and Sexual Aggression. Are There Reliable Effects and Can We Understand Them?' (2000) 11 *Annual Review of Sex Research* 26; V Vega and N Malamuth, 'Predicting Sexual Aggression: The Role of Pornography in the Context of General and Specific Risk Factors' (2007) 33 *Aggressive Behaviour* 104.

[10] Ana Bridges et al, 'Aggression and Sexual Behaviour in Best-Selling Pornography Videos: A Content Analysis Update' (2010) 16 *Violence Against Women* 1065. The authors found that of the 304 mainstream scenes analysed,

88.2 per cent contained physical aggression, while 48.7 per cent of scenes contained verbal aggression.

[11] Ibid 1080.

[12] Ibid 1077.

[13] Elisabet Le Roux, 'Pornography: Human Right or Human Rights Violation?' (2010) 66 *HTS Teologiese Studies/Theological Studies* 1.

[14] D Zillmann and J Weaver, 'Pornography and Men's Sexual Callousness Toward Women' in D Zillman and J Bryant (eds), *Pornography: Recent Research, Interpretations, and Policy Considerations* (Lawrence Erlbaum, 1989) 107.

[15] Several non experimental, experimental, and meta-analysis studies (which include both laboratory and naturalistic studies) have found that pornography consumption significantly predicted sexual aggression and attitudes supporting violence against women, even when controlling for other relevant individual characteristics that have predicted aggression in other studies. See, eg, Allen et al, above n 9; Hald et al, above n 9; Malamuth et al, 'Pornography and Sexual Aggression. Are There Reliable Effects and Can We Understand Them?', above n 9; Vega and Malamuth, above n 9; Malamuth et al, 'Pornography, Individual Differences in Risk and Men's Acceptance of Violence Against Women in a Representative Sample', above n 9.

[16] Chyng Sun et al, 'A Comparison of Male and Female Directors in Popular Pornography: What Happens When Women are at the Helm?' (2008) 32 *Psychology of Women Quarterly* 312.

[17] See Terrie Schauer, 'Women's Porno: The Heterosexual Female Gaze in Porn Sites "For Women"' (2005) 9 *Sexuality & Culture* 42, 58. Analysing pornography specifically advertised as 'made for women', Schauer notes that the content appears 'engineered similarly to those in heterosexual-male pornography [whereby] the visual material assembled for women's pleasure has yet to exhibit unique visual tags or coding that signify an erotic female gaze'. Interestingly, in Kendall, above n 8, 146, Kendall argues that gay pornography also reflects the power inequalities present in heterosexual sex, whereby male power through sex is gained through control and domination. This, he merits, results in condoms not being promoted, since their use imposes a limit on the right to do anything, anywhere, and with anyone sexually.

[18] Sun et al, above n 16.

[19] Daniel Bernardi, 'Interracial Joysticks: Pornography's Web of Racist Attractions' in Peter Lehman (ed), *Pornography: Film and Culture*, (Rutgers University Press, 2006) 222.

[20] Ibid 223–4.

[21] Ibid 231.

[22] Gloria Cowan et al, 'Racism and Sexism in Interracial Pornography' (1994) 18 *Psychology of Women Quarterly* 323, 335.

[23] Ibid.

[24] Vednita Carter, 'Prostitution and the New Slavery' in C Stark and R Whisnant (eds), *Not for Sale: Feminists Resisting Pornography and Prostitution* (Spinifex, 2004).

[25] Mireille Miller-Young, 'Putting Hypersexuality to Work: Black Women and Illicit Eroticism in Pornography' (2010) 13 *Sexualities* 219, 231.

[26] Bernardi, above n 19.

[27] Ibid 235.

[28] Ibid 236.

[29] Ibid 240.

[30] See, eg, Jason Carroll et al, 'Generation XXX: Pornography Acceptance and Use Among Emerging Adults' (2008) 23 *Journal of Adolescent Research* 6. It should be noted that while some couples might watch pornography together in order to improve their own sexual relationship, this particular case is not the norm in our current cultural landscape, as alluded to in Jill Manning, 'The Impact of Internet Pornography on Marriage and the Family: A Review of Research' (2006) 13 *Sexual Addiction & Compulsivity* 131; Ana Bridges et al, 'Romantic Partners' Use of Pornography: It's Significant for Women' (2003) 29 *Journal of Sex & Marital Therapy* 1.

[31] See Jill Manning, 'The Impact of Internet Pornography on Marriage and the Family: A Review of Research' (2006) 13 *Sexual Addiction & Compulsivity* 131; Bridges et al, 'Romantic Partners' Use of Pornography', above n 30.

[32] Green, above n 7, 208.

[33] Isabella Laws, 'Better Sex Education for Children is Needed to Combat Dangers of Pornography' (2013) 347 *British Medical Journal* f5764.

The oppression that dare not speak its name? Silences around heterosexuality in contemporary feminism

Julia Long

[1] J Armstrong and H Rudúlph, *Sexy Feminism: A Girl's Guide to Love, Success, and Style* (Mariner Books, 2013) 166.

[2] Mainstream feminist groups and campaigns that have gained particular media attention include OBJECT, UK Feminista, No More Page 3 and the Everyday Sexism Project.

[3] Adrienne Rich, 'Compulsory Heterosexuality and Lesbian Existence' in *Blood, Bread and Poetry: Selected Prose 1975–1985* (Virago Press, 1986).

[4] Ginny Berson, 'The Furies' (1972) 1 *The Furies* 18.

[5] *Domestic Violence*, End Violence Against Women Coalition <http://www.endviolenceagainstwomen.org.uk/domestic-violence/>.

[6] Rebecca Solnit, *Men Explain Things to Me* (Haymarket Books, 2014); Stacy Feder, 'Gender inequality: three phrases most men need to get used to hearing', *Guardian Liberty Voice* (online), 11 May 2014, <http://guardianlv.com/2014/05/gender-inequality-three-phrases-most-men-need-to-get-used-to-hearing/>.

[7] Laura Bates, 'How to have a feminist wedding', *The Guardian* (London), 28 June 2014.

[8] Sheila Jeffreys, *Unpacking Queer Politics: A Lesbian Feminist Perspective* (Polity Press, 2003).

[9] Stephanie Theobald, 'Lesbianism: sexual fluidity is a fact of life for women', *The Guardian* (London), 26 November 2013.

[10] See, eg, <http://radicallesbianfeminists.wordpress.com/about/>; <http://anntagonist.wordpress.com/tag/lesbian/>; <http://thearcticfeminist.wordpress.com/>.

[11] It is significant that both of these conferences – like others that have taken an uncompromisingly women-only stance – came under serious attack from transgender activists and men's rights activists, with both events having to relocate to alternative venues in the wake of this harassment. Such attacks clearly create a hostile climate for women-only organising, which is likely to be a factor in the reluctance of other feminist groups to adopt a women-only stance.

Political not generational: getting real about the second wave

Finn Mackay

[1] Shelley Budgeon, *Third Wave Feminism and the Politics of Gender in Late Modernity* (Palgrave Macmillan, 2011) 16.

[2] S Mann and D Huffman, 'The Decentring of Second Wave Feminism and the Rise of the Third Wave' (2005) 69 *Science & Society* 56.

[3] Sylvia Walby, *The Future of Feminism* (Polity Press, 2011) 19.

[4] J Baumgardner and A Richards, *Manifesta: Young Women, Feminism and the Future* (Farrar, Straus and Giroux, 2000).

[5] Finn Mackay, 'Political Not Generational: Getting Real About Contemporary UK Radical Feminism' (2014) *Social Movement Studies* 1.

[6] Andrea Dworkin, *Letters From a War Zone* (Lawrence Hill Books, 1993) 112.

[7] Lynnette Mitchell, 'Letter' (1981) 7 *Revolutionary and Radical Feminist Newsletter* 1.

[8] Patrick Califia, *Sex Changes: The Politics of Transgenderism* (Cleiss Press, 1997).

[9] Catherine M. Orr, 'Charting the Currents of the Third Wave' (1997) 12 *Hypatia* 29.

[10] Rebecca Walker (ed), *To Be Real: Telling the Truth and the Changing Face of Feminism* (Anchor Books, 1995).

[11] See Michaele L. Ferguson, 'Choice Feminism and the Fear of Politics' (2010) 8 *Perspectives on Politics* 247.

[12] Kimberlé Crenshaw, 'Demarginalising the Intersection of Race and Sex: A Black Feminist Critique of Antidiscrimination Doctrine, Feminist Theory, and Antiracist Politics' (1989) *University of Chicago Legal Forum* 139.

[13] Ferguson, above n 11.

[14] Julia Long, *Anti-Porn: The Resurgence of Anti-Pornography Feminism* (Zed Books, 2012).

Abuse masked as a 'cultural practice': speaking out against female genital mutilation

Naela Rose

[1] Martine Lefeuvre, as quoted in Bronwyn Winter, 'Women, the Law and Cultural Relativism in France: The Case of Excision' (1994) 19 *Signs: Journal of Women in Culture and Society* 939, 951.

[2] *Female Genital Mutilation (FGM) at a Glance,* The National Society for the Prevention of Cruelty to Children <http://www.nspcc.org.uk/ preventing-abuse/child-abuse-and-neglect/female-genital-mutilation-fgm/#factors?affId=1991357/>.

[3] Alexandra Topping, 'Ban Ki-moon backs campaign to tackle FGM through education', *The Guardian* (London), 19 February 2014.

[4] Alexandra Topping, 'Malala Yousafzai backs campaign against FGM', *The Guardian* (London), 25 February 2014.

[5] Carla AbouZahr, 'Women's Health Meeting: Trends And Projections For Mortality And Morbidity' (Paper presented at International Conference on Empowerment and Development Beyond 2014 Expert Meeting on Women's Health – Rights, Empowerment and Social Determinants, Mexico City) 30 September – 2 October 2014, 7.

[6] Kira Cochrane, 'The fourth wave of feminism: meet the rebel women', *The Guardian* (London), 11 December 2013.

For the sake of equality: moving towards the Nordic Model of prostitution law in Canada

Teresa Edwards

[1] *Bedford v Canada (Attorney General)* [2013] SCC 72.

[2] L Barnett and L Casavant, 'Prostitution: A Review of Legislation in Selected Countries' (Research Paper No 2011-115-E, Parliamentary Information and Research Services, Parliament of Canada, 2011).

[3] New Zealand Law Review Committee, New Zealand Government, *Report of the Prostitution Law Review Committee on the Operation of the Prostitution Reform Act 2003* (2008) 58.

[4] Ibid 57.

[5] Ibid 45–6.

[6] Julie Bindel, 'Why even Amsterdam doesn't want legal brothels', *The Spectator* (online), 2 February 2013, <http://www.spectator.co.uk/features/8835071/flesh-for-sale/>.

[7] Feargus O'Sullivan, 'Amsterdam's latest quest to tame legalised prostitution', *CityLab* (online), 25 March 2013, <http://www.citylab.com/politics/2013/03/amsterdams-latest-quest-tame-legalised-prostitution/5072/>.

[8] Seo-Young Cho et al, 'Does Legalised Prostitution Increase Human Trafficking? (2013) 41 *World Development* 67, 72.

[9] *Speaking of Prostitution: Arguments, Counterarguments About Prostitution* (2013) Women's Front in Sweden <http://www.kvinnofronten.nu/pdf/SoP.pdf/>.

[10] *Demand Change: Understanding the Nordic Approach to Prostitution* (2013) Coalition Against Trafficking in Women Australia <http://www.catwa.org.au/files/images/Nordic_Model_Pamphlet.pdf/>.

[11] Janine Benedet, *For the Sake of Equality: Arguments for Adapting the Nordic Model of Prostitution Law to Canada* (23 March 2014) Women's Coalition for the Abolition of Prostitution <http://www.abolitionprostitution.ca/english/useful-links>.

[12] Ibid.

[13] Barnett and Casavant, above n 2, 10.

[14] Ibid 18.

[15] *Bedford v Canada (Attorney General)* [2013] SCC 72 (20 December 2013) [134], [164].

[16] Ibid [2].

[17] *Understanding NWAC's Position on Prostitution* (November 2012) Native Women's Association of Canada <http://www.nwac.ca/sites/default/files/imce/Understanding%20NWAC's%20Position%20on%20Prostitution%20-%20Nov%202012.pdf>.

[18] *Demand Change,* above n 10.

[19] *What We Know About the Nordic Model,* Women's Coalition for the Abolition of Prostitution <http://www.abolitionprostitution.ca/downloads/what-we-know-about-the-nordic-model.pdf/>.

[20] *Speaking of Prostitution*, above n 9, 40.

[21] Yolande Geadah, *Prostitution: Time to Take Action* (31 May 2012) Women's Coalition for the Abolition of Prostitution <http://www.abolitionprostitution.ca/downloads/prostitution-time-to-take-action.pdf/>.

[22] Benedet, above n 11.

[23] *What We Know About the Nordic Model*, above n 19.

[24] Benedet, above n 11.

[25] Geadah, above n 21, 20.

[26] *Understanding NWAC's Position on Prostitution*, above n 17.

[27] *National Action Plan to Combat Human Trafficking – 2012–2013 Annual Report on Progress* (2012) Public Safety Canada <http://www.publicsafety.gc.ca/cnt/rsrcs/pblctns/2013-ntnl-ctn-pln-cmbt-hmn/index-eng.aspx/>.

[28] Nicole Barrett, *An Exploration of Promising Practices in Response to Human Trafficking in Canada* (2010) International Centre for Criminal Law Reform and Criminal Justice Policy <http://www.gov.mb.ca/msw/publications/human_trafficking.pdf/>.

[29] Geadah, above n 21, 19.

[30] *What We Know About the Nordic Model*, above n 19.

[31] *Understanding NWAC's Position on Prostitution*, above n 17, 2.

[32] Cherry Smiley, 'Real change for aboriginal women begins with the end of prostitution', *The Globe and Mail* (online), 14 January 2015, <http://www.theglobeandmail.com/globe-debate/real-change-for-aboriginal-women-begins-with-the-end-of-prostitution/article22442349/>.

[33] Chris Montanini, 'Debate of prostitution bill continues', *Londoner* (online), 12 September 2014, <http://www.thelondoner.ca/2014/09/10/debate-on-prostitution-bill-continues/>.

Saying 'I don't': moving beyond marriage

Meagan Tyler

[1] Jessica Valenti, 'My big feminist wedding', *The Guardian* (London), 24 April 2009.

[2] Megan Neil, 'IBISWorld finds average cost of a wedding in Australia is

greater than the cost of a Ford Falcon XR6 Limited Edition', *The Daily Telegraph* (Sydney), 28 September 2011.

[3] Elly Michelle Clough, 'Why are feminists judging their friends?' *SBS News* (online), 14 January 2014, <http://www.sbs.com.au/news/article/2014/01/14/comment-why-are-feminists-judging-their-friends>.

[4] Laura Bates, 'How to have a feminist wedding', *The Guardian* (London), 28 June 2014; Valenti, above n 1.

[5] Audrey Bilger, 'Marriage equality is a feminist issue', *Ms. Magazine* (online), 11 December 2012, <http://msmagazine.com/blog/2012/12/11/marriage-equality-is-a-feminist-issue/>.

[6] Carole Pateman, *The Sexual Contract* (Polity Press, 1988).

[7] Claudia Card, 'Gay Divorce: Thoughts on the Legal Regulation of Marriage' (2007) 22 *Hypatia* 24.

[8] Ibid 33.

[9] Chris Berg, *Quotable Quotes* (2012) Australian Marriage Equality <http://www.australianmarriageequality.org/quotable-quotes/>.

[10] Jonathan Rauch, *Gay Marriage: Why it is Good for Gays, Good for Straights and Good for America* (MacMillan, 2004).

[11] Ann Ferguson, 'Gay Marriage: An American and Feminist Dilemma' (2007) 22 *Hypatia* 39, 40.

[12] Meagan Tyler, 'No Means Yes? Perpetuating Myths in the Sexological Construction of Women's Desire' (2009) 32 *Women and Therapy* 40.

[13] *Criminal Code, Evidence Act and Other Acts Amendment Act 1989* (Qld) s 31; Kate Painter, 'Wife Rape in the United Kingdom' (Paper presented at the American Society of Criminology 50th Anniversary Meeting, San Francisco, 20–23 November 1991) 3–4.

[14] Meagan Tyler, 'Sex Self-Help Books: Hot Secrets for Great Sex or Promoting the Sex of Prostitution?' (2008) 31 *Women's Studies International Forum* 363.

[15] David Schnarch, *Passionate Marriage* (Norton, 1997) 304.

[16] A. James Hammerton, *Cruelty and Companionship: Conflict in Nineteenth-Century Married Life* (Routledge, 1992) 148.

[17] Claudia Card, 'Against Marriage and Motherhood' (1996) 11 *Hypatia* 1, 11.

[18] Iris Marion Young, *Intersecting Voices: Dilemmas of Gender, Political Philosophy,*

and Policy (Princeton University Press, 1997).

[19] C Delphy and D Leonard, *Familiar Exploitation: A New Analysis of Marriage in Contemporary Western Societies* (Polity Press, 1992).

[20] Pateman, above n 6.

[21] Zoe Holman, 'Why are my feminist friends still taking their husband's surnames?', *The Guardian* (online), 10 January 2014, <http://www.theguardian.com/commentisfree/2014/jan/10/marriage-feminism-weddings/>.

[22] Janeen Baxter, 'To Marry or Not to Marry: Marital Status and the Household Division of Labour' (2005) 26 *Journal of Family Issues* 300; Janeen Baxter et al, 'Pathways into Marriage: Cohabitation and the Domestic Division of Labour' (2010) 31 *Journal of Family Issues* 1507; B Shelton and D John, 'Does Marital Status Make a Difference? Housework Among Married and Cohabiting Men and Women' (1993) 14 *Journal of Family Issues* 401.

[23] W Brown and S Trost, 'Life Transitions and Changing Physical Activity Patterns in Young Women' (2003) 25 *American Journal of Preventive Medicine* 140.

[24] Baxter, 'To Marry or Not to Marry', above n 22.

[25] Stevi Jackson, *Heterosexuality in Question* (Sage, 1999); Sheila Jeffreys, *The Lesbian Heresy: A Feminist Perspective on the Lesbian Sexual Revolution* (Spinifex, 1993).

Building feminism, resisting porn culture: where to from here?

Rebecca Whisnant

[1] Andrea Dworkin, 'Women in the Public Domain: Sexual Harassment and Date Rape' in *Life and Death: Unapologetic Writings on the Continuing War Against Women* (Free Press, 1997)199.

[2] Andrea Dworkin, 'Feminism: An Agenda' in *Letters From a War Zone* (Lawrence Hill Books, 1993) 133.

BIOGRAPHIES OF CONTRIBUTORS

Meghan Donevan is currently working towards master's degrees in both economics (Stockholm University) and political science (Uppsala University). Her research interests include pornography, prostitution, human trafficking, and violence against women in general, as well as issues related to global development and political economy.

Teresa Edwards, legal counsel, has worked for more than 20 years to advance the needs and rights of Aboriginal peoples, with a particular focus on addressing Aboriginal women's human rights in Canada. Teresa is the director of international affairs and human rights with the Native Women's Association of Canada ('NWAC'). NWAC, founded in 1974, is based on the collective goal to enhance, promote, and foster the social, economic, cultural and political wellbeing of First Nations and Métis women within First Nation, Métis and Canadian societies. NWAC is also a member of the Women's Coalition for the Abolition of Prostitution.

Kate Farhall is a PhD candidate in the School of Social and Political Sciences at the University of Melbourne. Her current research investigates compulsory heterosexuality and the treatment of sexual minorities in the Australian women's lifestyle magazines *Cleo* and *Cosmopolitan*, as well as analysing the construction of heterosex within the magazines with a focus on pornification.

Dr Shakira Hussein is a research fellow at the Asia Institute at the University of Melbourne. Her work has been published in outlets including *The Australian*, *The Age*, *Crikey*, *The Griffith Review* and *The Best Australian Essays* (Black Inc. Publishing, 2011).

Natalie Jovanovski is a PhD candidate and feminist researcher from Melbourne, Australia. Her research interests include the harms of sexual objectification, the cultural reinforcement of eating disorders, and the discursive portrayal of food in contemporary Western media.

Miranda Kiraly is an editor, writer and law tutor from Melbourne, Australia. She has authored publications on law and politics, including 'Bittersweet Charity' in *Really Dangerous Ideas* (Connor Court, 2013) and 'Where Does the Private Domain Start and the Public End' in *Turning Left and Right: Values in Modern Politics* (Connor Court, 2013). Miranda previously worked in federal politics as a speechwriter and researcher. From 2009–2013, she was a leading discussant for the Liberal Book Club.

Dr Julia Long is a lecturer in sociology at Anglia Ruskin University, with a professional background in equalities and the women's sector. She is a lesbian feminist and the author of *Anti-Porn: The Resurgence of Anti-Pornography Feminism* (Zed Books, 2012).

Dr Finn Mackay founded the London Feminist Network in 2004 and the revived London Reclaim the Night march. She has been involved in feminist activism for 20 years and after a career in policy and training on domestic violence prevention education she returned to academia and is now a lecturer in sociology at the University of the West of England in Bristol, United Kingdom. Finn is the author of *Radical Feminism: Feminist Activism in Movement* (Palgrave Macmillan, 2015).

Laura McNally is a psychologist, consultant, writer and PhD candidate. Her research examines the social implications of cultural, political and economic trends. She is the chairperson of Endangered Bodies Australia, a global non-profit organisation founded by Susie Orbach that advocates for a world where women are more than the sum of their body parts.

Meghan Murphy is the founder and editor of *Feminist Current*, Canada's leading feminist website. She is a freelance writer and journalist from Vancouver, B.C. and holds a master's degree in women's studies from Simon Fraser University. Her work has been published in numerous places, including: *New Statesman*, *Al Jazeera English*, *Vice* and *Ms. Magazine*.

Dr Caroline Norma is a lecturer in the School of Global, Urban and Social Studies at RMIT University, Australia. She researches radical feminist approaches to prostitution, pornography and trafficking.

Dr Camille Nurka is an independent scholar in gender studies. She has published articles on gendered embodiment in a range of women's and gender studies journals, including *Women's Studies International Forum*, *Australian Feminist Studies*, and *Feminist Media Studies*.

Dr Helen Pringle works in the Faculty of Arts and Social Sciences at the University of New South Wales. Her research has been widely recognised by awards from Princeton University, the Fulbright Foundation, the Australian Federation of University Women, and the Universities of Adelaide, Wollongong and New South Wales. Her main fields of expertise are human rights, ethics in public life, and political theory, with particular attention to issues of sexual equality and discrimination, and of freedom of expression. She is the author of the most recent edition of *Australian Protocol & Procedures* (University of New South Wales Press, 2008).

Dr Kaye Quek is a lecturer and tutor in political science at the University of Melbourne and RMIT University, Australia. Her research examines state approaches to dealing with abuses of women's human rights, particularly those that occur in harmful forms of marriage.

Naela Rose is a writer, blogger and English teacher based in Istanbul, Turkey. She has also worked with Integrate Bristol since 2007 as a youth worker and production co-ordinator. Integrate Bristol is a charity formed to assist young people and children who have arrived in the United Kingdom from other countries and cultures, and campaigns against all forms of violence and abuse against women and girls.

Dr Laura Tarzia is a sociologist and research fellow at the

General Practice and Primary Health Care Academic Centre at the University of Melbourne, Australia. She is deputy lead of the Abuse and Violence research programme, and her current work focuses on domestic violence, unwanted sexual contact and sexual violence against women, and the response to these issues in primary care and health settings.

Professor Margaret Thornton FAASA FAAL is professor of law and ANU public policy fellow at the Australian National University. She is a barrister of the High Court of Australia and has degrees from Sydney, New South Wales and Yale. Her research interests include feminist legal theory, discrimination law, legal education, the legal profession and the corporatisation of universities. Her most recent book is *Privatising the Public University: The Case of Law* (Routledge, 2012).

Dr Meagan Tyler is a vice-chancellor's research fellow at RMIT University, Australia. Her research focuses on the social construction of gender and sexuality. Her work has been published in *Rural Studies*, *Women's Studies International Forum* and *Women and Therapy* as well as several edited collections, including *Everyday Pornography* (Routledge, 2010) and *Prostitution, Harm and Gender Inequality* (Ashgate, 2012). Meagan is also the author of *Selling Sex Short: The Pornographic and Sexological Construction of Women's Sexuality in the West* (Cambridge Scholars Press, 2011).

Dr Rebecca Whisnant is associate professor of philosophy and director of women's and gender studies at the University of Dayton. She co-edited *Not For Sale: Feminists Resisting Prostitution and Pornography* with Christine Stark (Spinifex, 2004) and *Global Feminist Ethics* with Peggy DesAutels (Rowman & Littlefield, 2010). She is a co-founder and board member of Stop Porn Culture, a non-profit organisation dedicated to challenging the porn industry through education and activism.

Lightning Source UK Ltd.
Milton Keynes UK
UKOW04f1623180716

278641UK00011B/374/P